Gilmore girls™

THE OFFICIAL KNITTING BOOK

Knit Your Way Through
Stars Hollow and Beyond

Gilmore girls™

THE OFFICIAL KNITTING BOOK

Knit Your Way Through Stars Hollow and Beyond

BY TANIS GRAY

Titan Books

London

An Insight Editions Book

Contents

6 INTRODUCTION

9 CHAPTER 1: HATS FROM THE HOLLOW

   11 Sookie's Bandana
   15 Daily News Hat
   21 Lorelai's Hat
   27 Emily's Golf Tam
   31 "I Smell Snow" Hat
   37 Jackson's Skullcap

41 CHAPTER 2: OY WITH THE COWLS AND SCARVES . . . AND MORE!

   43 "Oy with the Poodles Already" Cowl
   47 Minutemen Scarf & Fingerless Mitts
   59 Rory's Prep School Cowl
   63 "You Jump, I Jump" Beaded Lace Scarf
   67 "If You're Out on the Road" Cowl
   71 Stars Hollow Scarf
   75 A Thousand Yellow Daisies Cowl
   79 Richard's Friday Night Dinner Bow Tie

83 CHAPTER 3: "I'LL LEAVE YOU TO MAKE OUT WITH YOUR SOCKS" AND MITTS

   85 Saddle Shoe Socks
   89 Life and Death Brigade Fingerless Mitts
   99 Coffee, Coffee, Coffee Socks
   107 Luke's Fingerless Mitts

Project Skill Levels

✱ BEGINNER
✱✱ INTERMEDIATE
✱✱✱ ADVANCED

111 CHAPTER 4: GILMORE GARMENTS

- 113 Rory's Argyle Vest
- 123 Luke's Diner Pullover
- 133 Rory's Debutante Tunic
- 141 Paris's Mac & Cheese Cardigan
- 149 Rory's Boyfriends Pullover

155 CHAPTER 5: HOMEY DECOR AND GIFTS

- 157 Lorelai and Rory Dolls
- 165 Lane's Drumstick Bag
- 169 Doose's Market Tote
- 175 "Babette Ate Oatmeal" Pillow
- 179 Sookie's Baby Blanket
- 185 Firelight Festival Blanket

188 GLOSSARY

195 ABBREVIATIONS

196 YARN RESOURCE GUIDE

199 WHERE YOU LEAD, I WILL FOLLOW

Introduction

We all have a favorite comfort show, one we come back to again and again. Sometimes we have it on in the background, and other times we stop what we're doing and hang on every word like it's the first time we've seen it. It doesn't matter where we jump in—whether it's mid-episode or mid-season—watching a comfort show is like wrapping up with a cozy handmade blanket next to an old friend. And for many, our comfort show is *Gilmore Girls*.

Debuting on the Warner Brothers (WB) network in October of 2000, *Gilmore Girls* was unlike any other series on television at the time. There had been TV shows in the past where the two protagonists were a mother and daughter duo, but this was fresh and new. Lorelai and Rory Gilmore lived in the postcard town of Stars Hollow, Connecticut, surrounded by an eclectic and charismatic cast of characters living their lives. Their close relationship felt more like a role reversal with witty dialogue, fast-paced banter, family drama, and relatable situations that made us all feel like we could fit right into their little corner of the world. We cried happy tears from our couches when Rory gave her Chilton valedictorian speech, celebrated with Sookie and Jackson when they got engaged, cheered when Lorelai's Dragonfly Inn opened, channeled courage to Lane when she left the safety of her childhood home, and ecstatically whooped when

Luke and Lorelai finally kissed on the front porch. Audiences and critics celebrated the show, and it quickly gained a massive following, running seven seasons and 153 episodes. Even now, over 20 years later, thanks to online streaming, the show is as popular as ever.

Autumn and winter seasons in *Gilmore Girls* seemed extra special, so knitters watched with keen eyes for knitted items popping up on our beloved cast. I'm delighted to share this carefully curated size-inclusive collection packed with garments, accessories, and home decor inspired by our favorite characters, festivals, secret societies, locations, ex-boyfriends, and caffeinated beverages from Stars Hollow. Knit yourself an elegant botanical-themed sleeveless top inspired by Rory's debutante ball gown on page 133, or a comfy cardi inspired by Paris's favorite illicit snack of mac and cheese on page 141. If accessories are what you crave, knit up the Coffee, Coffee, Coffee Socks on page 99, Lorelai's "I Smell Snow" Hat on page 31, the Firelight Festival Blanket on page 185, or an exact replica of the golf tam Emily gave Rory on page 27. Packed with 29 projects, this book has enough to keep you knitting if you find yourself out on the road, feeling lonely and so cold.

If you like coffee with your oxygen, fiber on your needles, and all things *Gilmore Girls*, pull up a diner chair and join us.

See you in Stars Hollow,
Tanis

Chapter 1

Hats from the Hollow

Sookie's Bandana

Designed by Carissa Browning
SKILL LEVEL: EASY

"You were a good cake, Clyde. I never should have named you."
—Sookie, Season 2, Episode 4

Fans can't imagine any other actress nailing the part of quirky bandana-wearing chef Sookie St. James the way Melissa McCarthy did. Surprisingly, she wasn't the casting director's first choice. Jackson Belleville actor Jackson Douglas's real-life wife at the time, Alex Borstein, was originally cast as Sookie. Due to prior commitments with *MADtv*, when the series she was working on was picked up, the role of Sookie was recast with Melissa McCarthy. Borstein made guest appearances as Emily's clothing designer the fabulous Miss Celine, Lorelai's neighbor Dwight's board game–loving ex-wife, and again as the Dragonfly Inn's harpist, Drella—but it was the on-screen chemistry between McCarthy and Douglas that made them believable as a couple. Casting director Jami Rudofsky said, "We read a lot of amazing women—a lot, but then Melissa McCarthy walked in, and it's *Melissa McCarthy*. She's comedy gold, and she brought things to the character that were so inventive. Her physical comedy, everything she did was above and beyond, and that was it."

Everyone's favorite quirky chef is seldom seen in the kitchen without a bandana, often accompanied by adorable pigtails peeking out. Worked side to side all in one piece, this knitted kerchief is sized for both children and adults, and begins with a simple i-cord, followed by increases that form a biased triangle of garter stitch fabric accented with basic lace. After the midpoint, each column of eyelets is exchanged for a partial row of eyelets, intersecting to form a series of symmetric Vs. When the triangle is complete, most of the stitches are bound off, leaving only a few to continue the i-cord for a second tie.

SIZES
Child (Adult)

FINISHED MEASUREMENTS
Width (not including ties):
13¾ (18) in. / 35 (45.5) cm
Depth: 6¾ (8¾) in. / 17 (22) cm
Length of Ties: 7 (8) in. / 18 (20.5) cm

YARN
DK weight yarn, shown in Wool and Vinyl *Hard Rock DK* (4-ply; 100% superwash merino wool; 250 yd. / 229 m per 4 oz. / 115 g hank) in color Valley Girl, 1 hank

NEEDLES
US 5 / 3.75 mm, circular needle, any length, or size needed to obtain gauge

NOTIONS
3 (4) stitch markers
Tapestry needle

GAUGE
16 sts and 34 rows = 4 in. / 10 cm over garter stitch worked flat, taken after blocking
Make sure to check your gauge.

PATTERN NOTES
- This bandana is worked side to side, beginning with an i-cord tie. Increases along one edge form the triangle, which is worked on the bias. When the triangle is complete, all but 3 stitches are bound off and the second i-cord tie is worked from those 3 stitches.
- One full hank of yarn (250 yd. / 229 m) is enough to make 2 adult-sized bandanas.
- Written instructions are provided for the entirety of the bandana.

FIRST TIE

Make a 3-stitch i-cord as follows:
Make a slipknot and place on LHN.
Rnd 1 (inc): (K1, yo, k1) into slipknot, slide—3 sts.
Rnd 2: K3, slide.
Rep Rnd 2 until the tie measures 7 (8) in. / 18 (20.5) cm.
Final Rnd (inc): K2, kfb, slide—4 sts.

TRIANGLE

Row 1 (RS, inc): K2, kfb, sl1 wyif, turn—5 sts.
Row 2 (WS, and all WS rows unless otherwise noted): Knit to last 3 sts, sl3 wyif, turn.
Row 3 (inc): K2, kfb, knit to last st, sl1 wyif, turn—1 st inc.
Row 4 (WS): Knit to last 3 sts, sl3 wyif, turn.
Rows 5–12: Rep [Rows 3–4] 4 more times—10 sts.
Row 13 (RS, inc): K2, kfb, pm, k2tog, yo, k4, sl1 wyif, turn—1 st inc.
Row 15 (inc): K2, kfb, knit to last st, sl1 wyif, turn—1 st inc.
Row 17 (inc): K2, kfb, knit to M, sm, k2tog, yo, k4, sl1 wyif, turn—1 st inc.
Row 19 (inc): Work as for Row 15—1 st inc.
Row 20 (WS): Knit to last 3 sts, sl3 wyif, turn.
Rows 21–24: Rep [Rows 17–20] 1 more time—16 sts.
Row 25 (RS, inc): K2, kfb, pm, k2tog, yo, k4, sm, k2tog, yo, k4, sl1 wyif, turn—1 st inc.
Row 27 (inc): K2, kfb, knit to last st, sl1 wyif, turn—1 st inc.
Row 29 (inc): K2, kfb, knit to M, *sm, k2tog, yo, k4; rep from * to last st, sl1 wyif, turn—1 st inc.
Row 31 (inc): Work as for Row 27—1 st inc.
Row 32 (WS): Knit to last 3 sts, sl3 wyif, turn.
Rows 33–36: Rep [Rows 29–32] 1 more time—22 sts.
Row 37 (RS, inc): K2, kfb, pm, k2tog, yo, k4, *sm, k2tog, yo, k4; rep from * to last st, sl1 wyif, turn—1 st inc.
Row 39 (inc): K2, kfb, knit to last st, sl1 wyif, turn—1 st inc.
Row 41 (inc): K2, kfb, knit to M, *sm, k2tog, yo, k4; rep from * to last st, sl1 wyif, turn—1 st inc.
Row 43: Work as for Row 39—1 st inc.
Row 44 (WS): Knit to last 3 sts, sl3 wyif, turn.
Rows 45–48: Rep [Rows 41–44] 1 more time—28 sts.
Adult Size Only:
Rep [Rows 37–48] 1 more time—34 sts.
Both Sizes:
Row 49 (RS, inc): K2, kfb, (k2tog, yo) to M, rm, k2tog, yo, k4, *sm, k2tog, yo, k4; rep from * to last st, sl1 wyif, turn—1 st inc.
Row 51 (inc): K2, kfb, knit to last st, sl1 wyif, turn—1 st inc.
Row 53 (inc): K2, kfb, knit to M, *sm, k2tog, yo, k4; rep from * to last st, sl1 wyif, turn—1 st inc.
Row 55 (inc): Work as for Row 51—1 st inc.
Row 56 (WS): Knit to last 3 sts, sl3 wyif, turn.
Rows 57–60: Rep [Rows 53–56] 1 more time—34 (40) sts.
Adult Size Only:
Rep [Rows 49–60] 1 more time—46 sts.
Both Sizes:
Row 61 (RS, inc): K2, kfb, (k2tog, yo) to M, rm, k2tog, yo, k4, sm, k2tog, yo, k4, sl1 wyif, turn—1 st inc.
Row 63 (inc): K2, kfb, knit to last st, sl1 wyif, turn—1 st inc.
Row 65 (inc): K2, kfb, knit to M, sm, k2tog, yo, k4, sl1 wyif, turn—1 st inc.
Row 67: Work as for Row 63—1 st inc.
Row 68 (WS): Knit to last 3 sts, sl3 wyif, turn.
Rows 69–72: Rep [Rows 65–68] 1 more time—40 (52) sts.
Row 73 (RS, inc): K2, kfb, (k2tog, yo) to M, rm, k2tog, yo, k4, sl1 wyif, turn—1 st inc.
Row 75 (inc): K2, kfb, knit to last st, sl1 wyif, turn—1 st inc.
Row 76 (WS): Knit to last 3 sts, sl3 wyif, turn.
Rows 77–80: Rep [Rows 75–76] 2 more times—44 (56) sts.
Row 81 (RS, inc): Work as for Row 75—45 (57) sts.
Row 82 (WS): BO all sts knitwise until 3 sts rem on LHN and 1 st on RHN, sl3 wyif, turn—4 sts.

SECOND TIE

Rnd 1 (dec): K2, k2tog, slide—3 sts.
Rnd 2: K3, slide.
Rep Rnd 2 until the tie measures 7 (8) in. / 18 (20.5) cm.
Final Rnd (dec): K3tog—1 st.
Cut yarn and fasten off.

FINISHING

Weave in ends inside i-cord ties.
Wet block to measurements.

Coffee Talk

Episodes of the show would film July through May, taking on average eight days to film one episode. The cast and crew would get major holidays off, as well as two months in the summer between seasons.

Daily News Hat

Designed by Alina Appasova
SKILL LEVEL: INTERMEDIATE

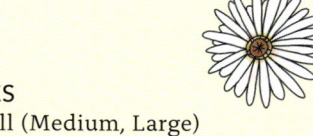

"Ladies and gentlemen, tonight represents a melding of the old and the new. For one night, identifying the two groups will be easy. The old will be the ones running around frantically trying to get out the latest issue of the Daily News, and the new will be the ones in the stupid hats."

—Doyle McMaster, Season 4, Episode 10

Wanting to become a journalist akin to CNN's Christiane Amanpour since she was a child, Rory goes from working on *The Franklin* newspaper at Chilton Prep School to working at the *Yale Daily News*, the oldest daily college newspaper in the United States, under Editor-in-Chief Doyle McMaster. Before passing muster to be officially on staff, new writers must have a certain number of articles published, and must participate in "heeling," a ritual involving making paper hats out of newspaper in a matter of minutes. Becoming the beat reporter for features and being called "an unflinchingly honest reviewer who shows no mercy, but a great deal of dark wit in her pieces" after writing a scathing review of a school ballet production, Rory eventually becomes the new editor-in-chief after the staff declares mutiny on current editor Paris Geller.

Alert the media! Knit in the round from the bottom up, this clever newsprint-covered hat begins with a corrugated ribbed brim. Newsprint "text" is worked in stranded colorwork across the body and modeled after the lyrics of the *Gilmore Girls* theme song formatted into columns. Topped with a newsworthy pom-pom, this hat can be made in multiple sizes by adjusting the number of text columns.

SIZES
Small (Medium, Large)

FINISHED MEASUREMENTS
Circumference: 16 (19¼, 22½) in. / 40.5 (49, 57) cm
Height: 8½ (9¼, 9¾) in. / 21.5 (23.5, 25) cm
The hat is designed to be worn with 2 in. / 5 cm of negative ease.

YARN
Fingering weight yarn, shown in Keenan Hand Dyed Yarn *Highland Fingering* (100% wool; 229 yd. / 209 m per 1¾ oz. / 50 g hank)

COLORWAYS
Main Color (MC): Irish Girl at North Ave Beach, 1 hank
Contrast Color (CC): Melancholy Oyster Boy, 1 hank

NEEDLES
US 1 / 2.25 mm, 16 in. / 40 cm long circular needle and set of 4 or 5 double-pointed needles or size needed to obtain gauge

NOTIONS
Stitch marker
Tapestry needle
Pom-pom maker, approx. 2⅛ in. / 5 cm diameter

GAUGE
30 sts and 40 rnds = 4 in. / 10 cm in stranded colorwork pattern in the round, taken after blocking
Make sure to check your gauge.

PATTERN NOTES
- The hat is worked in the round from the bottom up. It may be helpful to place a marker between pattern repeats in the colorwork portion of the hat.
- Instructions are provided for size Small first, with larger sizes in parentheses. When only one set of numbers is provided, it applies to all sizes.
- When working the stranded colorwork chart, catch floats longer than 5 stitches.

Continued on page 16

- When working the corrugated rib, be sure to move the MC yarn to the back between the needles after completing the purl stitch so all floats are on the WS of the hat.
- When the circumference of the hat becomes too small for the circular needle during the crown shaping, change to dpns to finish the hat.

PATTERN STITCHES
Corrugated Rib (worked over a multiple of 2 sts)
All Rnds: *K1 with CC, p1 with MC; rep from * to end of rnd.

CAST ON & BRIM
With circular needle and MC, CO 114 (138, 162) sts using the Twisted German cast on method. Pm for BOR and join to work in the rnd, being careful not to twist the sts.
Join CC.
Work in Corrugated Rib for 8 rnds. Do not break CC; carry it loosely up the inside of the hat until it is used again.

BODY
Setup Rnd 1: With MC, *k1, p1; rep from * to end of rnd.
Setup Rnd 2 (inc): With MC, *k18 (22, 26), kfb; rep from * to end of rnd—120 (144, 168) sts.

Next 2 Rnds: With MC, knit.
Begin Daily News Charts, reading all rows from right to left as for working in the rnd. Work Rnds 1–52 (1–58, 1–64) once, working each row as follows:
Size Small Only: Work Columns 1, 2, and 3 once, then Columns 1 and 2 once more (5 columns total).
Size Medium Only: Work Columns 1, 2, and 3 twice (6 columns total).
Size Large Only: Work Columns 1, 2, and 3 twice, then Column 1 once more (7 columns total).

CROWN SHAPING
Begin Crown Shaping Chart, reading all rows from right to left as for working in the rnd.

The chart is worked 5 (6, 7) times across each rnd—10 (12, 14) sts rem. Break yarn, pull tail through remaining live sts and cinch closed. Secure tails to WS.

FINISHING

Weave in all ends and block to measurements. Allow to dry completely. Trim all ends. Using both yarns, make pom-pom and attach to crown.

Coffee Talk

The *Yale Daily News*, the real newspaper, was first published in January 1878. Published Monday through Friday during the academic year only, it circulates throughout Yale and New Haven, Connecticut.

KEY

- ▨ No stitch
- ☐ MC
- ■ CC
- ☐ knit
- ╱ k2tog
- ╲ ssk
- ⋏ sk2p
- ▭ Pattern repeat

CROWN SHAPING CHART

CHART COLUMN 3

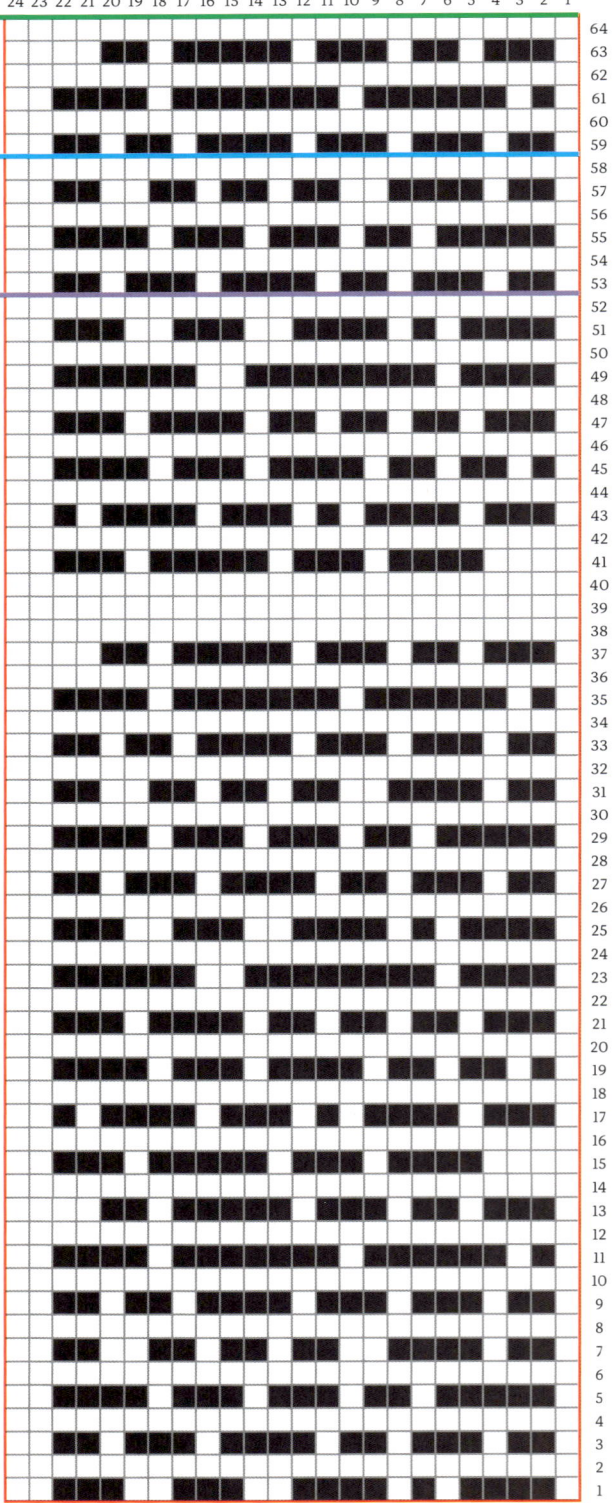

CHART COLUMN 2

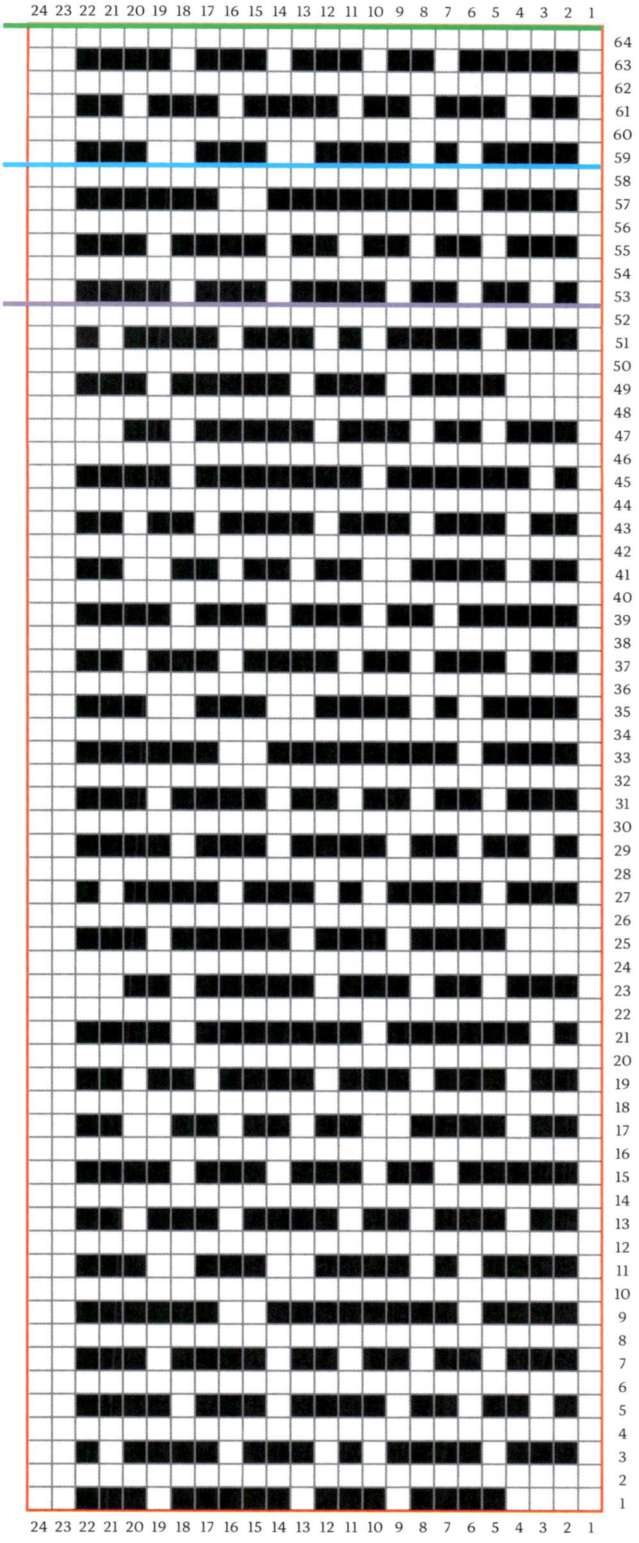

CHART COLUMN 1

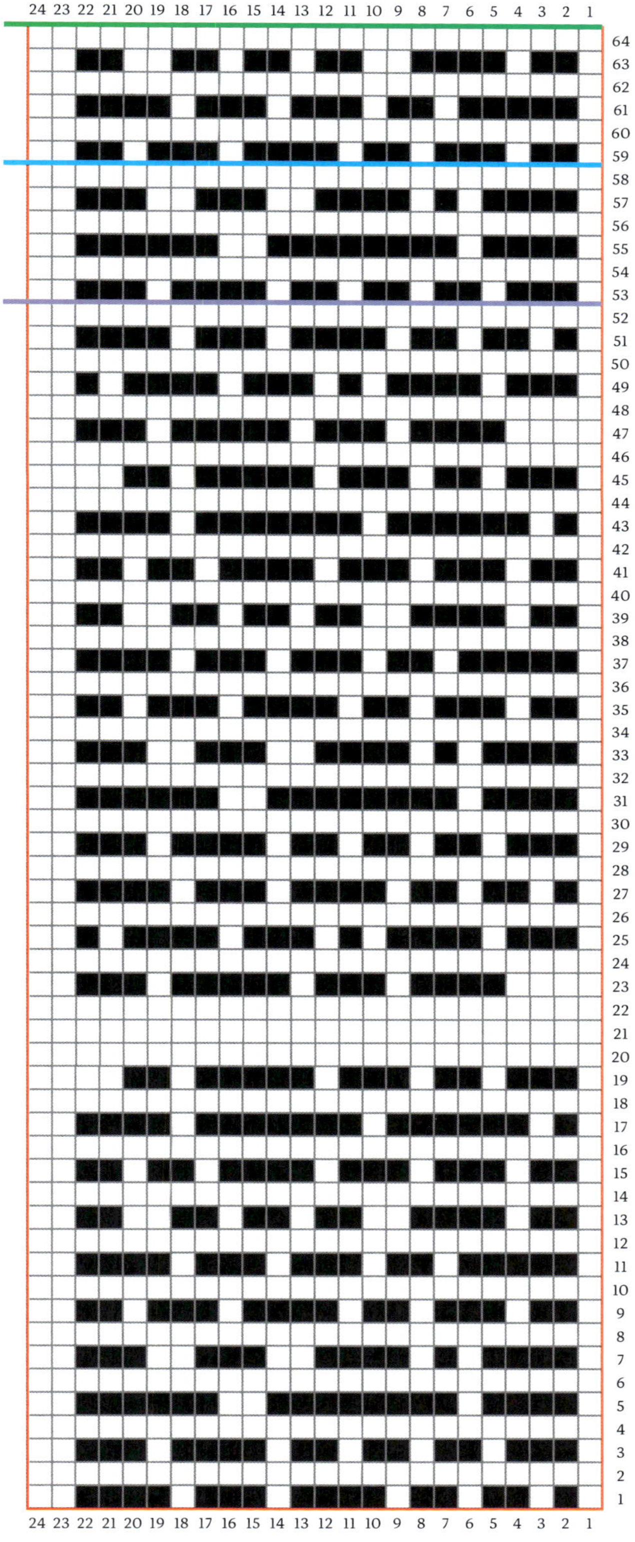

Lorelai's Hat

Designed by Arianna Soloway
SKILL LEVEL: INTERMEDIATE

"It takes a remarkable person to inspire all of this."
—Richard, Season 7, Episode 22

While many actresses auditioned for the part of Lorelai, Lauren Graham didn't know until right before the pilot began filming whether she would be able to execute the part. Wanting the role, but unsure of her availability, she recalls, "In life, nothing's all funny or all dramatic—it's both. I thought [*Gilmore Girls*] didn't sound like anything else. I had never read anything like it. That dialogue and intelligence really jumped out at me." While the casting directors loved her, creator Amy Sherman-Palladino didn't want to even hear her read because Graham was already tied to another show at NBC and was waiting to see whether it had been picked up. Sherman-Palladino remembers, "When it was clear that we weren't finding that magical Lorelai to walk in and be everything that we needed, it was like, 'Fine, bring Lauren in. Let me fall in love with somebody I can't have.' And I got lucky because the other show got canceled, and then I got her." Fortunately for *Gilmore* fans everywhere, Graham stayed in the role for all seven seasons and became a fashion role model for many, especially regarding her winter hats.

Every *Gilmore* fan knows how much Lorelai loves to wear hats! Worked from the bottom up in the round, the hat features a folded brim containing a secret message inside. Stranded colorwork motifs representing Lorelai's request to Max for a thousand yellow daisies, gently falling snow that only Lorelai can smell, the coffee cup from the Luke's Diner sign, crisp autumn leaves, and dragonflies circle around the body. Topped with a pom-pom, this cute beanie is an ode to many favorite episodes and icons from the series.

SIZES
Child (Adult Small, Adult Large)

FINISHED MEASUREMENTS
Circumference: 17½ (19½, 21¾) in. / 44.5 (49.5, 55.5) cm
Height: 8.5 in. / 21.5 cm**
Hat is designed to be worn with very little ease. Choose the size closest to your head circumference for the best fit.
**The height of hat is the same across all sizes. As a result, the Child sized hat will fit slightly slouchier than the Adult sizes.

YARN
Fingering weight yarn, shown in Hazel Knits *Artisan Sock Minis* (90% superwash merino, 10% nylon; approx. 100 yd. / 91 m per 1 oz. / 30 g mini hank)

COLORWAYS
Color A: Cinnabar, 1 hank
Color B: Silica, 1 hank
Color C: Lichen, 1 hank
Color D: Guac, 1 hank
Color E: Viviane, 1 hank

NEEDLES
US 3 / 3.25 mm, 16 in. / 40 cm long circular needle and set of 4 or 5 double-pointed needles or size needed to obtain gauge

NOTIONS
Stitch marker
Tapestry needle
Pom-pom maker (optional; 1⅝–2 in. / 4–5 cm diameter)

GAUGE
22 sts and 32 rows = 4 in. / 10 cm in stranded colorwork pattern in the round, taken after blocking
Make sure to check your gauge

Continued on page 22

PATTERN NOTES

- This hat is worked in the round from the bottom up, beginning with the folded brim. The brim is folded under and knit into the body of the hat to create a secured double-thick brim.
- It may be helpful to place a marker between pattern repeats in the body colorwork portion of the hat.
- When working the stranded colorwork charts, catch floats longer than 5 stitches.
- Carry unused yarn loosely up the inside of the hat until it is used again to save on yardage and ends to weave in. Break yarn only when instructed.
- Instructions are provided for the Child size first, with larger sizes in parentheses. When only one set of numbers is provided, it applies to all sizes.
- When the circumference of the hat becomes too small for the circular needle during the crown shaping, change to dpns to finish the hat.
- Once the Body Chart is complete, final decreases are worked using Color D only.

CAST ON & INSIDE BRIM

With circular needle and Color A, CO 96 (108, 120) sts using the Long Tail cast on method. Pm for BOR and join to work in the rnd, being careful not to twist the sts.

Cont with Color A, knit 6 rnds.

Break Color A; join Color B.

Begin Optional Brim Chart for the size of hat being made, reading all rows from right to left as for working in the rnd, joining Color E on Rnd 3 and breaking it again after completing Rnd 10. Work Rnds 1–12 once.

If you prefer not to work the Optional Brim Chart, knit 12 rnds with Color B only.

Break Color B; rejoin Color A and knit 7 rnds.

BODY OF HAT

Begin Body Chart, reading all rows from right to left as for working in the rnd, joining colors as necessary. Work Rows 1–24 once. The chart is worked 8 (9, 10) times across each rnd.

Rnd 25: Using Color A only, join the cast on edge to the current row as follows:

Fold the cast on edge to the inside of the hat with wrong sides facing together.

Be sure to align the first stitch of your cast on edge (immediately left of your cast on tail) with the first stitch of your current round (immediately to the left of the BOR M).

*Pick up the first stitch from your cast on edge and place it on the

LHN; knit the CO edge st together with the live st from the body of the hat; rep from * to end of rnd. When this process is complete, the cast on edge will be firmly connected to the inside of your hat and you will have the same number of sts as you originally cast on. Resume Body Chart. Work Rows 26–64 once—48 (54, 60) sts rem. Break all yarns except Color D.

CROWN SHAPING

Rnd 1 (dec): *K1, k2tog; rep from * to end of rnd—32 (36, 40) sts.
Rnd 2: Knit.
Rnd 3 (dec): *K2tog; rep from * to end of rnd—16 (18, 20) sts.
Rnd 4: Knit.
Rnd 5 (dec): *K2tog; rep from * to end of rnd—8 (9, 10) sts. Break yarn, pull tail through remaining live sts, and cinch closed. Secure tails to WS.

FINISHING

Weave in all ends and block to measurements. Allow to dry completely. Trim all ends. If desired, using Color E, make pom-pom and attach to crown.

BODY CHART

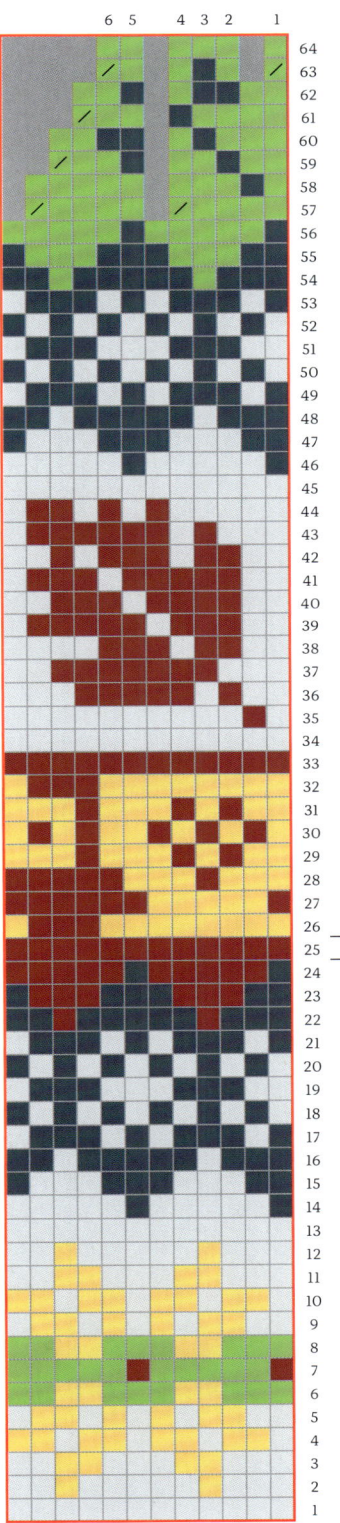

KEY

- No stitch
- Color A
- Color B
- Color C
- Color D
- Color E
- knit
- k2tog
- Pattern repeat

Brim Joining Row

Coffee Talk

Lorelai's childhood dollhouse remains a fixture throughout the show. It is originally in her parents' house, but Richard hand delivers it to Lorelai so it's not destroyed. This intricate prop wasn't only used in *Gilmore Girls*, it was also used in *Friends*.

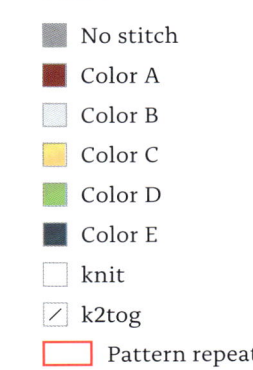

OPTIONAL BRIM CHART - CHILD

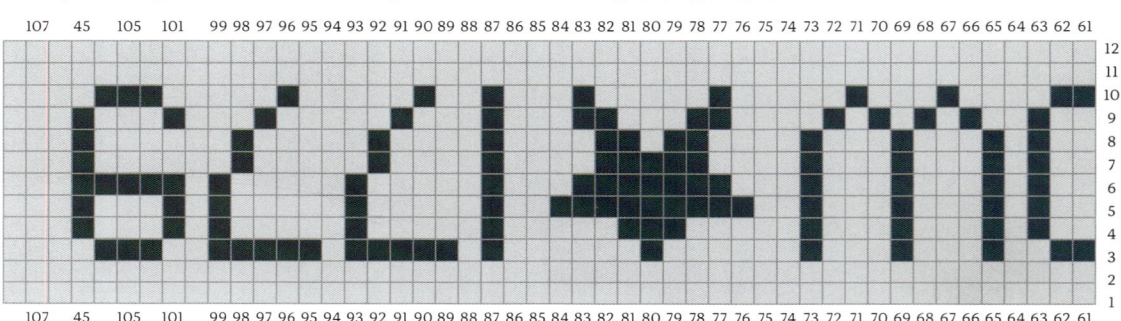

OPTIONAL BRIM CHART - ADULT SMALL

OPTIONAL BRIM CHART - ADULT LARGE

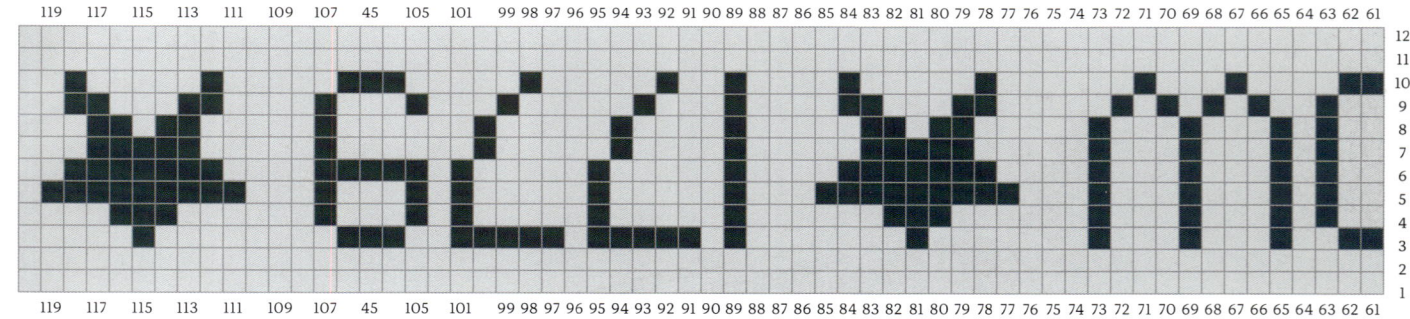

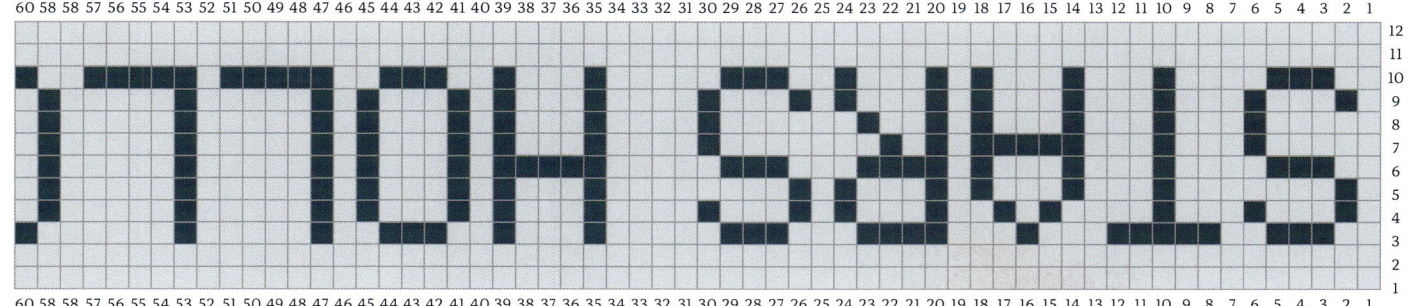

Emily's Golf Tam

Designed by Tanis Gray

SKILL LEVEL: EASY

Lorelai: "I told her she should go out for the debating team."

Rory: "It's not a sport."

Lorelai: "It is the way the Gilmores play."

—*Gilmore Girls*, Season 1, Episode 3

Determined to indoctrinate Rory into their high-society lifestyle, Emily Gilmore, played by Kelly Bishop, persuades Richard to take their granddaughter to their country club after discovering she's required to participate in a school sport. Despite protests from Lorelai, accusing them of pushing the life she ran away from onto her daughter, Rory discovers that while she may be terrible at golf (and the hat Emily provided makes her a target for teasing), getting to know her grandfather, his world, and his friends is worth exploring. Contrary to what they anticipated, both Richard and Rory have a wonderful time and begin to understand that they are more alike than they realized. This relationship continued offscreen, with Edward Herrmann saying about Alexis Bledel, "There is something about Audrey Hepburn, too, which is not actorish, it is simply this 'presence.' Alexis has this transparency about her—there's no character except this extraordinary presence. It's raw. Whatever is said to her has this ripple that goes through her. She's extraordinary." The two actors continued their friendship until Herrmann passed away in 2014.

Fore! Beginning with a 2x2 ribbed brim, this costume replica hat is worked in a traditional tam shape and topped with a jaunty pom-pom. A drastic increase round pushes out the body of the hat, then evenly spaced decreases rein it back in. Bands of color are worked with jogless stripes, creating unbroken and bold patterning throughout. Block it over a pie plate to exaggerate the shape, and you'll be ready to hit the links!

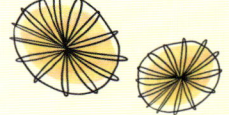

SIZES
One size; fits most adult heads

FINISHED MEASUREMENTS
Brim Circumference: 18½ in. / 47 cm (unstretched)
Body of Hat Circumference: 28 in. / 71 cm (at widest point)
Height: 8 in. / 20.5 cm
Recommended fit is 1–4 in. / 2.5–10 cm of negative ease.

YARN
DK weight yarn, shown in Berroco *Vintage DK* (52% acrylic, 40% wool, 8% nylon; 290 yd. / 266 m per 3½ oz. / 100 g hank)

COLORWAYS
Color A: #2145 Cast Iron, 1 hank
Color B: #2193 Yukon Green, 1 hank
Color C: #2122 Banane, 1 hank
Color D: #2150 Berries, 1 hank
Color E: #2100 Snow Day, 1 hank

NEEDLES
Size US 2 / 2.75 mm, 16 in. / 40 cm long circular needle
Size US 3 / 3.25 mm, 16 in. / 40 cm long circular needle and set of 4 or 5 double-pointed needles or size needed to obtain gauge

NOTIONS
Stitch marker
Tapestry needle
3 in. / 7.5 cm diameter pom-pom maker

GAUGE
24 sts and 32 rows = 4 in. / 10 cm in striped pattern in the round on larger needles, taken after blocking
Make sure to check your gauge.

PATTERN NOTES
- The tam is worked from the brim up, beginning with smaller circular needles for the ribbing, changing to the larger circular needles to work the body of the hat. When the circumference of the hat becomes too small during the crown shaping, switch to dpns for comfort.

Continued on page 28

- The apex of the hat is topped with a pom-pom.
- As you change colors between the stripes in the body of the tam, use the Jogless Stripes method for stripes that are 2 or more rows tall to avoid jogs at the beginning of round.
- Carry Color A loosely up the inside of the tam when not in use to save on ends to weave in. You may cut or carry Colors B, C, and D as desired between the large stripes. Cut Color E when the single round is complete.

CAST ON & BRIM

Using the smaller needle and Color A, CO 112 sts using the Long Tail cast on method. Pm for BOR and join to work in the rnd, being careful not to twist the sts.

Rib Rnd: (K2, p2) to end of rnd.
Drop, do not cut, Color A.
With Color B, work Rib Rnd 8 times total.
Cut Color B.
With Color A, knit 1 rnd.

BODY

Switch to larger circular needles.
Inc Rnd (with Color A): K1, *M1L, k2; rep from * to last st, M1L, k1—168 sts.

Begin Chart A, reading all rows from right to left as for working in the rnd. Work [Rows 1–57] 1 time (chart is worked 7 times across each rnd).

When the chart is complete, 14 sts rem. Break all yarns; leave a 6 in. / 15 cm tail of Color D.

Thread the tapestry needle with Color D, pull tail through rem live sts, and cinch closed. Secure tails to WS.

FINISHING

Weave in all loose ends to WS.
Wet block the tam over a plate to exaggerate the traditional tam shaping.
Using all 5 colors, make one 3 in. / 7.5 cm pom-pom and secure to the top of the hat, alternating the colors wrapped around the pom-pom maker to create chunks of color.

Coffee Talk

Although *Gilmore Girls* takes place in the fictional town of Stars Hollow, Connecticut, most of the series was filmed on studio lots in Burbank, California. The golf course where Richard teaches Rory to play golf is Brookfield Farms in Thousand Oaks, California—the same location where exterior shots of the Independence Inn were filmed.

CHART A

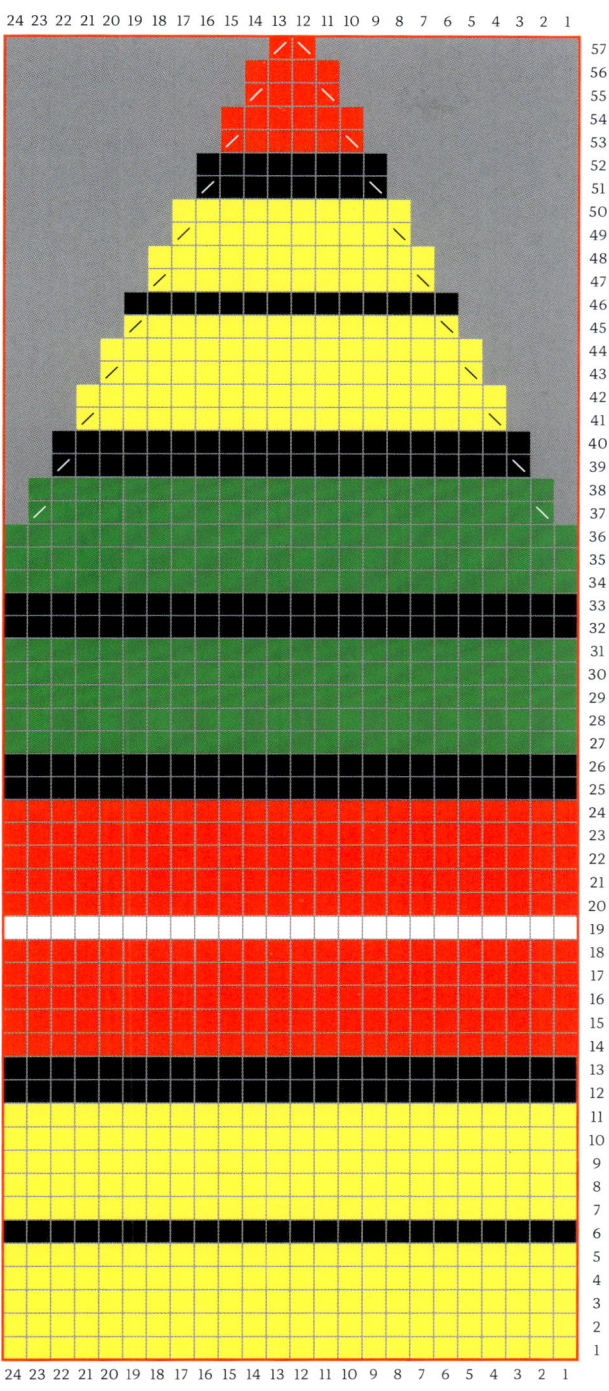

KEY

- No stitch
- knit
- Color A
- Color B
- Color C
- Color D
- Color E
- / k2tog
- \ ssk
- Pattern repeat

"I Smell Snow" Hat

Designed by Nikita Goodman
SKILL LEVEL: INTERMEDIATE

Lorelai: "I feel good. Tingly."

Rory: "That's called frostbite."

—*Gilmore Girls*, Season 1, Episode 8

Lorelai's love for snow and ability to smell it just before it starts is made official by her iconic line, "I smell snow," said throughout the series. In Connecticut, New England, snow is a common occurrence in the winter, yet because *Gilmore Girls* was filmed in sunny Burbank, California, that made things tricky for the cast and crew. A combination of snow blankets, finely cut paper, gently falling potato flakes, and soap-based foam blown out from a machine was used to simulate fresh flurries. Actor Scott Cohen, who plays Max Medina, said, "It was a big mess because the snow machine made so much noise, we had to rerecord dialogue for all our scenes." The costume department had to put the actors in scarves, hats, and gloves, and actress Melissa McCarthy (who played Sookie) recalls, "Sometimes we were like crammed into small things with coats on but it was actually like 112 degrees in Burbank." Despite the cast and crew's discomfort, snow represents important moments to Lorelai, who says, "You know that the best things in my life have happened when it snowed."

Do you smell snow? The hat is worked in the round from the bottom up starting with a simple 1x1 ribbed brim, with stranded colorwork snowflakes and letters that spell out Lorelai's iconic proclamation. Quick decreases close up the crown, which is then topped with a generous pom-pom. Everything is sure to be more magical when you wear this hat!

SIZES
One size; fits most adult heads

FINISHED MEASUREMENTS
Circumference: 18 in. / 45.5 cm, unstretched
Height: 8¾ in. / 22 cm
Recommended fit is 1–4 in. / 2.5–10 cm of negative ease.

YARN
DK weight yarn, shown in Yarn Café Creations Americano DK (4-ply; 100% superwash merino wool; 231 yd. / 211 m per 3½ oz. / 100 g hank)

COLORWAYS
Main Color (MC): Gothic Burgundy, 1 hank
Contrast Color (CC): Mist, 1 hank

NEEDLES
US 6 / 4 mm, 16 in. / 40 cm long circular needle
US 8 / 5 mm, 16 in. / 40 cm long circular needle and set of 5 double-pointed needles or size needed to obtain gauge

NOTIONS
Stitch markers (9; 1 unique for BOR)
Tapestry needle
Pom-pom maker, approx. 3½ in. / 9 cm diameter
US size G / 4.25 mm crochet hook (optional)
Metal aglets (optional)
Needle-nose pliers (optional)

GAUGE
20 sts and 22.5 rows = 4 in. / 10 cm over stranded colorwork pattern in the round on larger needle, taken after blocking
Make sure to check your gauge.

PATTERN NOTES
- This hat is worked in the round from the brim up, using the smaller needle for the brim, changing to the larger needle for the body of the hat.

Continued on page 32

- The small needle should be 2 needle sizes smaller than the large needle when gauge is met.
- Written instructions are provided for the brim and crown decreases of the hat. A chart is provided for the colorwork body of the hat.
- When the circumference of the hat becomes too small for the circular needle during the crown shaping, change to dpns to finish the hat.

CAST ON & BRIM

Using smaller circular needle and CC, CO 90 sts using the Cable cast on method. Pm for BOR and join to work in the rnd, being careful not to twist the sts.

Rib Rnd: *K1, p1; rep from * to end of rnd.

Rep Rib Rnd 4 more times.
Break CC.
Join MC.
Knit 1 rnd.
Work Rib Rnd 5 times.

BODY OF HAT

Switch to larger needles.
Knit 1 rnd.
Begin Chart A, reading all rows from right to left as for working in the rnd, joining CC as required. Work [Rows 1–33] 1 time (chart is worked 1 time across each rnd). As you work Rnd 33, place a marker every 9th stitch to prepare for the crown shaping. When chart is complete, break CC. The remainder of the hat is worked with MC only.

CROWN SHAPING

Rnd 1 (dec): *Ssk, k5, k2tog, sm; rep from * to end of rnd—70 sts.
Rnd 2 (dec): *Ssk, k3, k2tog, sm; rep from * to end of rnd—50 sts.
Rnd 3 (dec): *Ssk, k1, k2tog, sm; rep from * to end of rnd—30 sts.
Rnd 4 (dec): *Sk2p; rep from * to end of rnd—10 sts.

Break yarn, leaving a 6 in. / 15 cm tail. Pull tail through remaining live sts and cinch closed. Secure tails to WS.

FINISHING

Weave in all ends and block to measurements. Allow to dry completely. Trim all ends.

POM-POM

Using both yarns, make pom-pom and attach to crown. If you do not want your pom-pom to be removable, attach finished pom-pom directly to your hat and weave in the ends.

TO MAKE YOUR POM-POM REMOVABLE (OPTIONAL):

Step 1: Tie one strand of yarn very tight after cutting around the pom-pom maker to secure all the strands but do not remove the pom-pom maker.
Step 2: Using your crochet hook and MC, chain a 16 in. / 40.5 cm length; break yarn.
Step 3: Tie the chain around the pom-pom; now remove the pom-pom maker.
Step 4: Fluff and trim your pom-pom.
Step 5: Attach one aglet to each end of the chain using your needle-nose pliers. Feed the ends through the top of the hat and tie a bow. You can now attach and remove the pom-pom easily for washing purposes.

Coffee Talk

When the cast gathered to shoot the promotional poster for Season 1 of *Gilmore Girls*, they were dressed for winter. Actress Melissa McCarthy revealed, "Someone passed out, like just out cold because we were all in coats and trying to look blustery."

CHART A

90 89 88 87 86 85 84 83 82 81 80 79 78 77 76 75 74 73 72 71 70 69 68 67 66 65 64 63 62 61 60 59 58 57 56 55 54 53 52 51 50 49 48 47 46 45 44 43 42 41

33
32
31
30
29
28
27
26
25
24
23
22
21
20
19
18
17
16
15
14
13
12
11
10
9
8
7
6
5
4
3
2
1

87 86 85 87 86 85 84 83 82 81 80 79 78 77 76 75 74 73 72 71 70 69 68 67 66 65 64 63 62 61 60 59 58 57 56 55 54 53 52 51 50 49 48 47 46 45 44 43 42 41

KEY

☐ knit
■ MC
☐ CC

34

CHART B

Jackson's Skullcap

Designed by Tanis Gray
SKILL LEVEL: EASY

> Sookie: "A zucchini tush?"
>
> Jackson: "Just a temporary name."
>
> Sookie: "You want me to serve my customers a genetically engineered vegetable that's named after a butt?"
>
> —*Gilmore Girls*, Season 1, Episode 11

In a part that was created for him "out of thin air," actor Jackson Douglas's role as farmer and produce supplier for the Independence and Dragonfly Inn, Jackson Belleville, was never meant to last more than a few episodes. He was married at the time to the original Sookie—Alex Borstein, who had worked with creator Amy Sherman-Palladino's husband, Dan, doing voiceover work for *Family Guy*. Sherman-Palladino created the role for Douglas, saying, "Oh, I'll write a part for you." Douglas recalls, "I was just gonna be the vegetable guy—just be some comic relief," but when working opposite Melissa McCarthy, it was clear they had excellent on-screen chemistry. A short character arc suddenly turned into a 57-epsiode run on the popular series, with his character eventually becoming Sookie's husband, a father, and the town selectman of Stars Hollow.

Heading out to sleep with the zucchinis? Don't forget to grab your hat! Begun at the apex, this classically Jackson skullcap is worked from the top down in the round. Lifted increases are worked to expand the circumference at four points, then the brim is worked on smaller needles and folded over twice.

SIZES
One size; fits most adult heads

FINISHED MEASUREMENTS
Circumference: 21¾ in. / 55 cm
Height: 10 in. / 25.5 cm (unrolled)

YARN
DK weight yarn, shown in SweetGeorgia *Mohair Silk DK* (12-ply; 90% superwash merino, 5% super kid mohair, 5% silk; 218 yd. / 200 m per 3½ oz. / 100 g hank) in color Winter Haven, 1 hank

NEEDLES
US 4 / 3.5 mm, 16 in. / 40 cm long circular needle
US 6 / 4 mm, 16 in. / 40 cm long circular needle and set of 5 double-pointed needles or size needed to obtain gauge

NOTIONS
Stitch markers (5; 1 unique for BOR)
Tapestry needle

GAUGE
22 sts and 26 rnds = 4 in. / 10 cm in St st in the round on larger needles, taken after blocking
Make sure to check your gauge.

PATTERN NOTES
- Hat is worked in the round from the top down, beginning with dpns.
- Lifted increases are worked to expand the circumference of the hat. As the circumference of the crown increases, change to a circular needle for comfort.
- A brim is worked at the end using smaller needles. The brim is folded over twice.

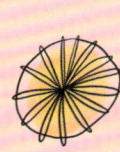

CAST ON & SETUP

CO 8 sts using the Circular cast on method. Divide sts evenly over 4 dpns, 2 sts per needle. Pm for BOR and join to work in the rnd, being careful not to twist the sts.

Setup Rnd: K1, pm, (k2, pm) 3 times, k1 (4 markers have been placed: one between the 2 sts on each dpn; the BOR marker remains between needles 1 and 4).

CROWN SHAPING

Rnd 1 (inc): *RLI, k1, sm, k1, LLI; rep from * to end of rnd—16 sts.
Rnd 2: Knit.
Rnd 3 (inc): *Knit to 1 st before M, RLI, k1, sm, k1, LL1; rep from * 3 more times, knit to end of rnd— 8 sts inc.
Rep [Rnds 2–3] 12 more times— 120 sts total; 30 sts on each dpn.

BODY OF HAT

Remove all markers except BOR M.
Cont in St st with no more increases until the hat measures 6 in. / 15 cm from the center top.

BRIM

Change to smaller needles.
Cont in St st for 4 in. / 10 cm.
BO all sts knitwise.

FINISHING

Weave in all ends to WS.
Fold brim up 2 in. / 5 cm, then another 1 in. / 2.5 cm to create a double folded brim.
Block lightly.

Coffee Talk

Actress Melissa McCarthy's Sookie St. James had two children, Davey and Martha, with Jackson Belleville during the first six seasons of the *Gilmore Girls*. When the actress got pregnant in real life for the first time during Season 7, it was written into the script as Sookie and Jackson's third child.

Chapter 2

Oy with the Cowls and Scarves... and More!

"Oy with the Poodles Already" Cowl

Designed by Jen Immer

SKILL LEVEL: INTERMEDIATE

> Dean: "So, it's a show?"
> Rory: "It's a lifestyle."
> Lorelai: "It's a religion."
> —*Gilmore Girls*, Season 1, Episode 14

One page of a standard television series script equates to roughly 60 seconds of speaking, but a *Gilmore Girls* script page covered only half that time, with an average scene page clocking in 20 to 25 seconds' worth of dialogue. At 65 to 80 pages long, each script was packed with pop culture references and a plethora of quotable lines. To help the cast meet the expectations of the show's tagline of "Life's short, talk fast," dialogue coach George Bell was brought in from Seasons 3 through 7. Creator and writer Amy Sherman-Palladino insisted the actors memorize each scene word for word with no improvising. Bell's job was to help the actors "*Gilmore*-ize," or speed up, what they had to say. He reveals, "What amazed me about Lauren is that she . . . would come to work without having even looked at the lines, but she could process it. She must have had a photographic memory or something. She was so quick with learning the lines."

Begun with a provisional or temporary cast on, this cowl is worked in stranded colorwork as a tube, then grafted together at the end with no visible wrong side. Sassy purple poodles parade across, with one of the show's most iconic lines, "Oy with the poodles already!" emblazoned across.

SIZES
One size

FINISHED MEASUREMENTS
Circumference: 31 in. / 79 cm
Height: 7 in. / 18 cm

YARN
DK weight yarn, shown in Teal Torch Knits *TTK DK* (80% U.S. superwash merino, 20% Cashstyle nylon; 245 yd. / 224 m per 3½ oz. / 100 g hank)

COLORWAYS
Main Color (MC): Afternoon Tea, 1 hank
Contrast Color (CC): Good 'til the Last Drop, 1 hank

NEEDLES
Two US 4 / 3.5 mm, 12 in. / 30 cm long circular needles or size needed to obtain gauge

NOTIONS
US size F-5 / 3.75 mm crochet hook for provisional cast on
Stitch marker
Tapestry needle
Smooth DK weight waste yarn

GAUGE
23 sts and 23 rows = 4 in. / 10 cm in stranded colorwork in the round, taken after steam blocking
Make sure to check your gauge.

PATTERN NOTES
- This cowl is worked in the round, as a tube.
- The project begins with a provisional cast-on and is worked in the round following the colorwork chart.
- Once the chart is complete, the tube is grafted closed for a seamless appearance.

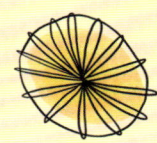
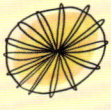

PROVISIONAL CAST ON

Using waste yarn, CO 80 sts using the Crochet Provisional cast on method. With MC, knit across all the provisionally cast on sts. Pm for BOR and join to work in the rnd, being careful not to twist the sts.

BODY

Begin Chart A, reading all rows from right to left as for working in the rnd, joining CC as necessary. Work Rows 1–60 once, then work Rows [61–75] 8 times total.

Leave the live sts on the working needle.

Break CC, leaving a tail for weaving in; break MC, leaving a 60 in. / 152.5 cm tail for grafting the cowl closed.

GRAFTING

Carefully remove the waste yarn at the cast on edge, placing each live stitch onto the second circular needle.

Bring the two ends of the tube together with the needle tips pointing in the same direction (to the right). There will be 80 sts on each needle.

Thread the tapestry needle with the long tail of MC yarn and graft the two sets of sts together.

FINISHING

Weave the ends into the hollow between the layers of the cowl.
Steam block your cowl (if desired).

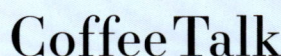

Coffee Talk

Episodes with town hall meetings would take over 20 hours to film. Because there were so many characters, multiple angles, and close-up dialogue shots that were needed, the cast would pass the time by making up games, like trying to guess what was inside Sally Struthers's character Babette Dell's purse.

Work [Rows 61–75] 8 times total.

CHART A

KEY

☐ knit

☐ MC

■ CC

▭ Pattern repeat

45

Minutemen Scarf & Fingerless Mitts

Designed by Jen Immer

SKILL LEVEL: INTERMEDIATE

Lane: "I did something really stupid today."
Lorelai: "Okay, what'd you pierce?"
Lane: "Nothing. I touched a boy's hair."

—*Gilmore Girls*, Season 1, Episode 8

While viewers only get the occasional glance inside Stars Hollow High, it remains an important location for many of the younger characters throughout the show. Before leaving for Chilton, Rory meets Dean for the first time in the hallway, and he continues his high school career there, playing on the hockey team until graduation. Rory's best friend Lane is secretly on the cheerleading squad—and her boyfriend Jess also attends the school when he bothers to shows up. Once Rory leaves for private school, she loses touch with much of the goings-on at Stars Hollow High. Between homework and spending much of her free time with Dean, she fails to be there for her best friend Lane and her "soulmate" crush. When Lane experiences extreme embarrassment at not being able to control herself by running her fingers through Rich's hair without permission, and Rory gets snowed in at her grandparents' house with no phone connection to talk her friend through it, the best friends realize they need to reconnect.

This fingerless mitt and matching scarf set has spirit! Cheer on Stars Hollow High with these fingerless mitts knit in the round starting with the bottom twisted rib cuff. Stranded colorwork stripes on the palm side and an "M" for Minutemen on the hand allow the wearer to wave their hands in support. An afterthought thumb is worked at the end. The accompanying scarf is worked as a tube in one piece with matching stranded colorwork motifs. The ends are closed with cheery tassels. Go Minutemen!

SIZES
Scarf
One size

Fingerless Mitts
Small (Medium, Large)

FINISHED MEASUREMENTS
Scarf
Length: 56 in. / 142 cm
(not including tassels)
Width: 6 in. / 15 cm

Fingerless Mitts
Circumference: 7 (7¾ 8½) in. /
18 (19.5, 21.5) cm
Length: 5½ (6, 6¾) in. / 14 (15, 17) cm

YARN
Fingering weight yarn, shown in Oink Pigments *Nimbus* (3-ply; 80% fine superwash merino, 10% cashmere, 10% nylon; 410 yd. / 375 m per 3½ oz. / 100 g hank)

Scarf
Main Color (MC): Redrum, 2 hanks
Contrast Color (CC): Birthday Suit, 1 hank

Fingerless Mitts
Main Color (MC): Redrum, 1 hank
Contrast Color (CC): Birthday Suit, 1 hank

NEEDLES
Scarf
US 2 / 2.75 mm, 12 in. / 30 cm long circular needles or size needed to obtain gauge

Fingerless Mitts
US 1 / 2.25 mm, 40 in. / 80 cm long circular needles *or* set of 5 dpns or size needed to obtain gauge

NOTIONS
Stitch marker
Tapestry needle
US size G-7 / 4.5 mm crochet hook (scarf only)
Smooth fingering weight waste yarn (fingerless mitts only)

Continued on page 48

GAUGE

Scarf
28 sts and 28 rows = 4 in. / 10 cm over stranded colorwork in the round, taken after steam blocking

Fingerless Mitts
Small: 34 sts and 42 rows = 4 in. / 10 cm over stranded colorwork in the round, taken after steam blocking

Medium: 31 sts and 38 rows = 4 in. / 10 cm over stranded colorwork in the round, taken after steam blocking

Large: 28 sts and 34.5 rows = 4 in. / 10 cm over stranded colorwork in the round, taken after steam blocking

Make sure to check your gauge.

PATTERN NOTES

Scarf
- This scarf is knit in the round as a tube.
- Alternating stripes of MC and CC are worked on either side of a colorwork chart that is mirrored at each end.
- When working the stripes at each end of the chart, carry the unused yarn loosely up the inside of the scarf to save on yardage and ends to weave in. Break yarn only when instructed.
- When working the MC-only length of the scarf (between Charts A and B), if you are using hand-dyed yarns, you may wish to alternate skeins.
- The tube will be closed at each end by attaching tassels.

Fingerless Mitts
- To honor the original design of these fingerless mitts and ensure a wider range of available fit, rather than compromise on the stitch pattern, these mitts have been graded using different gauges for each size. To achieve the gauge for your finished size of mitts, adjust your needle size as needed.
- The mitts are worked in the round from the bottom up using stranded knitting. Most of the pattern is charted; written instructions are not provided for colorwork or thumb shaping.
- The mitts can be worked using a long circular needle for the Magic Loop method or dpns. If using the Magic Loop method, divide the sts evenly over 2 needle tips; if using dpns, divide the sts evenly over 4 needles.
- Increases indicated on the chart create shaping for the thumb. Thumb stitches are then placed on waste yarn to be picked up and finished later.
- When knitting the colorwork, catch floats longer than 5 stitches.

SCARF

CAST ON

Using MC, CO 84 sts using the Long Tail cast on method. Pm for BOR and join to work in the rnd, being careful not to twist the sts.

With MC, knit 7 rnds.
Join CC.
With CC, knit 3 rnds.
With MC, knit 3 rnds.
With CC, knit 3 rnds.

BODY— FIRST CHART

Begin Chart A, reading all rows from right to left as for working in the rnd. Work Rows 1–37 once (chart is worked 2 times across each rnd).

With CC, knit 3 rnds.
With MC, knit 3 rnds.
With CC, knit 3 rnds.
Once complete, break CC yarn.
Cont in St st with MC only until the scarf measures approx. 38.5 in. / 98 cm from the end of the most recent CC stripe.
Join CC.
With CC, knit 3 rnds.
With MC, knit 3 rnds.
With CC, knit 3 rnds.

BODY— SECOND CHART

Begin Chart B, reading all rows from right to left as for working in the rnd, joining CC as necessary. Work Rows 1–37 once (chart is worked 2 times across each rnd).

With CC, knit 3 rnds.
With MC, knit 3 rnds.
With CC, knit 3 rnds. Break CC.
With MC, knit 7 rnds.
BO all sts loosely knitwise.

FINISHING

Weave in all loose ends to the WS / inside of the tube.
Steam block your scarf (if desired). Complete all blocking before attaching the tassels.

ADDING TASSELS

Cut fifty-four 10 in. / 25.5 cm lengths of MC yarn.
Placing the first tassel in the 2nd stitch in from the edge, and every 5th stitch after, make and place tassels as follows:
*Holding 3 strands together, fold in half. Using the crochet hook, pull the loop of the folded strands through the edge of the scarf (making sure the two edges are held together to close the scarf end). Pass the 6 tails (2 from each folded strand) through the loop and cinch down to complete 1 section of fringe.
Rep from * until 9 evenly spaced tassels have been placed along one edge.
Repeat the above instructions from * at the other end of the scarf.
Trim all tassel ends to the same length if desired.

FINGERLESS MITTS

CAST ON & RIBBED EDGE— BOTH MITTS

With MC, CO 60 sts using the Long Tail cast on method. Pm for BOR (if desired) and join to work in the rnd, being careful not to twist the sts.
Rib Rnd: *K1tbl, p1; rep from * to end of rnd.
Rep [Rib Rnd] 9 more times (10 rnds total).

FIRST MITT

Begin Left Mitt Chart, reading all rows from right to left as for working in the rnd, joining CC as required.
Work Rows 1–29 once—81 sts at completion.
Rnd 30: Work 30 sts in patt as per Row 30 of chart, place the next 21 thumb sts on waste yarn, work the remaining 30 sts of Row 30 of the chart to end of rnd—60 sts rem.
Work Rows 31–42 once.
Break CC. Proceed to Finish Mitt.

SECOND MITT

Begin Right Mitt Chart, reading all rows from right to left as for working in the rnd, joining CC as required.
Work Rows 1–29 once—81 sts at completion.
Rnd 30: Work 30 sts in patt as per Row 30 of chart, place the next 21 thumb sts on waste yarn, work the remaining 30 sts of Row 30 of the chart to end of rnd—60 sts rem.
Work Rows 31–42 once.
Break CC. Proceed to Finish Mitt.

FINISH MITT— BOTH MITTS

Rib Rnd: *K1tbl, p1; rep from * to end of rnd.
Rep [Rib Rnd] 5 more times (6 rnds total).
BO all sts loosely in patt.

THUMB— BOTH MITTS

Carefully remove waste yarn and place 21 live sts on the needles, distributing sts for comfort.
Rejoin MC yarn to the right edge of the gap between the needles at the inside edge of the thumb hole. Pick up and knit 5 sts across the gap— 26 sts. Pm for BOR (if desired) and join to work in the rnd.
Rib Rnd: *K1tbl, p1; rep from * to end of rnd.
Rep [Rib Rnd] 5 more times (6 rnds total).
BO all sts loosely in patt.

FINISHING

Weave in all ends and steam block. Allow to dry completely. Trim all ends.

Coffee Talk

The name of the show, *Gilmore Girls*, was inspired by the Gilmore Bank in Los Angeles and was briefly changed to *The Gilmore Way* in order to be more inclusive to encompass all the townspeople and focus less on Lorelai and Rory, before being changed back.

SCARF CHART A

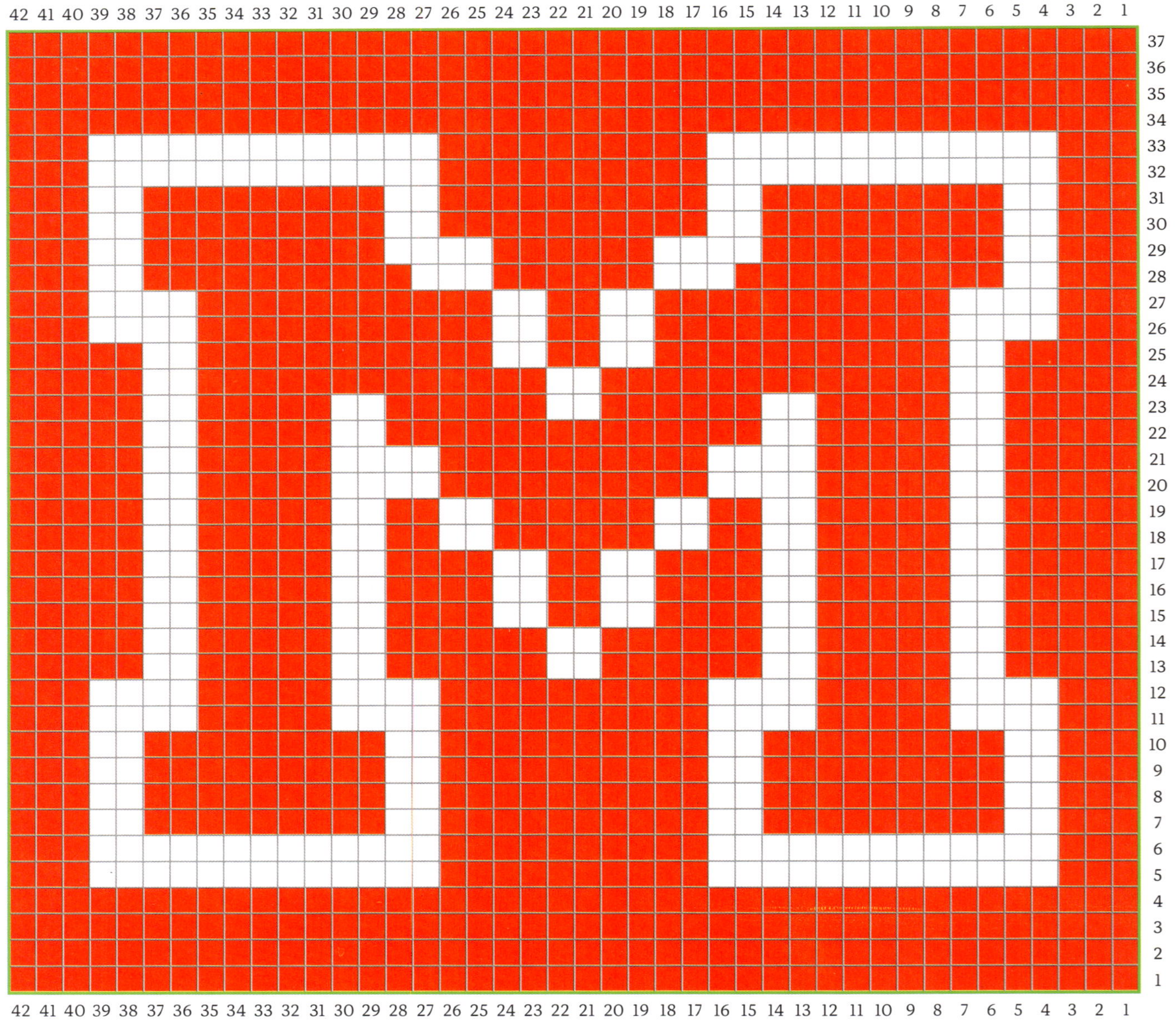

KEY

- ☐ knit
- ▨ No stitch
- ▥ MC
- ☐ CC
- ◥ M1L
- ◤ M1R
- ▢ Pattern repeat
- — Place sts below on waste yarn

SCARF CHART B

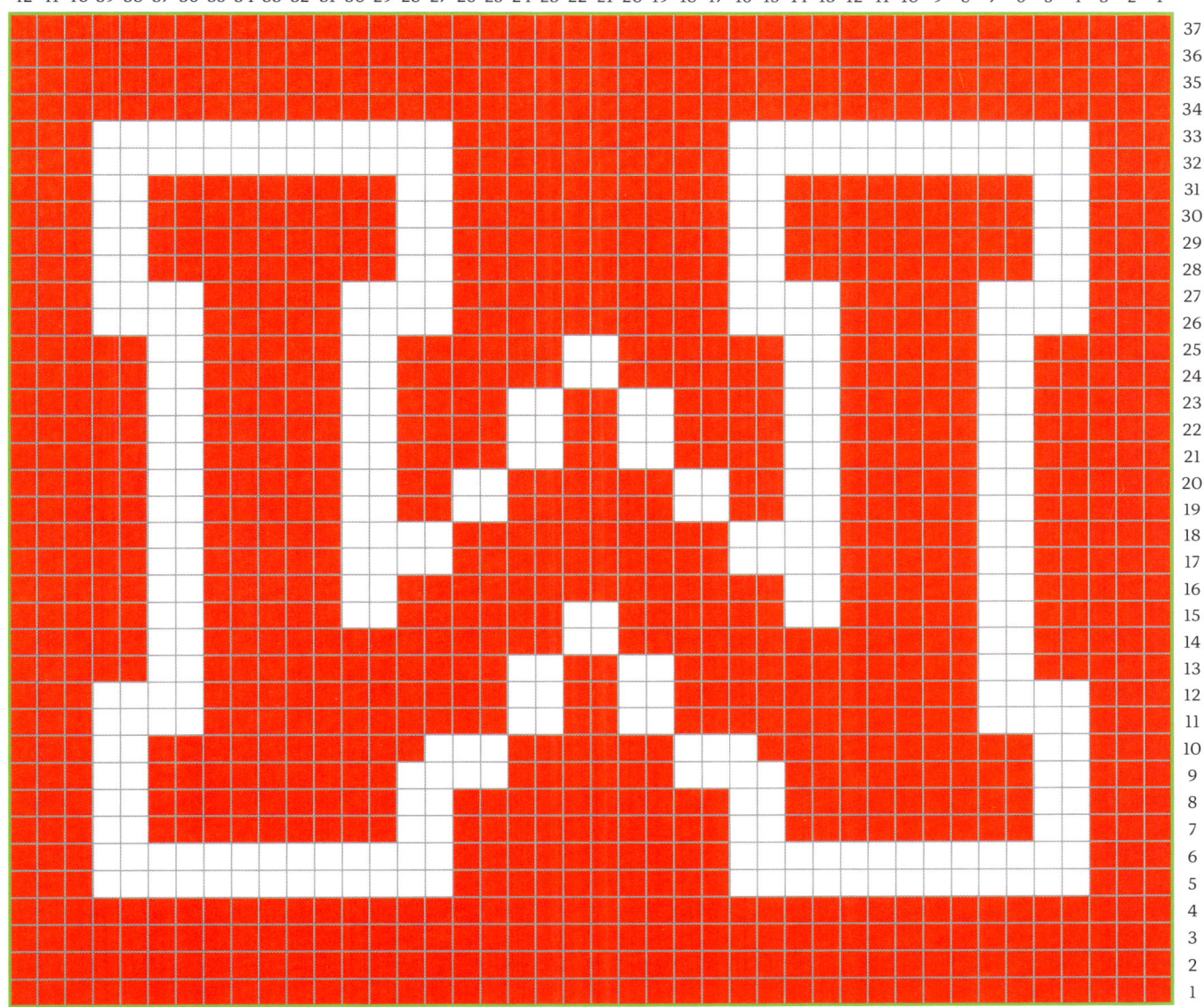

LEFT MITT CHART

KEY

- knit
- No stitch
- MC
- CC
- M1L
- M1R
- Pattern repeat
- Place sts below on waste yarn

55

RIGHT MITT CHART

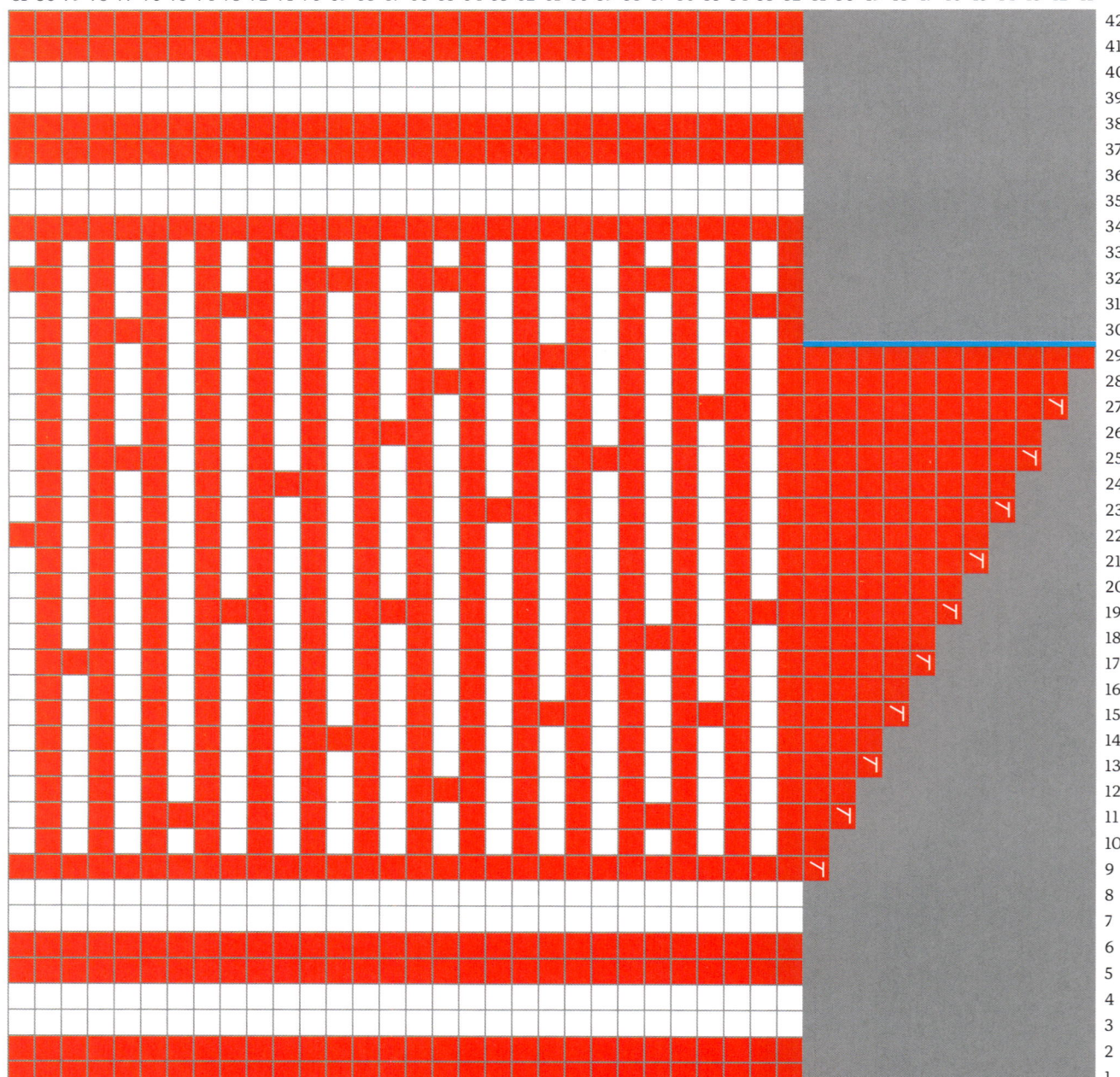

KEY

- knit
- No stitch
- MC
- CC
- M1L
- M1R
- Pattern repeat
- Place sts below on waste yarn

Rory's Prep School Cowl

Designed by Carissa Browning

SKILL LEVEL: INTERMEDIATE

"You may have been the smartest girl in Stars Hollow, but this is a different place. The pressures are greater, the rules are stricter, and the expectations are higher."

—Headmaster Charleston, Season 1, Episode 2

Chilton Prep School is the catalyst for bringing together the Gilmore family—estranged for years after Lorelai skipped town with her infant daughter at sixteen years old. Determined to ensure her intelligent daughter gets a spot at the coveted co-ed, plaid uniform–wearing private school Chilton, Lorelai visits her parents in Hartford to ask for a loan for the tuition. The loan agreements include regular Friday night dinners and a weekly phone call with updates about both Rory's and Lorelai's lives. While scary and overwhelming at first, it's at Chilton that Rory begins to hone her talent as a writer for *The Franklin* newspaper, embarks on her roller-coaster friendship with Paris, (almost) joins the secret society, meets her future almost-stepfather, Max Medina, and goes on to eventually become valedictorian.

Plaid fabric within the confines of a knitted construction can have its limitations but also its advantages, like reversibility! This cowl is worked in the round using double knitting to create a double-layered, double-sided fabric with different plaid patterns on each face. Although three colors are used in this multisized project, each individual round uses only two colors at a time, making it easier than it looks!

SIZES
Small (Large)

FINISHED MEASUREMENTS
Circumference: 21 (42) in. / 53.5 (107) cm
Height: 9¾ in. / 25 cm

YARN
DK weight yarn, shown in Fiber Seed *Sprout DK* (3-ply; 90% superwash merino wool, 10% nylon; 250 yd / 229 m per 3½ oz. / 100 g hank)

COLORWAYS
Color A: Navy, 1 hank
Color B: Blue Bird, 1 (2) hank(s)
Color C: Natural, 1 hank
See Pattern Notes for information on selecting colors.

NEEDLES
US 5 / 3.75 mm, 16 (32) in. / 40 (80) cm long circular needle or size needed to obtain gauge

NOTIONS
4 (8) stitch markers (1 unique for BOR)
Tapestry needle

GAUGE
19 sts and 26 rows = 4 in. / 10 cm over double knitting worked in the round, taken after blocking
Make sure to check your gauge.

PATTERN NOTES
- This cowl is worked in the round from the bottom up using double knitting.
- Careful consideration should be given to color choices as the plaid illusion depends on Color B truly looking like a mixture of Colors A and C.
- The original size Large cowl used just less than a full skein of Color A. It is therefore recommended to swatch with Colors B and C for the Large cowl. If you have concerns about running out of Color A due to variances in row gauge, purchase an additional

Continued on page 60

skein of Color A. Size Small can be completed with a single skein of each color.
- You may wish to use a needle 1 or 2 sizes smaller than the gauge-size needle for the Italian cast on, then change to the main needle size for the remainder of the cowl.
- Written instructions are provided for the entirety of the cowl.
- Although this is a 3-color double knitting pattern, only 2 colors are used at a time.

CAST ON & SETUP

Using Two-Color Italian cast on method and alternating knit sts in Color B and purl sts in Color A, CO 200 (400) sts, turn.

Setup Row 1 (RS): *KApB 10 times, kBpA, kApB 2 times, kBpA 3 times, kApB 3 times, kBpA 3 times, kApB 2 times, kBpA, pm; rep from * to end of row, do not turn.

Pm for BOR and join to work in the rnd, being careful not to twist the sts.

PLAID PATTERN

Patt Rnd 1: *KApB 10 times, kBpA, kApB 2 times, kBpA 3 times, kApB 3 times, kBpA 3 times, kApB 2 times, kBpA, sm; rep from * to end of rnd.

Patt Rnds 2–6: Rep [Patt Rnd 1] 5 more times.

Join Color C, but do not cut Colors A and B. Allow Color A to hang to back of work.

Patt Rnd 7: *KBpC 10 times, kCpB, kBpC 2 times, kCpB 3 times, kBpC 3 times, kCpB 3 times, kBpC 2 times, kCpB, sm; rep from * to end of rnd.

Pick up Color A and allow Color C to hang to back of work.

Patt Rnd 8: Work as for Patt Rnd 1.

Note: When repeating the same Patt Rnd two or more times consecutively, you will want to hide the third (unused) color between the layers of double knitting. To do this, bring Color B under the unused color, and bring the other active color over the unused color before beginning the next repetition of the Patt Rnd.

Patt Rnd 9: Work as for Patt Rnd 1.

Patt Rnds 10–13: Work [Patt Rnd 7] 4 times, hiding Color A between rnds.

Patt Rnds 14–17: Work [Patt Rnd 1] 4 times, hiding Color C between rnd.

Patt Rnds 18–21: Work [Patt Rnd 7] 4 times, hiding Color A between rnds.

Patt Rnds 22–23: Work [Patt Rnd 1] 2 times, hiding Color C between rnds.

Patt Rnd 24: Work as for Patt Rnd 7.

Patt Rnds 25–30: Work [Patt Rnd 1] 6 times, hiding Color C between rnds.

Rep [Patt Rnds 1–30] 1 more time.

BIND OFF

Break Color C.

Setup Rnd: With Color A only, (k1, sl1 wyif) around, rm as you come to them.

Break Color A.

Cut Color B, leaving a tail approx. 75 (150) in. / 190.5 (381) cm long (or roughly 3.5 times the circumference of the cowl).

Thread the tapestry needle with the Color B long tail and seam the live sts of front and back layers together using the Sewn Tubular bind off method.

FINISHING

Weave in the ends carefully by threading the tapestry needle with the tail and weaving the tail into the hollow of the double knitting. Gently block to measurements.

Coffee Talk

Actor Scott Cohen— who plays Rory's teacher Max Medina, and later, Lorelai's fiancé—was a substitute teacher in Queens, New York, before pursuing acting full time.

"You Jump, I Jump" Beaded Lace Scarf

Designed by Tanis Gray

SKILL LEVEL: ADVANCED

"It'll be fun, it'll be a thrill. Something stupid, something bad for you. Just something different. Isn't this the point of being young? It's your choice, Ace. People can live a hundred years without really living for a minute. You climb up here with me, it's one less minute you haven't lived."

—Logan Huntzberger, Season 5, Episode 7

When Logan Huntzberger first waltzes into Rory's life, she's unimpressed, pegging him as a spoiled, privileged, frat boy type. But he becomes more of a presence when she begins working at the *Yale Daily News* and finds he is also on staff. As he is the heir to his father Mitchum's newspaper empire, Rory begins to empathize with him. Contrary to his upbringing and parents' influence, Logan embraces his wilder side, pulling stunts with the Life and Death Brigade, going on poorly planned adventures with his friends Colin and Finn, and throwing crazy parties. He encourages Rory to explore her less sheltered side, allowing her access to Yale's secret society and participating in one of their biggest stunts yet: leaping off a seven-story-high scaffold with a harness and umbrella while wearing a ball gown and scarf around her neck. Embracing the thrill, Rory tells Logan, "You jump, I jump, Jack."

Made in the traditional Shetland lace style, this beaded lace scarf is worked in two identical pieces, then grafted together at the center to allow the lace to mirror image itself. Begun with garter edges, the scarf showcases lace hearts that move up the body. Beads are added as you go with a small crochet hook. Every other row is purled across, and length can be added or taken away in full repeats. Choose a color to match your favorite ball gown!

SIZES
One size

FINISHED MEASUREMENTS
Width: 9 in. / 23 cm
Length: 92 in. / 234 cm

YARN
Sport weight yarn, shown in Queen City Yarn *Latta Classic* (3-ply; 100% non-superwash merino / Rambouillet wool; 312 yd. / 285 m per 3½ oz. / 100 g hank) in color Cornflower, 3 hanks

NEEDLES
Two US 3 / 2.75 mm, 16 in. / 40 cm long circular needles or size needed to obtain gauge

NOTIONS
US size 14/10 / 0.75 mm crochet hook
140 beads, size 6/0 / 4 mm seed beads in silver-lined sapphire
Stitch markers
Tapestry needle

GAUGE
24.5 sts and 28 rows = 4 in. / 10 cm in lace pattern worked flat, taken after blocking
Make sure to check your gauge.

PATTERN NOTES
- Scarf is worked flat, back and forth in rows.
- Beads are added with a crochet hook as you go—it is recommended that you do not pre-string.
- Scarf is worked in the traditional Shetland lace style, with two identical pieces worked separately and grafted together in the middle so the lace is mirror imaged.
- The lace pattern is charted only. Written instructions are provided for the construction of the scarf.

CAST ON—FIRST HALF

Using the first circular needle, CO 55 sts using the Long Tail cast on method. Do not join to work in the rnd.

Beginning with a RS row, knit 4 rows.

BODY OF SCARF

Begin Chart A, reading all RS (odd-numbered) rows from right to left, and all WS (even-numbered) rows from left to right. Work [Rows 1–32] 10 times (the pattern repeat is worked 2 times across each row).

Do not bind off; break yarn and set aside.

CAST ON—SECOND HALF

Using the second circular needle, CO 55 sts using the Long Tail cast on method. Do not join to work in the rnd.

Beginning with a RS row, knit 4 rows.

BODY OF SCARF

Begin Chart A, reading all RS (odd-numbered) rows from right to left, and all WS (even-numbered) rows from left to right. Work [Rows 1–32] 9 times, then [Rows 1–31] 1 more time (the pattern repeat is worked 2 times across each row).

Do not bind off; leave live sts on the needle. Break yarn, leaving a 36 in. / 91.5 cm tail.

GRAFTING

Bring the two sets of live sts together with the RS facing up; the working yarn should be at the right edge of the work.

Thread the tapestry needle with the long tail from the second half of the scarf and graft the two sets of sts together.

FINISHING

Weave in all ends. Wet block to dimensions.

Coffee Talk

The ball gowns worn by the women in the Life and Death Brigade were originally from Season 2 of the show. Bright white and worn by Rory's fellow debutantes, the gowns were later dyed by key costumer Valerie Campbell in a rainbow of colors for the big stunt in Season 5.

CHART A

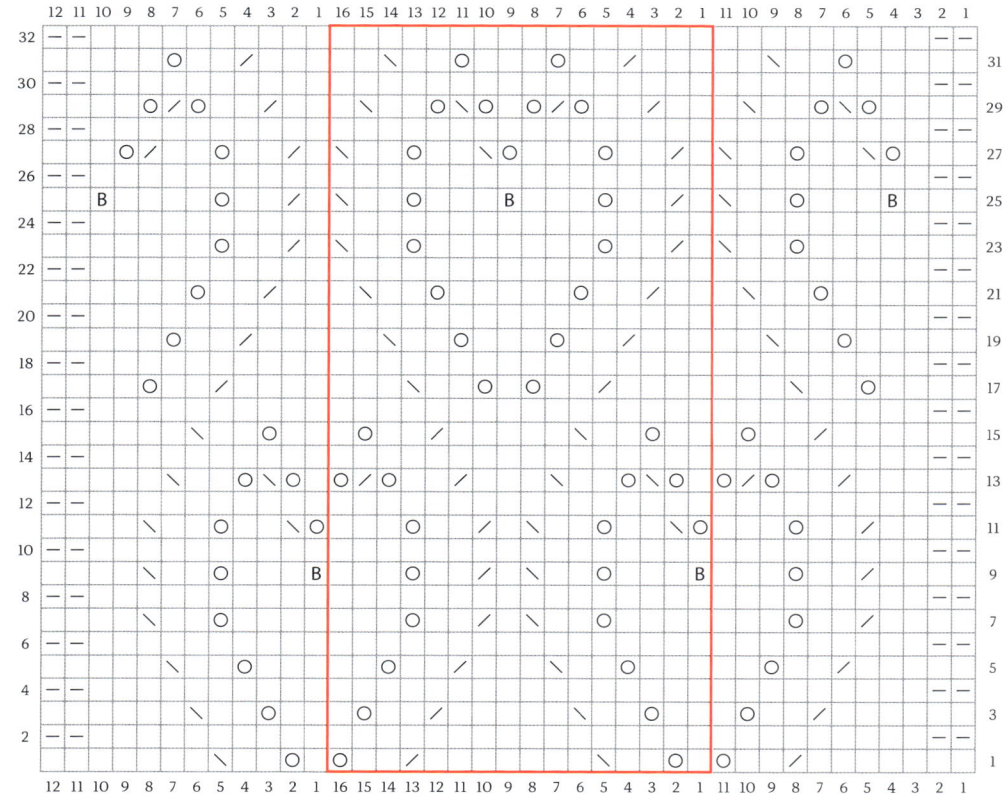

KEY

- ☐ k on RS, p on WS
- – p on RS, k on WS
- B Place bead
- O yo
- ╱ k2tog
- ╲ skp
- ▭ Pattern repeat

65

"If You're Out on the Road" Cowl

Designed by Nicole Coutts
SKILL LEVEL: INTERMEDIATE

"We're almost there, but nowhere near it. All that matters is that we're going."
—LORELAI, Season 2, Episode 4

Across seven seasons and 153 episodes of *Gilmore Girls*, each begins the same way: with the theme song, "Where You Lead," originally written in 1973 by Carole King and featured on her *Tapestry* album. Carole was approached to re-record the song with her daughter for the show. Creator Amy Sherman-Palladino wanted a theme "that felt classic, and you just don't get more classic than Carole King." Even though the original song was written about a woman's love for a man, King and her daughter, Louise Goffin, were happy to change the lyrics to be more empowering for women and give it "a new lease on life." According to the show's creator, "It's the greatest theme song in the entire world."

Nothing makes you ready for a fall binge-watching session of *Gilmore Girls* cozied up on the couch than this crisp autumn cowl. Worked seamlessly in the round, the cowl features stranded colorwork falling leaves that circle around facing different directions, sandwiched by corrugated ribbing. The autumnal palette ebbs in and out, making it a perfect fall wardrobe staple.

SIZES
One size

FINISHED MEASUREMENTS
Circumference: 22 in. / 56 cm
Height: 9¾ in. / 25 cm

YARN
Fingering weight yarn, shown in Jamieson's of Shetland *Spindrift* (2-ply; 100% pure Shetland wool; 115 yd. / 105 m per 1 oz. / 25 g skein)

COLORWAYS
Color A: #880 Coffee, 2 skeins
Color B: #794 Eucalyptus, 1 skein
Color C: #789 Marjoram, 1 skein
Color D: #230 Yellow Ochre, 1 skein
Color E: #478 Amber, 1 skein
Color F: #870 Cocoa, 1 skein

NEEDLES
US 3 / 3.25 mm, 16 in. / 40 cm long circular needle or size needed to obtain gauge

NOTIONS
Stitch marker
Row counter (optional)
Tapestry needle

GAUGE
30 sts and 37 rows = 4 in. / 10 cm over stranded colorwork in the round, taken after blocking
Make sure to check your gauge.

PATTERN NOTES
- This cowl is worked in the round from the bottom up using stranded colorwork for the body of the cowl, and corrugated ribbing at the top and bottom edges.
- When working the corrugated rib, be sure to move the Color A yarn to the back between the needles after completing the purl stitch so all floats are on the WS of the cowl.
- Written instructions are provided for the construction of the cowl. Charts are provided for all colorwork.
- Cut Color B–F yarn between rounds when it is not being worked.

Continued on page 68

CAST ON & BOTTOM EDGE

Using Color A, CO 150 sts using the Long Tail cast on method. Pm for BOR and join to work in the rnd, being careful not to twist the sts.

Begin Chart A, reading all rows from right to left as for working in the rnd, joining and breaking Colors B–F as required. Work Rnds 1–10 once (chart is worked 75 times across each rnd).

Rnd 11 (inc): Using Color A, k6, *k7, kfb; rep from * to end of rnd—168 sts.
Rnd 12: Using Color A, knit.

BODY OF COWL

Begin Chart B, reading all rows from right to left as for working in the rnd, joining and breaking Colors B–F as required. Work [Rnds 1–32] 2 times, then Rnds 1–2 once more (66 rnds total; chart is worked 12 times across each rnd).

TOP EDGE

Setup Rnd 1: Using Color A, knit.
Setup Rnd 2 (dec): Using Color A, k6, *k7, k2tog; rep from * to end of rnd—150 sts rem.

Begin Chart C, reading all rows from right to left as for working in the rnd, joining and breaking Colors B–F as required. Work Rnds 1–10 once (chart is worked 75 times across each rnd).

Using Color A, BO all sts loosely knitwise.

FINISHING

Weave in ends. Wet block to dimensions and allow to dry completely. Trim all ends.

To further smooth and finish the fabric, steam the cowl, if desired.

Coffee Talk

Real-life friends Carole King and Amy Sherman-Palladino worked together on *Gilmore Girls* for more than just the theme song. King was cast as Sophie Bloom, the Stars Hollow music store owner, a character instrumental in Lane Kim's journey to becoming a drummer.

CHART A

CHART B

CHART C

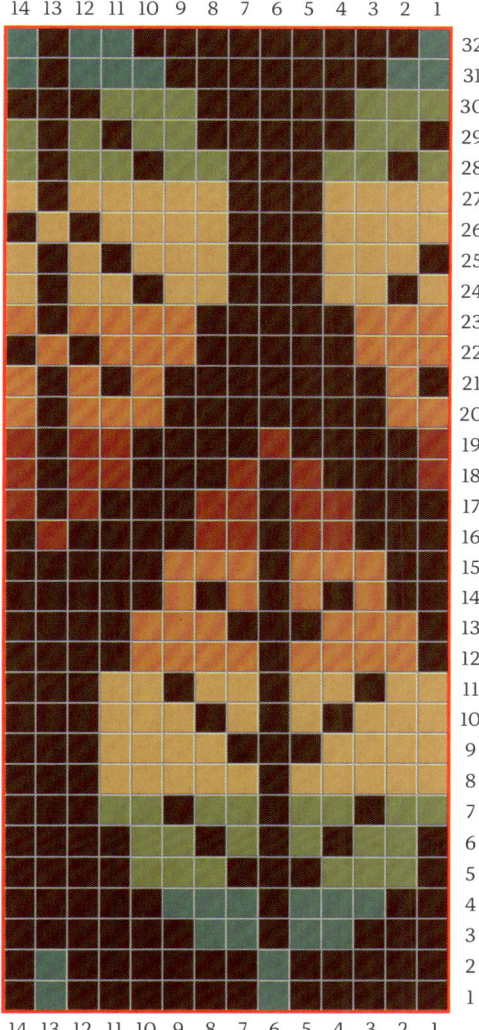

KEY

☐ knit
− purl
■ Color A
■ Color B
■ Color C
■ Color D
■ Color E
■ Color F
▭ Pattern repeat

Stars Hollow Scarf

Designed by Jenny Noto
SKILL LEVEL: ADVANCED

"This is Stars Hollow. You take three left turns and you're back in the center of town."
—Luke, Season 2, Episode 5

While still in the early planning stages of *Gilmore Girls*, California native creator Amy Sherman-Palladino traveled to New York with her husband. Wanting to visit Mark Twain's house in Hartford, Connecticut, the two took a drive and stayed at The Mayflower Inn in Washington Depot. Unbeknownst to her, this would be the town that inspired Stars Hollow. She recalls, "We're driving by, and people are slowing down, saying, 'Excuse me, where is the pumpkin patch?' And everything is green, and people are out, and they're talking. And we went to a diner, and everyone knew each other, and someone got up and they walked behind the [counter], and they got their own coffee because the waitress was busy, and I'm, like, 'Is this out of central casting? Who staged this thing for me?'" After spending a day in the town, she had worked out much of the show in her head and began writing the script for the pilot that very evening. She remembers, "If I can make people feel this much of what I felt walking around this fairy town, I thought that would be wonderful."

Twinkle like the stars in Stars Hollow with this elegant beaded stranded colorwork scarf. It's worked in two identical pieces, then grafted in the center so the motif will mirror image. Delicate graphic snowflakes fall gently in each direction with sparkling beads added as you go.

SIZES
One size

FINISHED MEASUREMENTS
Width: 7⅛ in. / 18 cm
Length: 54 in. / 137 cm
The length of scarf may vary due to minor differences in row gauge and the total yardage in your CC skeins.

YARN
Fingering weight yarn, shown in A Whimsical Wood Yarn Co. *Serotonin Sock* (3-ply; 75% extra fine superwash merino, 25% nylon; 463 yd. / 423 m per 3½ oz. / 100 g hank)

COLORWAYS
Main Color (MC): Coal Dust, 1 hank
Contrast Color (CC): Lush Lavender, 1 hank

NEEDLES
US 4 / 3.5 mm, 16 in. / 40 cm long circular or size needed to obtain gauge
US 6 / 4 mm, 16 in. / 40 cm long circular needle

NOTIONS
1 spare gauge-size or smaller 16 in. / 40 cm long circular needle
Stitch markers (6; 1 unique for BOR)
Row counter (optional)
Tapestry needle
US 12 / 1.00 mm crochet hook
180 beads, size 6/0 / 4 mm seed beads, color of your choosing
Scale that weighs in grams

GAUGE
27 sts and 32 rows = 4 in. / 10 cm over St st worked in the round on smaller needles, taken after steam blocking
Make sure to check your gauge.

PATTERN NOTES
- This tubular scarf is worked in the round from the cast on edge to the center, twice, then grafted together for a seamless finish.

Continued on page 72

- Use MC yarn to swatch for your project. This will allow you to maximize the use of the CC yarn for the length of the scarf.
- Weigh your CC yarn before starting. As you work the 1-color CC sections of the scarf, periodically weigh your skein before you start a round, and after you complete a round, to determine how much weight you need to complete 1 full round. This will help maximize the length of your scarf.
- When transitioning between 1-color stockinette stitch and the stranded colorwork, adjust needle size as necessary to maintain gauge. The original design used a needle 2 sizes larger than the gauge-size needle to maintain gauge.
- This pattern includes both written and charted instructions. The stranded colorwork portion of the scarf is charted only.

BEFORE YOU CAST ON

Weigh both skeins of yarn in grams and write down their weights.

CAST ON— FIRST HALF

Using the smaller needle and MC, CO 96 sts using the Cable cast on method. Do not join to work in the round.

Setup Row (RS): Knit.

Pm for BOR and join to work in the rnd, being careful not to twist the sts.

BODY OF SCARF

Rnds 1–59: Knit.

Rnd 60: *K16, pm; rep from * to end of rnd (the final M will be the existing BOR M).

Switch to larger needle, if necessary, to maintain gauge.

Begin Chart A, reading all rows from right to left as for working in the round, joining CC as necessary. Work Rnds 1–39 once (chart is worked 6 times across each rnd). Once complete, break MC and change back to smaller needle (if necessary).

Cont in St st until you have used almost half of the CC yarn.

Break CC yarn, leaving a 6 in. / 15 cm tail for weaving in. It may be helpful to make a note about how many CC rows you worked beyond the chart so the Second Half will match.

Transfer all live sts to the spare 16 in. / 40 cm circular needle.

CAST ON— SECOND HALF

Work as for the First Half, leaving the live sts on the working needle. Leave a tail of CC yarn approx. 42 in. / 106.5 cm long (or approx. 3 times the length of the circumference of your scarf) for grafting.

GRAFTING

Bring the two sets of live sts together with the needle tips pointing in the same direction (to the right). There will be 96 sts on each needle.

Thread the tapestry needle with the long tail of CC yarn and graft the two sets of sts together.

FINISHING

Weave in all ends. Steam block flat to relax the sts, straighten the edges, and adjust beads.

Coffee Talk

The Hickory Stick Bookshop in Washington Depot, Connecticut, has a section of books with "Rory Reads," including many of the tomes Rory reads in the show, as well as *Gilmore Girls*–inspired books on display.

CHART A

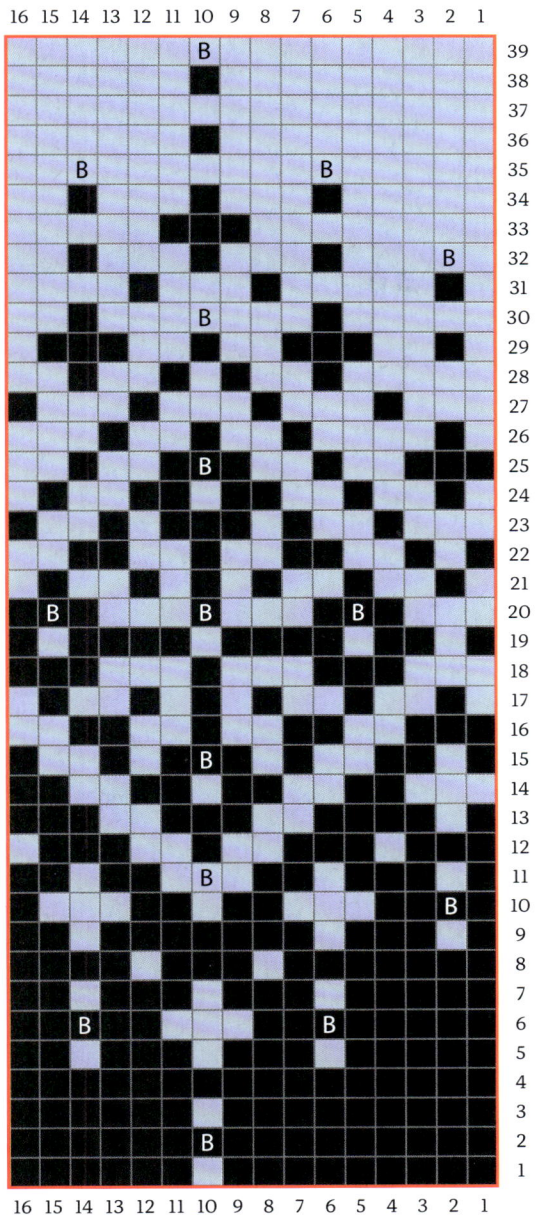

KEY

- ☐ knit
- ■ MC
- ░ CC
- B Place bead
- ▭ Pattern repeat

SCHEMATIC

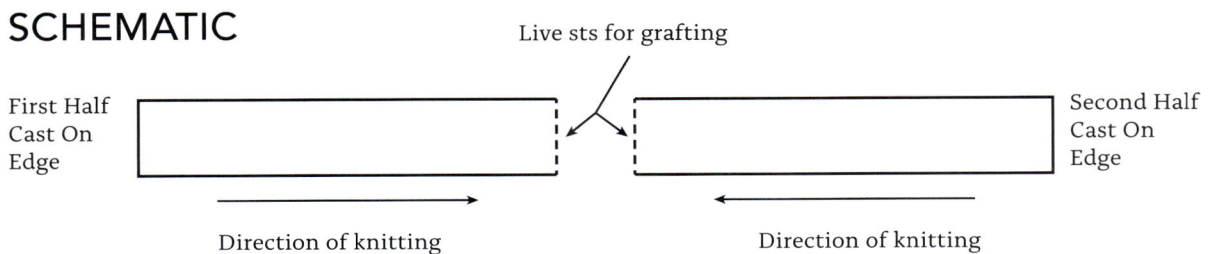

A Thousand Yellow Daisies Cowl

Designed by Beth Leath
SKILL LEVEL: INTERMEDIATE

"I woke up this morning and I realized that I studied and taught the great literature all my life. And those stories are replete with characters that let opportunities slip by, but what I teach is more than literature, it's lessons in life."

—Max, Season 1 Episode 21

When writing the Max Medina proposal scene for the finale of Season 1 of *Gilmore Girls*, creator and writer Amy Sherman-Palladino put a lot of thought into which flower they would use. She said, "It wouldn't be roses. Daisies are such a hardy, everyday-Joe kind of flower, a flower you can really get behind. A blue-collar flower. We didn't want it to be daffodils, or something sort of wispy and too Jane Austen-y. We wanted it to be something really real. I think we wiped out yellow daisies on the West Coast." Despite 1,000 yellow daisies sounding like a lot of flowers, they didn't have the visual impact needed on-screen. Production designer Sandy Veneziano said, "We cheated a little bit on some of the shots. We would push the background daisies—if it wasn't a wide shot—further in and put some on apple boxes so they were a little higher and filled the space."

Worked the long way in the round, this large circumference cowl features sections of the daisy stitch flanked by four-stitch cabled columns and sections of reverse stockinette. Created by wrapping the yarn twice around the needle for multiple stitches, then dropping the extra wraps on the following round, the daisy stitch is a beautiful and unique way to symbolize Lorelai and Max's relationship.

SIZES
One size

FINISHED MEASUREMENTS
Circumference: 46 in. / 117 cm
Height: 7½ in. / 19 cm

YARN
DK weight yarn, shown in Urban Girl Yarns *Boston DK* (3-ply; 100% superwash merino wool; 230 yd. / 210 m per 3½ oz / 100 g hank) in color Madam Whistledown, 2 hanks

NEEDLES
US 6 / 4 mm, 32 in. / 80 cm long circular needle or size needed to obtain gauge

NOTIONS
Stitch marker
Cable needle
Row counter
Tapestry needle

GAUGE
24 sts and 32 rows = 4 in. / 10 cm over Daisy Stitch pattern worked in the round, taken after blocking
Make sure to check your gauge.

PATTERN NOTES
- This cowl is worked in the round from the bottom up.
- The pattern repeat is a multiple of 35 stitches; to increase or decrease the circumference of your cowl, add or subtract stitches in multiples of 35. If you increase the circumference or height of the cowl, you will need more yarn.
- Written instructions are provided for the entirety of the cowl.

PATTERN STITCHES
Daisy Stitch (worked over 5 sts)
Sl5 knitwise to RHN (dropping extra wraps), sl5 purlwise back to LHN (this reorients the direction of your sts), (k1 tbl, yo, k1 tbl, yo, k1 tbl) into all 5 sts together.

Continued on page 76

PATTERN STITCHES FOR SWATCHING

Daisy Stitch Pattern (worked over a multiple of 6 + 1 sts)

Rnd 1: K1, *(k1 wrapping the yarn twice around the needle) 5 times, k1; rep from * to end.
Rnd 2: K1, *Daisy Stitch, k1; rep from * to end.
Rnd 3: K4, *(k1 wrapping the yarn twice around the needle) 5 times, k1; rep from * to last 3 sts, k3.
Rnd 4: K4, *Daisy Stitch, k1; rep from * to last 3 sts, k3.

CAST ON & BOTTOM BORDER

CO 245 sts using the Long Tail cast on method. Pm for BOR and join to work in the rnd, being careful not to twist the sts.

Rnd 1: Knit.
Rnd 2: Purl.
Rep [Rnds 1–2] 2 more times.

BODY OF COWL

Setup Rnd: *P3, k4, p3, k25; rep from * to end of rnd.
Rnd 1: *P3, k4, p3, k1, [(k1 wrapping the yarn twice around the needle) 5 times, k1] 4 times; rep from * to end of rnd.
Rnd 2: *P3, k4, p3, k1, (Daisy Stitch, k1) 4 times; rep from * to end of rnd.
Rnd 3: *P3, 2/2 RC, p3, k4, [(k1 wrapping the yarn twice around the needle) 5 times, k1] 3 times, k3; rep from * to end of rnd.
Rnd 4: *P3, k4, p3, k4, (Daisy Stitch, k1) 3 times, k3; rep from * to end of rnd.
Rep [Rnds 1–4] 7 more times.

TOP BORDER

Rnd 1: Knit.
Rnd 2: Purl.
Rep [Rnds 1–2] 2 more times.
BO all sts using the Icelandic bind off method.

FINISHING

Weave in ends. Wet block to dimensions and allow to dry completely. Trim all ends.

CoffeeTalk

Creator and writer Amy Sherman-Palladino said about Lauren Graham that the 1,000 yellow daisies scene "might have been one of her favorite scenes ever because it's one of the few times she didn't have to say anything."

Richard's Friday Night Dinner Bow Tie

Designed by Tanis Gray

SKILL LEVEL: EASY

"Rory, you're a person of great heart and great character, and that combination will always win the day."
—Richard Gilmore, Season 7, Episode 12

A driving force in both Lorelai and Rory's life, Richard Gilmore—played by Edward Herrmann—is a smartly dressed international insurance consultant, lover of literature, former Whiffenpoof, grandfather, golfer, vintage car lover, and Yale alum. Notwithstanding their difficult past with Lorelai, Richard and Emily savor their Friday night dinners—a by-product of a loan agreement made to pay for Chilton, then later when Rory attends Yale—with their daughter and granddaughter, eager to forge a relationship. These Friday night dinners became an important theme throughout the series, showing the contrast between Lorelai and Rory's relationship, Emily and Lorelai's relationship, and the bond that formed between grandparents and grandchild.

Dress to impress with this simple garter stitch bow tie worked flat back and forth in rows. It's designed to standard bow tie measurements, and the neck size is easily adjustable by adding or removing length in the straight section. Straightforward increases and decreases make this the perfect project for beginner knitters. Stripe it in your alma mater's colors like Richard's version, use a gradient for pizzazz, or keep it effortless with a solid color.

SIZES
One size

FINISHED MEASUREMENTS
Length: 33 in. / 84.5 cm
Width (at widest point): 3¼ in. / 8 cm

YARN
Sport weight yarn, shown in Kim Dyes Yarn *Tartlet Sport Mini* (100% superwash merino; 100 yd. / 91.5 m per mini)

COLORWAYS
Main Color (MC): Starless Night, 1 mini
Contrast Color (CC): Silver Lining, 1 mini

NEEDLES
US 2 / 2.75 mm, 16 in. / 40 cm long circular needles or size needed to obtain gauge

NOTIONS
Locking stitch marker
Tapestry needle

GAUGE
28 sts and 57 rows = 4 in. / 10 cm in garter st worked flat, taken after blocking
Make sure to check your gauge.

PATTERN NOTES
- Bow tie is worked flat, from end to end, in garter stitch. Use a locking stitch marker to differentiate RS from WS.
- As the striping begins, the color used on each row (MC or CC) will be provided in the row indicator. Carry the unused color up the edge of the work.
- The strap section determines the fit of the bow tie. Add or remove length as necessary in this section.

CAST ON & SETUP

With MC, CO 22 sts using the Long Tail cast on method.
Setup Row 1 (WS, MC): Knit.
Setup Row 2 (RS, CC): Knit.
Setup Row 3 (WS, CC): Knit.

FIRST NECK & LEAF

Row 1 (RS, dec, MC): Ssk, knit to last 2 sts, k2tog—2 sts dec.
Row 2 (WS, MC): Knit.
Row 3 (CC): Knit.
Row 4 (CC): Knit across.
Rep [Rows 1–4] 5 more times—10 sts rem.
Row 25 (RS, MC): Knit.
Row 26 (WS, MC): Knit.
Row 27 (CC): Knit.
Row 28 (CC): Knit.
Rep Rows 25–28 once more.
Row 33 (RS, inc, MC): Kfb, knit to last st, kfb—2 sts inc.
Row 34 (WS, MC): Knit.
Row 35 (CC): Knit.
Row 36 (CC): Knit.
Rep [Rows 33–36] 5 more times—22 sts.
Rows 57–64: Work Rows [25–28] 2 times.
Rows 65–96: [Work Rows 1–4] 8 times—6 sts rem.

STRAP

Row 1 (RS, MC): Knit.
Row 2 (WS, MC): Knit.
Row 3 (CC): Knit.
Row 4 (CC): Knit.
Rep Rows 1–4 until the strap measures 19 in. / 48.5 cm, or to desired length, ending with Row 4.

SECOND NECK & LEAF

Row 1 (RS, inc, MC): Kfb, knit to last st, kfb—2 sts inc.
Row 2 (WS, MC): Knit.
Row 3 (CC): Knit.
Row 4 (CC): Knit.
Rep [Rows 1–4] 7 more times—22 sts.
Row 33 (RS, MC): Knit.
Row 34 (WS, MC): Knit.
Row 35 (CC): Knit.
Row 36 (CC): Knit.
Rep Rows 33–36 once more.
Row 41 (RS, dec, MC): Ssk, knit to last 2 sts, k2tog—2 sts dec.
Row 42 (WS, MC): Knit.
Row 43 (CC): Knit.
Row 44 (CC): Knit.
Rep [Rows 41–44] 5 more times—10 sts rem.
Rows 65–72: Work Rows [33–36] 2 times.
Rows 73–92: Work [Rows 1–4] 5 times—20 sts.
Break CC.
Row 93 (RS, Inc, MC): Kfb, knit to last st, kfb—22 sts.
Row 94 (WS, MC): Knit.
With RS facing, BO all sts knitwise.

FINISHING

Weave in all ends and block to measurements.

SCHEMATIC

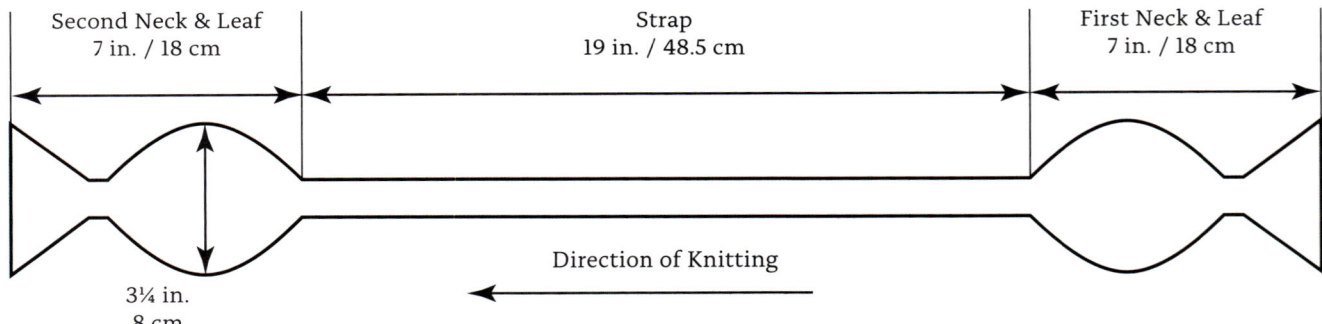

Second Neck & Leaf 7 in. / 18 cm
Strap 19 in. / 48.5 cm
First Neck & Leaf 7 in. / 18 cm
3¼ in. 8 cm
Direction of Knitting

CoffeeTalk

In a 2016 *Vanity Fair* interview, costume designer Brenda Maben told readers that Richard Gilmore had over fifty bow ties in his wardrobe, including one with the Yale logo on it.

Chapter 3

"I'll Leave You to Make Out with Your Socks" and Mitts

Saddle Shoe Socks

Designed by Karen Hickland
SKILL LEVEL: INTERMEDIATE

> "And we get to wear uniforms. No more having people check you out to see what jeans you're wearing 'cause everyone's dressed alike in boring clothes and just there to learn."
>
> —Rory, Season 1, Episode 1

Bringing a character to life is about so much more than casting the perfect actor, writing in their voice, or doing their hair and makeup. Costumes are such an integral part of each character's individuality. Before an episode is filmed, production meetings with the directors, designers, producers, and writers take place to be sure everyone is on the same page regarding character development. *Gilmore Girls* costume designer Brenda Maben says, "It's about matching the clothes to the words," with the show having "racks and racks of clothes for most of these characters." Additional meetings take place with the rest of the wardrobe department to carry that vision across. Key costumer Valerie Campbell states, "The moment the designer hands it off to us, we establish it, we follow the continuity, and when the episode and outfit are done, we put it away and archive it." Some of the actors were allowed to provide input into their costumes, picking and choosing from their character's racks. Some wardrobe choices were difficult, like Rory's handmade blue off-the-shoulder Chilton dance dress (crafted by costume tailor Ian Carter), while some choices were easy, like Rory's plaid Chilton uniform paired with classic saddle shoes.

Worked in the round from the cuff down, these classic saddle shoe ankle socks are the perfect accessory for your next *Gilmore Girls* marathon. They begin with a 2x2 ribbed cuff, and then a German short row heel is followed by short rows to create the saddle, ending with wedge toe shaping and grafting.

SIZES
Small (Medium, Large)

FINISHED MEASUREMENTS
Circumference: 7 (8, 9) in. / 18 (20.5, 23) cm
Designed to be worn with 1 in. / 2.5 cm of negative ease.

YARN
Fingering weight yarn, shown in Emma's Yarn *Practically Perfect Sock* 2-ply (80% superwash merino, 20% nylon; 400 yd. / 366 m per 3½ oz. / 100 g hank)

COLORWAYS
Color A: Whisper, 1 hank
Color B: Navy Blazer, 1 hank
Color C: After Dark, 1 hank

NEEDLES
US 1.5 / 2.5 mm, set of 5 double-pointed needles or size needed to obtain gauge
See Pattern Notes for information about needle alternatives.

NOTIONS
Stitch markers (5)
Row counter (optional)
Tapestry needle

GAUGE
32 sts and 48 rnds = 4 in. / 10 cm in St st in the round, taken after blocking
Make sure to check your gauge.

PATTERN NOTES
- The socks are ankle-height, worked from the cuff down. The foot length is adjustable after the saddle motif is complete.
- As an alternative to dpns, you may use two circulars for the 2 Circular method or a 32 in. / 80 cm long circular needle for the Magic Loop method.

Continued on page 86

- German short rows are used to create the gusset shaping and to shape the saddle motif. When working the short rows, all DS are worked and counted as 1 stitch.
- Slip markers as encountered unless otherwise noted.
- Instructions for size Small are provided first, with instructions for sizes Medium and Large provided in parentheses. When only one set of numbers is provided, it applies to all sizes.

CAST ON & CUFF

Using Color B, CO 56 (64, 72) sts using the Long Tail cast on method. Distribute sts evenly over the needles: If using dpns, you will have 14 (16, 18) sts on each needle; if using 2 circs or Magic Loop, you will have 28 (32, 36) sts on each needle. Pm for BOR and join to work in the rnd, being careful not to twist the sts.
Rnds 1–24: *K2, p2; rep from * to end of rnd.
Break Color B.
Join MC.
Rnds 25–26: Knit.
Rnd 27: Purl.
Remove BOR M. Do not break MC.

SOCK HEEL

HEEL FLAP

Join Color C.
The Heel Flap is worked flat over the last 28 (32, 36) st of the rnd only; the sts for the top of the sock will remain unworked.
Turn the sock so the WS is facing.
Row 1 (WS): Sl1 wyif, purl to end.
Row 2 (RS): *Sl1 wyib, k1; rep from * to end.
Rep [Rows 1–2] 14 (15, 16) more times. There will be 15 (16, 17) slipped sts up each edge of the Heel Flap.

HEEL TURN

Cont to work flat. The provided st counts in this section are for the heel only.
Setup Short Row (WS, dec): Sl1 wyif, p14 (16, 18), p2tog, p1, turn—27 (31, 35) sts rem.
Short Row 1 (RS, dec): Sl1 wyib, k3, ssk, k1, turn—26 (30, 34) sts rem.
Short Row 2 (dec): Sl1 wyif, purl to 1 st before gap, p2tog across the gap, p1, turn—1 st dec.
Short Row 3 (dec): Sl1 wyib, knit to 1 st before gap, ssk across the gap, k1, turn—1 st dec.
Rep [Short Rows 2–3] 4 (5, 6) more times ending with Short Row 3 (all sts have been used). Do not turn after last row—16 (18, 20) sts rem.

GUSSET

Cont to work flat. The provided st counts in this section are for the heel only.
Rotate sock so right edge (as worn) of Heel Flap is up and the sts from the final repeat of Row 3 of the Heel Turns are on the RHN.
Setup Row 1 (RS): Using Color C, pick up and knit tbl 15 (16, 17) sts along the right Heel Flap edge (1 st for each slipped stitch). Turn.
Break Color C.
Resume using MC.
Setup Row 2 (WS): Sl1 wyif, purl to end of row, pick up and purl tbl 15 (16, 17) sts along the left Heel Flap edge (1 st for each slipped stitch). Turn—46 (50, 54) heel sts.
Short Row 1 (RS, dec): Sl1 wyib, knit to last 4 sts, k2tog, k1, turn—45 (49, 53) sts rem.
Short Row 2 (WS, dec): DS, purl to last 4 sts, ssp, p1, turn—44 (48, 52) sts rem.
Short Row 3 (dec): DS, knit to 3 sts before prev DS, k2tog, k1, turn—1 st dec.
Short Row 4 (WS): DS, purl to 3 sts before prev DS, ssp, p1, turn—1 st dec.
Rep [Short Rows 3–4] 7 more times—28 (32, 36) sts rem. There will be 9 DS down the right side of the gusset and 8 DS down the left side of the gusset (as worn).

FOOT

ABOVE SADDLE

Cont with MC.
Setup Row 1 (RS): DS, k4 (5, 6), pm for new BOR. The BOR is at the center of the sole.
Resume working in the rnd.
Setup Rnd 2: Knit, resolving each DS as kDS as encountered.
Rnd 1: K24 (27, 30), pm-A, k8 (10, 12), pm-B, knit to end of rnd.
Rnds 2–9: Knit.

SADDLE SETUP

Begin working flat; cont with MC.
Short Row 1 (RS): Knit to M-A, turn.
Short Row 2 (WS): DS, purl to M-B (passing the BOR M), turn.
Short Row 3: DS, knit to 1 st before prev DS, turn.
Setup Row 4: DS, purl to 1 st before prev DS, turn.
Rep [Short Rows 3–4] 2 more times.
Short Row 9 (RS): DS, knit to BOR.

SADDLE

Resume working in the rnd.
Rnd 1: Knit, resolving each DS as kDS as encountered. Drop MC.
Rnds 2–3: Using Color C, knit.
Rnd 4: *K3 with Color C, k1 with MC; rep from * to end of rnd.
Break MC. Cont with Color C only.
Rnds 5–6: Knit.
Rnd 7: K14 (16, 18), p28 (32, 36), knit to end of rnd.
Rnd 8: Knit.
Begin working flat.
Short Row 9 (RS): Knit to M-B, sm, k1, turn.
Short Row 10 (WS): DS, purl to M-A, sm, p1, turn.
Short Row 11: DS, knit to prev DS, kDS, k2, turn.
Short Row 12: DS, purl to prev DS, pDS, p2, turn.

Rep [Short Rows 11–12] 2 more times.
Short Row 17 (RS): DS, knit to BOR. Resume working in the rnd.
Rnd 18: Knit, resolving rem DS as kDS as encountered.
Rnds 19–25: Knit.
Begin working flat.
Short Row 26 (RS): Knit to M-B, sm, k6 (7, 8), turn.
Short Row 27 (WS): DS, purl to M-A, sm, p6 (7, 8), turn.
Short Row 28: DS, knit to 1 st before prev DS, turn.
Short Row 29: DS, purl to 1 st before prev DS, turn.
Rep [Rows 28–29] 2 more times.
Short Row 34 (RS): DS, knit to BOR. Resume working in the rnd.
Rnd 35: Knit, resolving each DS as kDS as encountered.
Rnd 36: K14 (16, 18), p28 (32, 36), knit to end of rnd.
Rnds 37–38: Knit.
Join MC.
Rnd 39: *K3 with Color C, k1 with MC; rep from * to end of rnd. Drop MC.
Rnds 40–41: Using Color C, knit.
Break Color C. The remainder of the sock is worked with MC only.

SADDLE RESOLUTION

Rnd 1: Knit.
Begin working flat.
Short Row 1 (RS): Knit to M-A, turn.
Short Row 2 (WS): DS, purl to M-B (passing the BOR M), turn.
Short Row 3: DS, knit to 1 st before prev DS, turn.
Short Row 4: DS, purl to 1 st before prev DS, turn.
Rep [Short Rows 3– 4] 2 more times.
Short Row 9 (RS): DS, knit to BOR. Resume working in the rnd.

FINISH THE FOOT

Resolve all DS as kDS as encountered on Rnd 1.
Rnd 1: K14 (16, 18), pm, (knit to M, rm) 2 times, k10 (11, 12), pm, knit to BOR.
Rnd 2: Knit.
Rep Rnd 2 until Foot measures 1¼ (1½, 1¾) in. / 3 (4, 4.5) cm shorter than desired length.

TOE

Rnd 1 (dec): *Knit to 3 sts before M, k2tog, k1, sm, k1, ssk; rep from * once more, knit to end of rnd— 4 sts dec.
Rnd 2: Knit.
Rep [Rnds 1–2] 4 (6, 7) more times— 36 (36, 40) sts rem.
Rep [Rnd 1] 4 more times—20 (20, 24) sts rem.
Adjustment Row (RS): Knit to first M, rm.

Redistribute the sts: The first 10 (10, 12) sts are on one needle; the rem 10 (10, 12) sts are on a second needle. Hold these two needles parallel.
Break yarn, leaving a 12 in. / 30.5 cm tail. Graft closed the toe of your sock.

FINISHING

Weave in ends.
Make a second sock identical to the first to complete a pair.
Wet block and allow to dry completely before wearing.
Trim ends.

Coffee Talk

The blue hues in the Chilton blue skirt were chosen specifically to match Alexis Bledel's eyes.

Life and Death Brigade Fingerless Mitts

Designed by Jacquline Rivera

SKILL LEVEL: INTERMEDIATE

Rory: "That was a once in a lifetime experience!"

Logan: "Only if you want it to be."

—*Gilmore Girls*, Season 5, Episode 7

While searching for her next article subject for The *Yale Daily News*, Rory stumbles across a gorilla-masked woman proclaiming, "*In omnia paratus*" (Latin for "prepared in all things"), which leads her down the rabbit hole searching for the Life and Death Brigade, a secret society at Yale. Although not much is known or written about the society, they have a reputation for pulling dangerous and elaborate stunts. Finding out that Logan Huntzberger's grandfather was a member, she confronts him. However, Logan won't give her information, and instead agrees to let her experience it if she accepts "unknown conditions." She finds herself gently kidnapped and taken to the 108th assembly deep in the woods, styled as a 1930s safari. While viewers never learn whether Rory becomes an official member, she is left with a bottle of champagne, a gorilla mask, her confiscated camera, and quite a story when she is returned home.

You won't have to pull a crazy stunt to knit up these fingerless mitts! Worked in the round starting from the bottom cuff edge, they feature elegant top hats and bow ties worked in stranded colorwork on the palm side, while the front of the mitts highlights the Life and Death Brigade's motto, "*In omnia paratus*," superimposed on the umbrella, evoking Rory's time participating in their games. Increases establish the afterthought polka-dot thumb, with the stitches put on waste yarn to be worked after the body of the mitt is completed.

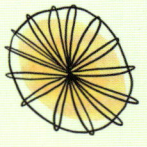
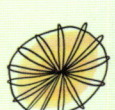

SIZES
1 (2, 3, 4)

FINISHED MEASUREMENTS
Circumference: 7½ (8, 8½, 9) in. / 19 (20.5, 21.5, 23) cm
Length: 9¾ (10¼, 10¾, 11½) in. / 25 (26, 27.5, 29) cm
Designed to fit with 0 in. / 0 cm of ease; choose the size closest to your hand circumference for the best fit.

YARN
Fingering weight yarn, shown in Lattes & Llamas *Vacation Yarn* (75% superwash merino, 25% nylon; 463 yd. / 423 m per 3½ oz. / 100 g hank)

COLORWAYS
Main Color (MC): Palpatine, 1 hank
Contrast Color (CC): Frost Giant, 1 hank

NEEDLES
US 2 / 2.75 mm, set of 5 double-pointed needles or size needed to obtain gauge

NOTIONS
Stitch marker (optional)
Row counter (optional)
Waste yarn
Tapestry needle

GAUGE
Size 1: 34 sts and 40 rows = 4 in. / 10 cm over stranded colorwork in the round, taken after blocking
Size 2: 32 sts and 38 rows = 4 in. / 10 cm over stranded colorwork in the round, taken after blocking
Size 3: 30 sts and 36 rows = 4 in. / 10 cm over stranded colorwork in the round, taken after blocking
Size 4: 28.5 sts and 34 rows = 4 in. / 10 cm over stranded colorwork in the round, taken after blocking
Make sure to check your gauge.

PATTERN NOTES
- To honor the original design of these fingerless mitts and ensure a

Continued on page 90

wider range of available fit, rather than compromise on the stitch pattern, these mitts have been graded using different gauges for each size. To achieve the gauge for your finished size of mitts, adjust your needle size as needed.

- The mitts are worked in the round from the bottom up using stranded knitting. Most of the pattern is charted; written instructions are not provided for colorwork or thumb shaping.
- Increases indicated on the chart create shaping for the thumb. Thumb stitches are then placed on waste yarn to be picked up and finished later.
- When knitting the colorwork, catch floats longer than 5 stitches.

CAST ON & RIBBED EDGE—BOTH MITTS

With MC, CO 56 sts using the Long Tail cast on method. Distribute sts evenly across 4 needles—14 sts per needle. Pm for BOR (if desired) and join to work in the rnd, being careful not to twist the sts.

Rnds 1–9: *K1, p1; rep from * to end of rnd.

Rnd 10 (inc): *Kfb, work est rib patt over next 5 sts, kfb, work in est rib patt over next 7 sts; rep from * to end of rnd—64 sts.

Rnd 11: Join CC; do not break MC. With CC only, knit.

FIRST MITT

Begin Left Mitt Chart, reading all rows from right to left as for working in the rnd.

Work Rows 1–53 once—82 sts at completion.

Row 54: Work 27 sts in patt as per Row 54 of chart, place the next 18 thumb sts on waste yarn, work the remaining 37 sts of Row 54 of the chart to end of rnd—64 st rem.

Work Rows 55–80 once.

Do not break either yarn. Proceed to Finish Mitt.

SECOND MITT

Begin Right Mitt Chart, reading all rows from right to left as for working in the rnd.

Work Rows 1–53 once—82 sts at completion.

Row 54: Work 37 sts in patt as per Row 54 of chart, place the next 18 thumb sts on waste yarn, work the remaining 27 sts of Row 54 of the chart to end of rnd—64 st rem.

Work Rows 55–80 once.

Do not break either yarn. Proceed to Finish Mitt.

FINISH MITT— BOTH MITTS

Setup Rnd: With CC only, knit. Break CC.

Rnd 1: Knit

Rnd 2 (dec): *K2tog, (p1, k1) 3 times, p2tog, (k1, p1) 3 times; rep from * to end of rnd—56 sts.

Rnds 3–6: *K1, p1; rep from * to end of rnd.

Bind off all sts loosely in patt.

THUMB— BOTH MITTS

Carefully remove waste yarn and place 18 live sts on dpns, distributing sts for comfort.

Rejoin CC yarn to the right edge of the live sts with the RS facing.

Setup Row (RS): K18, pick up and knit 4 sts to close the gap. Pm for BOR (if desired) and join to work in the rnd—22 sts total.

Rnds 1–2: Knit.

Rnd 3 (dec): (K1, p1) to last 4 sts, k2tog, p2tog—20 sts.

Rnds 4–6: *K1, p1; rep from * to end of rnd.

BO all sts loosely in patt.

FINISHING

Weave in all ends and wet block. Allow to dry completely. Trim all ends.

Coffee Talk

The Life and Death Brigade evening tent scenes were shot in one night at Griffith Park just outside the Warner Bros. studio lot. After the cast and crew relocated twenty miles away to the Disney Ranch, the scaffolding jump stunt, outdoor games, and human paintball game were shot over the next two days.

LEFT MITT CHART

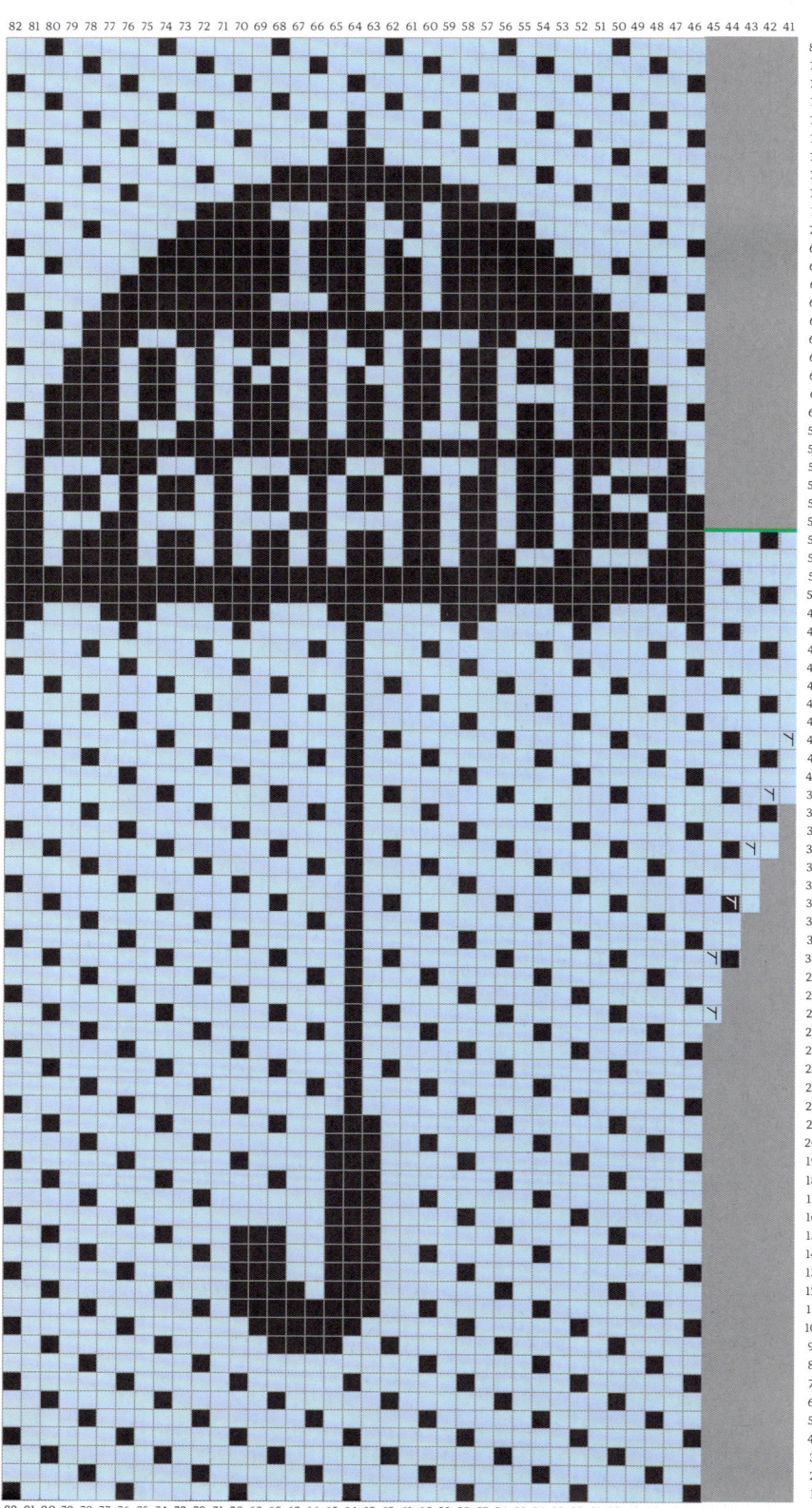

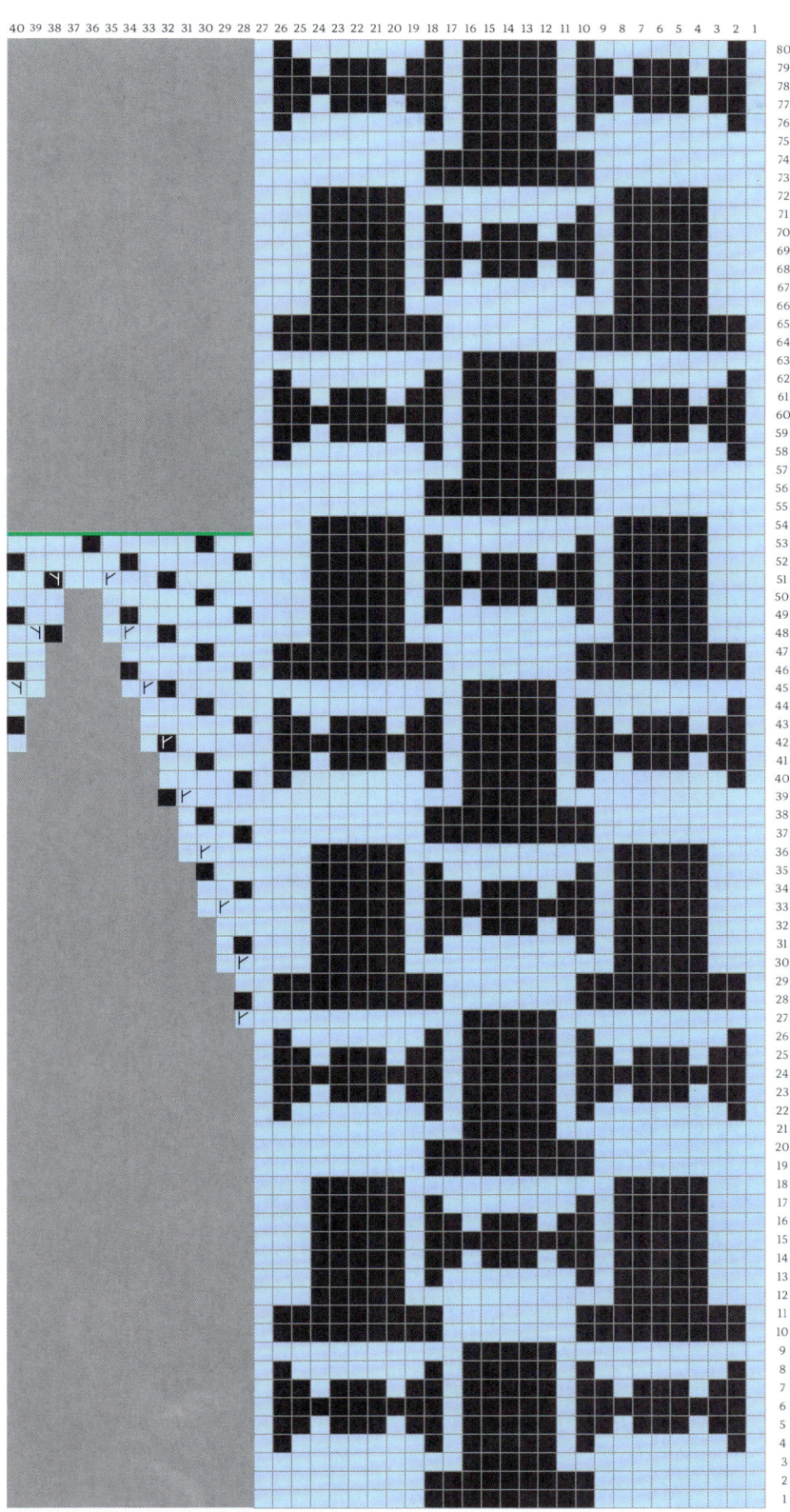

KEY

☐ knit
▨ No stitch
■ MC
▨ CC
⌐ M1L
¬ M1R
── Place sts below on waste yarn

RIGHT MITT CHART

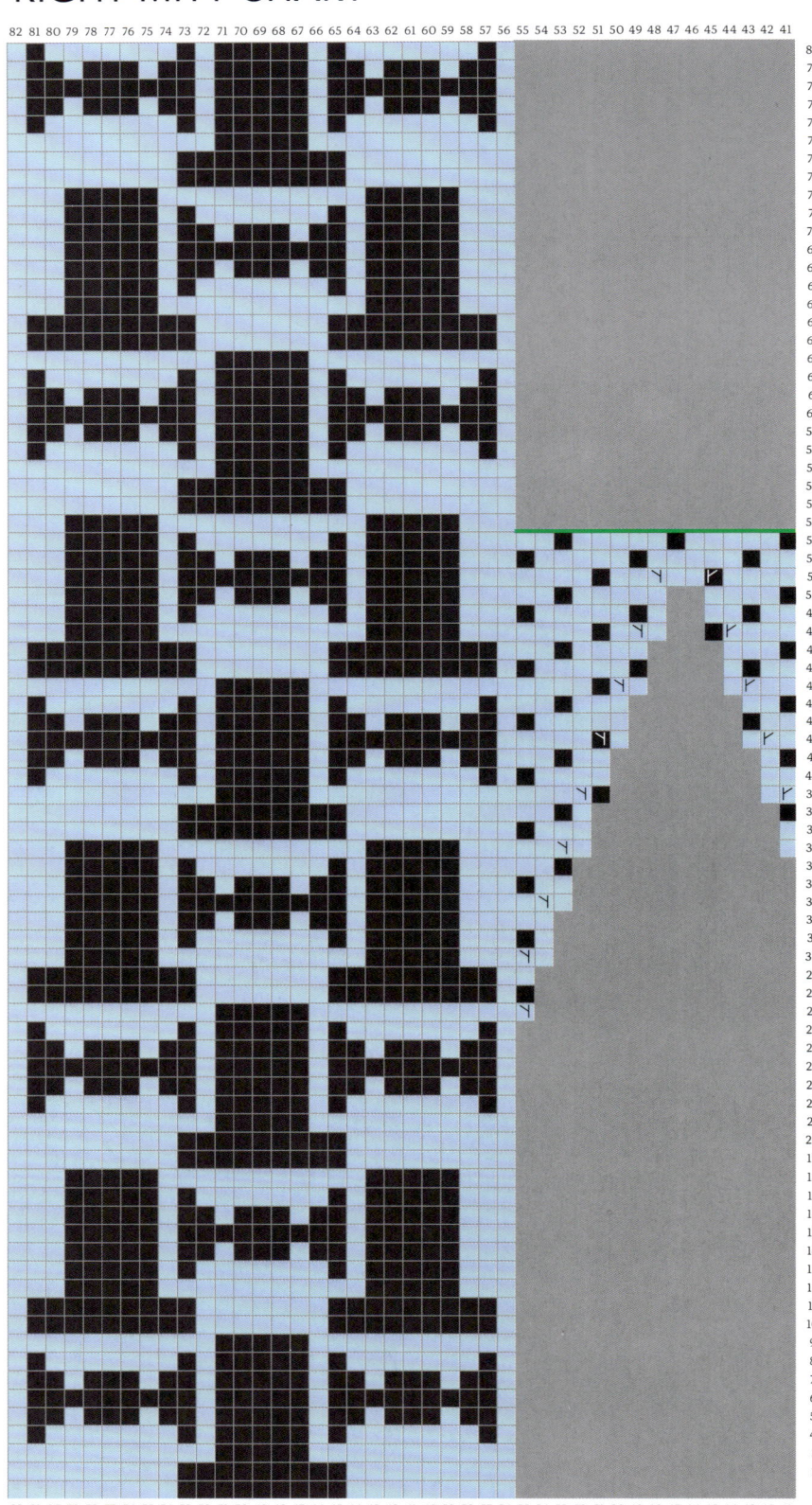

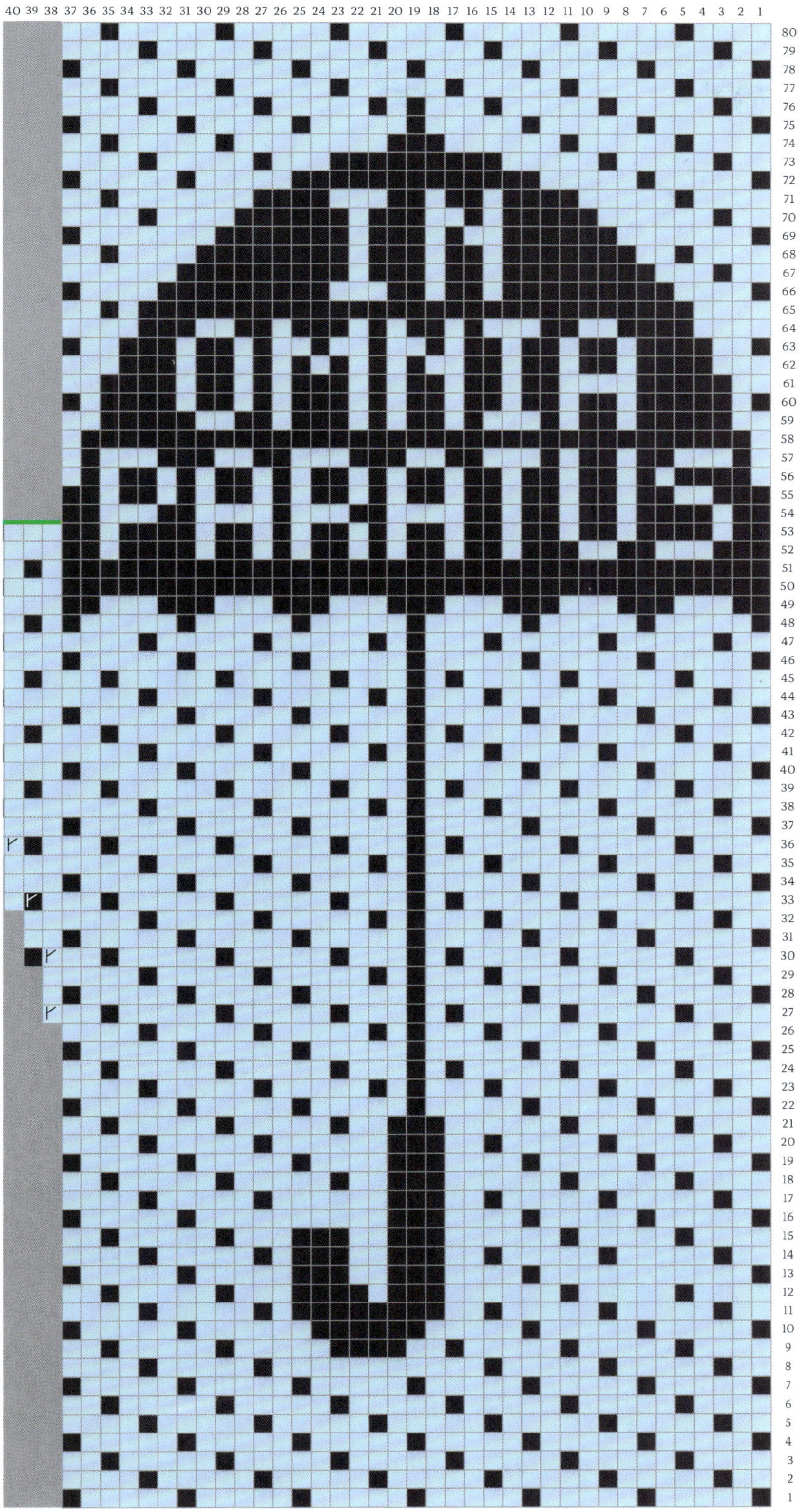

KEY

- ☐ knit
- ▨ No stitch
- ■ MC
- ☐ CC
- ⌐ M1L
- ¬ M1R
- ━ Place sts below on waste yarn

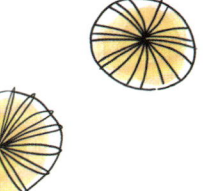

Coffee, Coffee, Coffee Socks

Designed by Spillyjane

SKILL LEVEL: INTERMEDIATE

Max: "Do you like coffee?"
Lorelai: "Only with my oxygen."

—*Gilmore Girls*, Season 1, Episode 5

A real-life coffee addict, actress Lauren Graham reveals, "I drink a lot of coffee. I would get to this place on-set [of *Gilmore Girls*] in real life where if I had any more, I was going to keel over dead, so sometimes there was water in there." Her costar, Alexis Bledel, however, is not a coffee drinker. In scenes where Rory needs to drink, Coke was put in her mug. Much of the beloved series revolves around not only America's favorite hot, caffeinated drink, but also food. Once the deal between Lorelai and her parents is struck for the Chilton tuition loan, Friday night dinners become an important part of the show, as do regular visits to Luke's Diner. Bledel said, "It really bothers me when actors don't eat the food that's in the scene. Like they're supposed to be having a meal but don't eat it, so we would go for it most of the time." Graham remembers spitting the food out when the camera stopped rolling so she wouldn't get sick if they had to do dozens and dozens of takes, whereas actor Jared Padalecki, who played Dean, would not only eat everything, but often take the leftovers home.

Whether you prefer a to-go cup or like to sit and sip, it doesn't matter how many cups you've consumed . . . if you're a coffee lover, these are the socks for you! Worked from the cuff down seamlessly in the round, the socks sport multicolored coffee mugs swirling around the leg in stranded colorwork. Both the heel and the gusset are worked in the main color only, then the colorwork resumes across the instep, stopping again before the toe decreases begin. Once the remaining stitches are grafted together, mug handles and "Y" for Rory's college are embroidered on post-knitting.

SIZES
Small (Medium, Large)

FINISHED MEASUREMENTS
Foot Circumference: 7 (8, 9) in. / 18 (20.5, 23) cm
Leg Length (from cuff to top of heel): 5.5 (6, 7) in. / 14 (15, 18) cm
Minimum Foot Length (from bottom of heel to toe tip): 8 (9, 10¼) in. / 20.5 (23, 26) cm
Adjustable foot length (can be made longer than the minimum foot length)
The sock is designed to be worn with ½–1 in. / 1–2.5 cm of negative ease.

YARN
Fingering weight yarn, shown in Emma's Yarn *Practically Perfect Sock* (2-ply; 80% superwash merino, 20% nylon; 400 yd. / 366 m per 3½ oz. / 100 g hank) in color Navy Blazer (Color A)
Fingering weight yarn, shown in Emma's Yarn *Practically Perfect Smalls* (2-ply; 80% superwash merino, 20% nylon; 81 yd. / 74 m per ¾ oz. / 20 g hank)

COLORWAYS
Color B: Sage Before Beauty, 1 hank
Color C: Whisper, 1 hank
Color D: Freshly Cut, 1 hank
Color E: Kisses, 1 hank
Color F: Limoncello, 1 hank
Color G: Stiletto, 1 hank
Color H: Forget Me Not, 1 hank

NEEDLES
US 2 / 2.75 mm, set of 5 double-pointed needles or size needed to obtain gauge

NOTIONS
Stitch marker (optional)
Tapestry needle

Continued on page 100

GAUGE

Small: 36 sts and 41.5 rows = 4 in. / 10 cm in stranded colorwork pattern, taken after steam blocking

Medium: 32 sts and 37 rows = 4 in. / 10 cm in stranded colorwork pattern, taken after steam blocking

Large: 28 sts and 32.5 rows = 4 in. / 10 cm in stranded colorwork pattern, taken after steam blocking

Make sure to check your gauge.

PATTERN NOTES

- To honor the original design of the socks and ensure a wider range of available fit, rather than compromise on the stitch pattern, these socks have been graded using different gauges for each size. To achieve the gauge for your finished size of socks, adjust your needle size as needed.
- These colorwork socks are worked from the cuff down in the round.
- A stitch marker may be used to mark the beginning of round, if desired.
- The pattern offers a break from the colorwork as both the heel and the gusset are worked with Color A alone. Colorwork knitting resumes across the instep once the gusset is complete and then stops again before the toe decreases begin.
- Both socks are worked identically. Work two to complete a pair.
- Each row of Chart A (Leg) will be worked twice per rnd. Each row of Chart B (Foot) will be worked once per rnd.
- Once the socks are finished and blocked, embroidered details will be added to each mug using simple straight embroidery. These details are the handles on the mugs and the "Y"s on each of the white mugs. While working, be sure to keep your embroidery loose enough so that the socks retain their elasticity. You may wish to use a separate length of yarn as you embellish each separate motif. There might be more ends to weave in this way, but the resulting socks will be more easily worn.
- Colorwork will be easier and faster to work if Color A is held with the right hand while Color B is held with the left. This will also improve the look of the resulting colorwork.

CAST ON & CUFF

Using Color A, CO 64 sts using the Long Tail cast on method. Divide sts evenly across 4 needles—16 sts per needle. Pm for BOR (if desired) and join to work in the rnd, being careful not to twist the sts.

Rib Rnd: *K2 tbl, p2; rep from * to end of rnd.

Rep Rib Rnd 9 more times for a total of 10 rnds.

LEG

Begin Chart A, reading all rows from right to left as for working in the rnd, joining Colors B–H as required. Work Rows 1–46 once (chart is worked 2 times across each rnd). Once complete, break all but Color A.

HEEL FLAP

The Heel Flap is worked flat with Color A only over 32 sts across N1 and N2.

Row 1 (RS): K16 across N1. K16 across N2 with the same needle. There are now 32 sts on N1 for the Heel Flap. The unworked 32 sts of N3 and N4 will remain on hold while the remainder of the heel is worked. Turn work.

Row 2 (WS): Sl1 wyif, purl to end of row. Turn work.

Row 3: Sl1 wyib, knit to end of row. Turn work.

Row 4: Sl1 wyif, purl to end of row. Turn work.

Rep Rows 3–4 until the Heel Flap measures 2 in. / 5 cm long, or to desired length, ending with Row 4. There are still 32 sts on N1.

TURN HEEL

Row 1 (RS, dec): Sl1 wyib, k18, ssk, k1. Turn work—31 sts.

Row 2 (WS, dec): Sl1 wyif, p7, p2tog, p1. Turn work—30 sts.

Row 3 (dec): Sl1 wyib, knit to 1 st before the gap, ssk across the gap, k1. Turn work—1 st dec.

Row 4 (dec): Sl1 wyif, purl to 1 st before the gap, p2tog across the gap, p1. Turn work—1 st dec.

Rep [Rows 3–4] 4 more times—20 sts rem on N1.

GUSSET

Resume working in the round.

With another dpn, pick up and knit tbl 1 st in each of the sl sts along the right edge of the Heel Flap leading toward the instep. The number of sts that will be picked up will vary based on the length of the Heel Flap. Pick up and knit 1 additional stitch in the gap between the sts just picked up and the start of the first instep needle. This is now N1.

With a new dpn, k16 from the first instep needle. This is now N2.

With a new dpn, k16 from the remaining instep needle. This is now N3.

With a new dpn, pick up and knit 1 stitch in the gap between the end of N3 and the first slipped stitch down the left edge of the Heel Flap. Then pick up and knit tbl 1 st in each of the slipped sts along the left edge of the Heel Flap. This number of sts should match those on N1. Finally, knit 10 sts from N1. This is now N4. The new BOR is located at the center of the bottom of the heel/sole.

Rnd 1:

N1 (dec)—Knit to the last 3 sts, k2tog, k1—1 st dec.

N2—Knit to end.

N3—Knit to end.

N4 (dec)—K1, ssk, knit to end—1 st dec.
Rnd 2 (all needles): Knit to end.
Rep Rnds 1–2 until 64 total sts rem (16 sts on each needle).
Next 2 rnds: Knit.

FOOT

Begin Chart B, reading all rows from right to left as for working in the rnd, joining Colors B–H as required. Work Rows 1–32 once (chart is worked 1 time across each rnd). Once complete, break all but Color A.

With Color A, knit 2 rnds, or cont in St st until foot is approx. 2 (2.5, 2.75) in. / 5 (6.5, 7) cm short of the desired total length.

TOE

Rnd 1:
N1 (dec)—Knit to the last 3 sts, k2tog, k1—1 st dec.
N2 (dec)—K1, ssk, knit to end—1 st dec.
N3 (dec)—Knit to the last 3 sts, k2tog, k1—1 st dec.
N4 (dec)—K1, ssk, knit to end—1 st dec.
Rnd 2 (all needles): Knit to end.
Rep [Rnds 1–2] 10 more times—20 sts rem (5 sts on each needle).
Sl 5 sts from N2 to N1 and sl 5 sts from N4 to N3 (10 sts on each needle).
Break yarn, leaving a 12 in. / 30.5 cm tail. Graft closed the toe of your sock.

FINISHING

Weave in all ends. Steam block and press if desired.

Working from Chart C, using a tapestry needle and the appropriate colors of yarn, use straight stitches to add handles to all mugs as well as "Y"s to the white ones. Weave in all ends from the embroidery process.

Coffee Talk

"The Rory," a signature drink Emily excitedly creates for Rory's twenty-first birthday party in Season 6, Episode 7, is a martini made with champagne, vodka, pineapple juice, and grenadine. The rim is dipped in pink edible glitter. Luke is less enthusiastic about it, claiming it "really tasted really pink, like *pink* pink. . . . It's like drinking a 'my little pony.'"

CHART A

Needles 2 & 4   Needles 1 & 3

CHART B

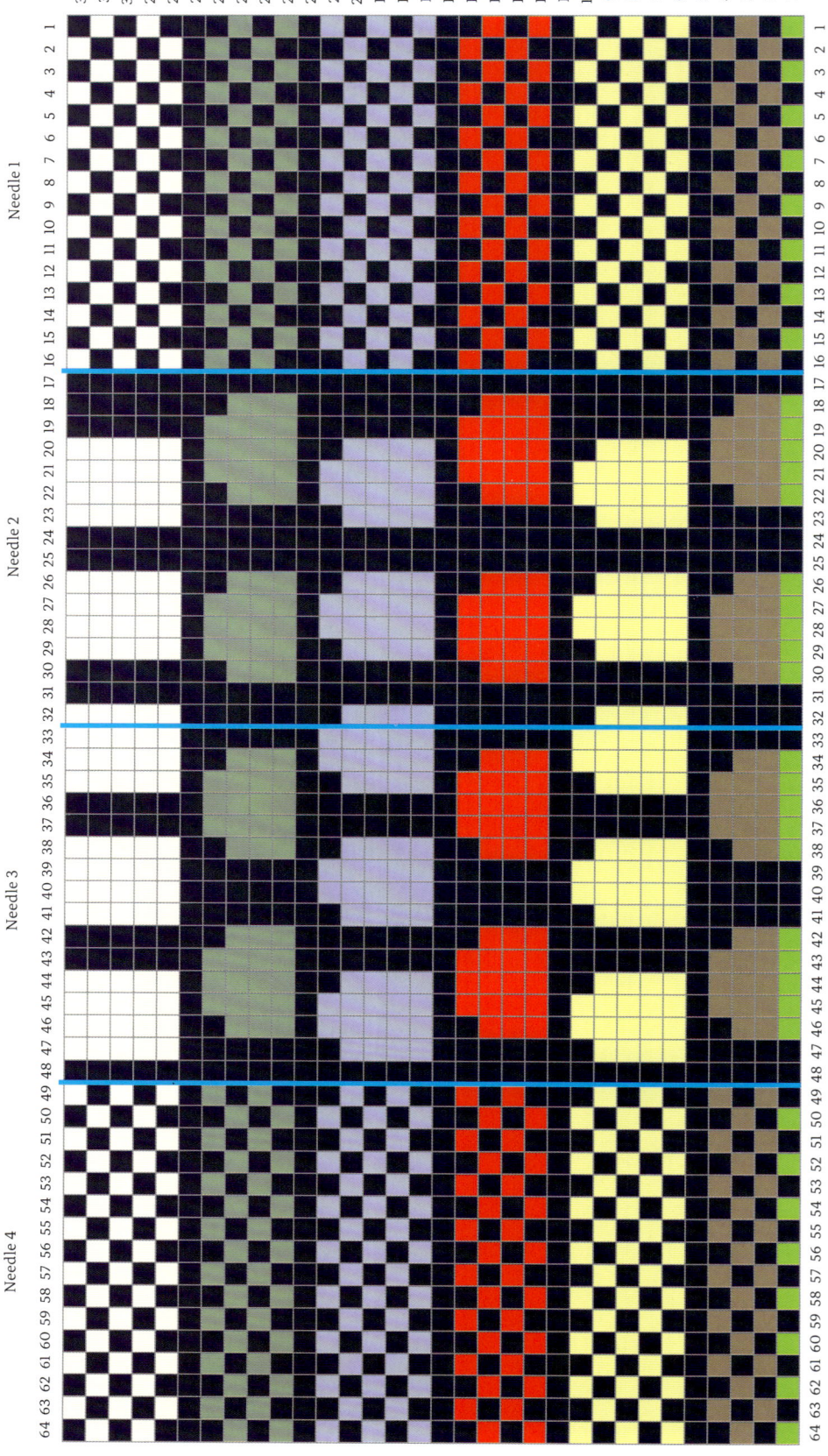

CHART C

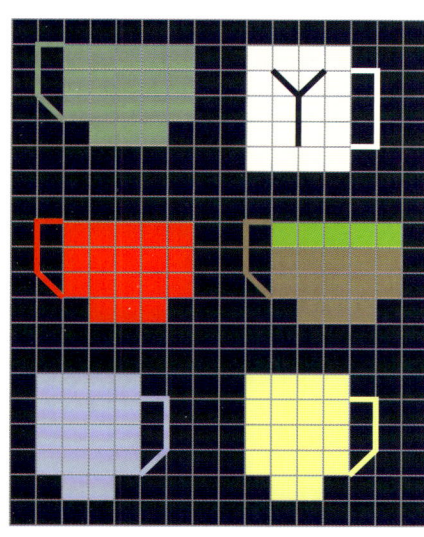

EMBROIDERY KEY

- Existing Color A
- Existing Color B
- Existing Color C
- Existing Color D
- Existing Color E
- Existing Color F
- Existing Color G
- Existing Color H
- Embroider with Color A
- Embroider with Color B
- Embroider with Color C
- Embroider with Color E
- Embroider with Color F
- Embroider with Color G
- Embroider with Color H

COLORWORK KEY

- knit
- Color A
- Color B
- Color C
- Color D
- Color E
- Color F
- Color G
- Color H
- Needle divider
- Pattern repeat

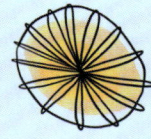

Luke's Fingerless Mitts

Designed by Paul Haesemeyer

SKILL LEVEL: INTERMEDIATE

*"Lorelai, this thing we're doing here, me, you—
I just want you to know I'm in. I am all in."*
—Luke, Season 5, Episode 3

With a large cast of female characters living in Stars Hollow, flannel-shirted, backwards–baseball capped, denim-clad Luke Danes wasn't always destined to become Lorelai's love interest. In fact, Luke was originally written as a gal pal to Lorelai named Daisy. Creator Amy Sherman-Palladino says, "Luke was originally a female character. [The network] came to me and said we need another guy, so I literally just took a character and changed the name." Actor Scott Patterson auditioned for the role, and Sherman-Palladino recalls, "I don't need to see anyone else. He's 100 percent it." Once actors Patterson and Lauren Graham began working together on set, their on-screen partnership was undeniable. Graham remembers, "It didn't seem like, 'Oh this is the definite love interest. . . .' It's just this funny, weird chemistry that we had in terms of being complete opposites and also this built-in conflict of he has the thing she wants—which is coffee. . . . It was just something about the two of those characters together that they kept going back to and then it kept growing." Though tested at times throughout the series, Luke and Lorelai remain one of TV's most beloved on-screen couples.

Whether you're serving up coffee, driving your truck around town, unpacking deliveries, or shoveling snow, these fingerless gloves are the perfect accessory to get your work done and keep your hands warm. The gloves are worked from the bottom up in the round beginning with a 2x2 ribbed cuff. A gusset is made to accommodate the thumb, with the rest of the body knit in stockinette to the knuckles. Fingers are then knit individually and topped with colors to match the Luke's Diner sign.

SIZES
1 (2, 3)

FINISHED MEASUREMENTS
Hand Circumference: 7 (7½, 8) in. / 18 (19, 20.5) cm
Gloves are designed to be worn with 1 in. / 2.5 cm of negative ease.

YARN
Fingering weight yarn, shown in Brooklyn Tweed *Loft* (2-ply woolen spun; 100% American Targhee-Columbia wool; 275 yd. / 251 m per 1¾ oz. / 50 g hank) in color Soot, 1 hank (Color A)

Fingering weight yarn, shown in Brooklyn Tweed *Tones Light* (2-ply woolen spun; 100% American Columbia wool; 225 yd. / 206 m per 1¾ oz. / 50 g hank)

COLORWAYS
Color B: Vacay Overtone, 1 hank
Color C: Persimmon Undertone, 1 hank
Color D: Goldfinch Undertone, 1 hank

NEEDLES
US 1 / 2.25 mm, set of 5 double-pointed needles and/or 32 in. / 80 cm long circular needle or size needed to obtain gauge

NOTIONS
Stitch markers
Row counter (optional)
Tapestry needle
Waste yarn

GAUGE
30 sts and 40 rows = 4 in. / 10 cm over St st worked in the round, taken after blocking
Make sure to check your gauge.

PATTERN NOTES
- These gloves are worked from the bottom up in the round. Make two to complete a pair. The gloves are knit with left and right hand in mind. Add a discrete marker,

Continued on page 108

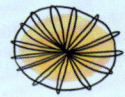

whether it's scrap yarn, adding or removing one row from the cuff stripes, or a purl stitch, to mark Left vs. Right.
- The same needle size is used throughout. Use dpns if not using Magic Loop for cuff and hand of glove. Use dpns to knit fingers.
- Written instructions are provided for the entirety of the pattern.
- All cast ons use the Backwards Loop cast-on method unless otherwise noted.

CAST ON & CUFF

With Color B, CO 52 (56, 60) sts using the Long Tail cast on method. Pm for BOR and join to work in the rnd, being careful not to twist the sts.

Rnds 1–2 (Color B): *K1, p1; rep from * to end of rnd.
Break Color B.
Join Color C.
Rnds 3–6 (Color C): *K1, p1; rep from * to end of rnd.
Break Color C.
Join Color D.
Rnds 7–10 (Color D): *K1, p1; rep from * to end of rnd.
Break Color D.
Join MC.
Rep Rnd 1 with MC until cuff measures 4 in. / 10 cm from the CO edge.

BEGIN HAND

Rnd 1: Knit.
Rnd 2 (inc): Knit to end of rnd (do not slip BOR M), pm-A, M1L—53 (57, 61) sts.
There is 1 st between M-A and BOR M.
Rnd 3 (inc): K26 (28, 30), M1L, knit to end of rnd—54 (58, 62) sts.

THUMB GUSSET

Rnds 1–4: Knit.
Rnd 5 (inc): Knit to M-A, sm, M1R, knit to BOR M, M1L, sm—2 sts inc.

Rep [Rnds 1–5] 6 (7, 8) more times—14 (16, 18) sts inc; 68 (74, 80) total sts.
Place 15 (17, 19) thumb gusset sts on waste yarn; remove M-A—53 (57, 61) sts rem.

FINISH HAND

Setup Rnd (inc): Knit to end of rnd (do not slip BOR M), CO 1 st, sm—54 (58, 62) sts.
Work in St st until hand measures 3¾ (4, 4¼) in. / 9.5 (10, 11) cm from the end of the MC ribbing.

LEFT HAND
Remove BOR M, k1, pm for new BOR.

RIGHT HAND
Remove BOR M, knit to last 2 sts, pm for new BOR.

FINGERS

LITTLE FINGER
Setup Rnd: K20 (22, 23), place just worked sts on waste yarn. K14 (14, 16), CO 2 (2, 3) sts. Place rem 20 (22, 23) sts on waste yarn. Do not tie off waste yarn. Additional sts for fingers will be used from held sts—16 (16, 19) sts on working needle.
Pm for BOR and join to work in the rnd.
Work in St st for ¾ in. / 2 cm.
Break MC, join Color B.
Sizes 1 & 2 Only:
Rnd 1: Knit.
Rnds 2–3: *K1, p1; rep from * to end of rnd.
Size 3 Only:
Rnd 1: Knit.
Rnd 2 (dec): *K1, p1; rep from * to last 3 sts, k1, p2tog—18 sts.
Rnd 3: *K1, p1; rep from * to end of rnd.
All Sizes:
BO all sts loosely in patt.
Base of Next 3 Fingers
With MC, starting where sts were cast on for Little Finger, pick up and knit 2 (2, 3) sts. Move 40 (44, 46) sts from waste yarn to working needles and knit across all sts. Pm for BOR and join to work in the rnd—42 (46, 49) sts.
Work in St st for ¼ (½, ½) in. / 0.5 (1.5, 1.5) cm from pick up.

RING FINGER
Cont with MC, k8 (9, 10), CO 2 (2, 3) sts. Place the next 28 (30, 32), sts on waste yarn. K6 (7, 7) rem sts—16 (18, 20) sts on working needle.
Pm for BOR and join to work in the rnd.
Work in St st for ¾ in. / 2 cm.
Break MC, join Color D.
Rnd 1: Knit.
Rnds 2–3: *K1, p1; rep from * to end of rnd.
BO all sts loosely in patt.

MIDDLE FINGER
With MC, starting where sts were cast on for Ring Finger, pick up and knit 2 (2, 3) sts. Move 7 (7, 8) sts from waste yarn to working needles and knit across these sts. CO 2 (2, 3) sts. Leaving the next 14 (16, 16) sts on waste yarn, move the last 7 (7, 8) sts from waste yarn to working needles and knit across these sts—18 (18, 22) sts on working needle.
Pm for BOR and join to work in the rnd.
Work in St st for ¾ in. / 2 cm.
Break MC, join Color C.
Rnd 1: Knit.
Rnds 2–3: *K1, p1; rep from * to end of rnd.
BO all sts loosely in patt.

INDEX FINGER
With MC, starting where sts were cast on for Middle Finger, pick up and knit 2 (2, 3) sts. Move the rem 14 (16, 16) sts from waste yarn to working needle and knit across these sts—16 (18, 19) sts total.
Pm for BOR and join to work in the rnd.
Work in St st for ¾ in. / 2 cm.
Break MC, join Color B.
Sizes 1 & 2 Only:
Rnd 1: Knit.

Rnds 2–3: *K1, p1; rep from * to end of rnd.

Size 3 Only:

Rnd 1: Knit.

Rnd 2 (dec): *K1, p1; rep from * to last 3 sts, k1, p2tog—18 sts.

Rnd 3: *K1, p1; rep from * to end of rnd.

All Sizes:

BO all sts loosely in patt.

THUMB

Place 15 (17, 19) thumb sts on needles.

Using MC, pick up and knit 3 sts along cast on st on hand—18 (20, 22) sts total.

Pm for BOR and join to work in the rnd.

Rnd 1: Knit.

Rnd 2 (dec): K1, k2tog, knit to last 2 sts, ssk—16 (18, 20) sts.

Work in St st for 1 in. / 2.5 cm. Break MC, join Color D.

Rnd 3: Knit.

Rnds 4–5: *K1, p1; rep from * to end of rnd.

BO all sts loosely in patt.

FINISHING

Weave in all ends, closing gaps along finger crooks as needed. Wet block to dimensions. Trim ends.

Coffee Talk

While Luke is almost always wearing a flannel shirt and backwards baseball cap, key set costumer Valerie Campbell shares that he had plenty of shirts, but only one signature hat. Actor Scott Patterson would often bring the hat home, causing an occasional baseball cap shortage for Luke.

Chapter 4

Gilmore Garments

Rory's Argyle Vest

Designed by Jenny Noto

SKILL LEVEL: ADVANCED

Lorelai: "Happy birthday, little girl. I can't believe how fast you're growing up."

Rory: "Really? Feels slow."

Lorelai: "Trust me, it's fast. What do you think of your life so far?"

—*Gilmore Girls*, Season 1, Episode 6

With only four and a half weeks to cast the pilot episode of *Gilmore Girls*, the casting directors looked to a fresh-faced actress, college student, and former model with only one uncredited role on her résumé. Alexis Bledel was their first choice for the leading role of Rory—despite being sick at the time of her audition! Casting director Jill Anthony told *Vanity Fair*, "Luckily, we had videotaped one of her early auditions. We popped that in, and they saw her on camera, and she just jumped off the screen, you know. Those blue eyes." Fans embraced Rory as a smart—and smartly dressed—teenager and the unusual combination of this young mother-daughter duo, earning *Gilmore Girls* praise across the globe, critical acclaim, a spot on *Time* magazine's "Best TV Shows of All-TIME," and the #12 ranking on *Empire*'s "The 100 Best TV Shows of All Time" list in 2021.

An ode to Rory's penchant for argyle, this vest—constructed in the round from the bottom up—knits up quickly in worsted weight. Steeks allow for the stranded colorwork to be knit in the round for ease. Once the body is complete, the arm and neck holes are cut and stitches are picked up for the finishing ribbing.

SIZES
1 (2, 3, 4, 5)[6, 7, 8, 9]{10, 11, 12, 13}

FINISHED MEASUREMENTS
Chest Circumference:
36 (38½, 40¾, 45½, 48)[50½, 52¾, 57½, 60]{62½, 64¾, 69½, 72} in.
91.5 (97.5, 103.5, 116, 122)[128, 134, 146.5, 152.5]{158.5, 164.5, 177, 183} cm
The vest is designed to be worn with 2–4 in. / 5–10 cm of positive ease.

YARN
Worsted weight yarn, shown in Little Fox Yarns *Fennec* (4-ply; 100% non-superwash merino wool; 218 yd. / 200 m per 3½ oz. / 100 g hank)

COLORWAYS
Main Color (MC): Pink Opal, 3 (3, 3, 3, 4)[4, 4, 4, 4]{5, 5, 5, 5} hanks
Contrast Color (CC): Smudge, 2 (2, 2, 2, 2)[2, 2, 3, 3]{3, 3, 3, 3} hanks

NEEDLES
US 6 / 4 mm, 16 in. / 40 cm and 32–40 in. / 80–100 cm long circular needles
US 8 / 5 mm, 16 in. / 40 cm and 24–40 in. / 60–100 cm long circular needles or size needed to obtain gauge

NOTIONS
Stitch markers (6; 1 unique for BOR)
Locking stitch marker (1)
Stitch holders or waste yarn
Row counter (optional)
Tapestry needle
Sewing needle and thread
Sewing machine (optional)

GAUGE
20 sts and 20 rows = 4 in. / 10 cm over stranded colorwork, worked in the round on larger needle, taken after blocking
Make sure to check your gauge.

PATTERN NOTES
- This vest is worked in the round from the bottom up. Neckline and armhole shaping occur

Continued on page 114

simultaneously while still working in the round. The neckline and armhole edges are then steeked before the ribbed finishings are added.

- All ribbing is worked with the smaller needle; the body is worked with the larger/gauge-size needle.
- When the circumference of the work becomes too small for the longer circular needle during the shaping of the upper body, change to the smaller circumference needles to finish.
- Non-superwash wool yarns are recommended for this project. Non-superwash wools allow the scales of the wool to "cling" to each other, preventing unraveling of the yarn during the steeking process.
- When choosing what size to make, if you fall between sizes, it is recommended to size up for the best fit.
- As you work Chart A up the length of the yoke (once the steek columns have been added to the neckline and armhole edges), be sure to line up the stitch pattern columns vertically. As stitches are removed for shaping, or added for the setup of the steek columns, your round may not begin at Column 1 of the chart.
- During the yoke shaping, some larger sizes may have a smaller number of sts remaining than smaller sizes at the end of a shaping section. When the shaping is complete, the number of remaining sts will be correct, from smallest to largest, relative to the size being made.
- When working the decreases in the yoke, work the decrease using the color that will allow you to remain in pattern.

CAST ON

Using the smaller needle and MC, CO 180 (192, 204, 228, 240)[252, 264, 288, 300]{312, 324, 348, 360} sts using the Cable cast on method. Do not join to work in the rnd.
Setup Row (RS): *K1, p1; rep from * to end of row.
Pm for BOR and join to work in the rnd, being careful not to twist the sts.

RIBBING

Rib Rnd: *K1, p1; rep from * to end of rnd.
Rep Rib Rnd until the hem measures 3 in. / 7.5 cm from the CO edge.

BODY

Switch to larger needle.
Using MC, knit 1 rnd.
Begin Chart A, reading all rows from right to left as for working in the rnd, joining CC as required. Rep Rows 1–10 until the garment measures 12.75 (12.75, 12.75, 12.75, 13)[13, 13, 13.25, 13.25]{13.25, 13.5, 13.5, 13.5} in. / 32.5 (32.5, 32.5, 32.5, 33)[33, 33, 33.5, 33.5]{33.5, 34.5, 34.5, 34.5} cm from the CO edge or to desired length for the body (chart is worked 15 (16, 17, 19, 20)[21, 22, 24, 25]{26, 27, 29, 30} times across each rnd). Once the target length is reached, break both yarns, leaving tails for weaving in.

STEEK SETUP

Remove BOR M.
Place the first 6 (7, 8, 8, 9)[10, 11, 13, 14]{15, 16, 16, 17} sts on a st holder or waste yarn for half of the left underarm.
Rejoin MC and CC.
Cont in est colorwork patt across the next 39 (41, 43, 49, 51)[53, 55, 59, 61]{63, 65, 71, 73} sts—these sts will make up the Left Front.
Place the next st on the locking marker for the center front st. Leave this st hanging to the front of the work. PM-A.
CO 8 steek sts using the Backwards Loop cast on method following the Steek Chart. PM-B.
Note: Each row of the Steek Chart is the same. It is 10 rows tall to match the number of rows in Chart A so that following the stitch pattern across multiple charts is made easier.
Cont in est colorwork patt across the next 39 (41, 43, 49, 51)[53, 55, 59, 61]{63, 65, 71, 73} sts—these sts will make up the Right Front. PM-C.
Place the next 12 (14, 16, 16, 18)[20, 22, 26, 28]{30, 32, 32, 34} sts on a st holder or waste yarn for the right underarm.
CO 8 steek sts using the Backwards Loop cast on method following the Steek Chart. PM-D.
Cont in est colorwork patt across the next 77 (81, 85, 97, 101)[105, 109, 117, 121]{125, 129, 141, 145} sts—these sts will make up the Back. PM-E.
Place the last 6 (7, 8, 8, 9)[10, 11, 13, 14]{15, 16, 16, 17} sts onto the first st holder or waste yarn to complete the left underarm.
CO 8 steek sts using the Backwards Loop cast on method following the Steek Chart. PM for new BOR.
179 (187, 195, 219, 227)[235, 243, 259, 267]{275, 283 307, 315} sts rem:
39 (41, 43, 49, 51)[53, 55, 59, 61]{63, 65, 71, 73} Left and Right Front sts each side
77 (81, 85, 97, 101)[105, 109, 117, 121]{125, 129, 141, 145} Back sts
24 steek sts—8 at each underarm and 8 at the center front

SHAPING FOR ARMHOLES AND NECKLINE

Read carefully through the following instructions to ensure you follow all instructions for your size. Change to smaller circumference needles for comfort as the circumference becomes smaller.

SHAPING PART 1—ALL SIZES:

Full Dec Rnd (dec): K2tog, work est patt to 2 sts before M-A, ssk, sm, work Steek Chart to M-B, sm, k2tog, work est patt to 2 sts before M-C, ssk, sm, work Steek Chart to M-D, sm, k2tog, work est patt to 2 sts before M-E, ssk, sm, work Steek Chart to BOR M—6 sts dec.

Rep Full Dec Rnd 2 (2, 2, 4, 4)[4, 4, 4, 5]{5, 5, 5, 5} more times.

18 (18, 18, 30, 30)[30, 30, 30, 36]{36, 36, 36, 36} sts dec; 161 (169, 177, 189, 197)[205, 213, 229, 231]{239, 247, 271, 279} sts rem:

33 (35, 37, 39, 41)[43, 45, 49, 49]{51, 53, 59, 61} Left and Right Front sts each side

71 (75, 79, 87, 91)[95, 99, 107, 109]{113, 117, 129, 133} Back sts

24 steek sts—8 at each underarm and 8 at the center front

SHAPING PART 2—ALL SIZES:

Rnd 1 (dec, armholes): K2tog, work est patt to M-A, sm, work Steek Chart to M-B, sm, work est patt to 2 sts before M-C, ssk, sm, work Steek Chart to M-D, sm, k2tog, work est patt to 2 sts before M-E, ssk, sm, work Steek Chart to BOR M—4 sts dec.

Rnd 2 (dec, full): K2tog, work est patt to 2 sts before M-A, ssk, sm, work Steek Chart to M-B, sm, k2tog, work est patt to 2 sts before M-C, ssk, sm, work Steek Chart to M-D, sm, k2tog, work est patt to 2 sts before M-E, ssk, sm, work Steek Chart to BOR M—6 sts dec.

Rep [Rnds 1–2] 1 (2, 3, 4, 5)[5, 6, 6, 6]{7, 7, 9, 9} more times.

20 (30, 40, 50, 60)[60, 70, 70, 70]{80, 80, 100, 100} sts dec; 141 (139, 137, 139, 137)[145, 143, 159, 161]{159, 167, 171, 179] sts rem:

27 (26, 25, 24, 23)[25, 24, 28, 28]{27, 29, 29, 31} Left and Right Front sts each side

63 (63, 63, 67, 67)[71, 71, 79, 81]{81, 85, 89, 93} Back sts

24 steek sts—8 at each underarm and 8 at the center front

SHAPING PART 3—SIZES 1 (2, -, 4, -) [-, -, -, -] {-, -, 12, 13} ONLY:

Rnd 1 (dec, armholes): K2tog, work est patt to M-A, sm, work Steek Chart to M-B, sm, work est patt to 2 sts before M-C, ssk, sm, work Steek Chart to M-D, sm, k2tog, work est patt to 2 sts before M-E, ssk, sm, work Steek Chart to BOR M—4 sts dec.

Rnd 2 (dec, neck): Work est patt to 2 sts before M-A, ssk, sm, work Steek Chart to M-B, sm, k2tog, work est patt to M-C, sm, work Steek Chart to M-D, sm, work est patt to M-E, sm, work Steek Chart to BOR M—2 sts dec.

Rep [Rnds 1–2] 2 (2, -, 2, -)[-, -, -, -]{-, -, 3, 3} more times.

18 (18, -, 18, -)[-, -, -, -]{-, -, 24, 24} sts dec; 123 (121, -, 121, -)[-, -, -, -]{-, -, 147, 155} sts rem:

21 (20, -, 18, -)[-, -, -, -]{-, -, 21, 23} Left and Right Front sts each side

57 (57, -, 61, -)[-, -, -, -]{-, -, 81, 85} Back sts

24 steek sts—8 at each underarm and 8 at the center front

SHAPING PART 3—SIZES - (-, 3, -, 5) [6, 7, 8, 9] {10, 11, -, -} ONLY:

Rnd 1: Work est patt to M-A, sm, work Steek Chart to M-B, sm, work est patt to M-C, sm, work Steek Chart to M-D, sm, work est patt to M-E, sm, work Steek Chart to BOR M.

Rnd 2 (dec, full): K2tog, work est patt to 2 sts before M-A, ssk, sm, work Steek Chart to M-B, sm, k2tog, work est patt to 2 sts before M-C, ssk, sm, work Steek Chart to M-D, sm, k2tog, work est patt to 2 sts before M-E, ssk, sm, work Steek Chart to BOR M—6 sts dec.

Rep [Rnds 1–2] - (-, 1, -, 1)[1, 1, 3, 3] {3, 3, -, -} more times.

- (-, 12, -, 12)[12, 12, 24, 24]{24, 24, -, -} sts dec; - (-, 125, -, 125)[133, 131, 135, 137]{135, 143, -, -} sts rem:
- (-, 21, -, 19)[21, 20, 20, 20]{19, 21, -, -} Left and Right Front sts each side
- (-, 59, -, 63)[67, 67, 71, 73]{73, 77, -, -} Back sts

24 steek sts—8 at each underarm and 8 at the center front

SHAPING PART 4—SIZES 1 (2, 3, 4, 5)[-, 7, -, -]{-, -, -, -} ONLY:

Rnd 1: Work est patt to M-A, sm, work Steek Chart to M-B, sm, work est patt to M-C, sm, work Steek Chart to M-D, sm, work est patt to M-E, sm, work Steek Chart to BOR M.

Rnd 2 (dec, neck): Work est patt to 2 sts before M-A, ssk, sm, work Steek Chart to M-B, sm, k2tog, work est patt to M-C, sm, work Steek Chart to M-D, sm, work est patt to M-E, sm, work Steek Chart to BOR M—2 sts dec.

Rep [Rnds 1–2] 6 (5, 6, 4, 4)[-, 3, -, -] {-, -, -, -} more times.

14 (12, 14, 10, 10)[-, 8, -, -]{-, -, -, -} sts dec; 109 (109, 111, 111, 115)[-, 123, -, -] {-, -, -, -} sts rem:

14 (14, 14, 13, 14)[-, 16, -, -]{-, -, -, -} Left and Right Front sts each side

57 (57, 59, 61, 63)[-, 67, -, -]{-, -, -, -} Back sts

24 steek sts—8 at each underarm and 8 at the center front

SHAPING PART 4—SIZES - (-, -, -, -)[6, -, 8, 9] {-, 11, -, -} ONLY:

Rnd 1: Work est patt to M-A, sm, work Steek Chart to M-B, sm, work est patt to M-C, sm, work Steek Chart to M-D, sm, work est patt to M-E, sm, work Steek Chart to BOR M.

Rnd 2 (dec, neck): Work est patt to 2 sts before M-A, ssk, sm, work Steek Chart to M-B, sm, k2tog, work est patt to M-C, sm, work Steek Chart to M-D, sm, work est patt to M-E, sm, work Steek Chart to BOR M—2 sts dec.

Rnd 3 (dec, armholes): K2tog, work est patt to M-A, sm, work Steek Chart to M-B, sm, work est patt to 2 sts before M-C, ssk, sm, work Steek Chart to M-D, sm, k2tog, work est patt to 2 sts before M-E, ssk, sm, work Steek Chart to BOR M—4 sts dec.

Rnd 4 (dec, neck): Work est patt to 2 sts before M-A, ssk, sm, work Steek Chart to M-B, sm, k2tog, work est patt to M-C, sm, work Steek Chart to M-D, sm, work est patt to M-E, sm, work Steek Chart to BOR M—2 sts dec.

8 sts dec; - (-, -, -, -)[125, -, 127, 129] {-, 135, -, -} sts rem:
- (-, -, -, -)[18, -, 17, 17]{-, 18, -, -} Left and Right Front sts each side
- (-, -, -, -)[65, -, 69, 71]{-, 75, -, -} Back sts

24 steek sts—8 at each underarm and 8 at the center front

SHAPING PART 4—SIZE 10 ONLY:

Rnd 1: Work est patt to M-A, sm, work Steek Chart to M-B, sm, work est patt to M-C, sm, work Steek Chart to M-D, sm, work est patt to M-E, sm, work Steek Chart to BOR M.

Rnd 2 (dec, neck): Work est patt to 2 sts before M-A, ssk, sm, work Steek Chart to M-B, sm, k2tog, work est patt to M-C, sm, work Steek Chart to M-D, sm, work est patt to M-E, sm, work Steek Chart to BOR M—2 sts dec.

Rnd 3 (dec, armholes): K2tog, work est patt to M-A, sm, work Steek Chart to M-B, sm, work est patt to 2 sts before M-C, ssk, sm, work Steek Chart to M-D, sm, k2tog, work est patt to 2 sts before M-E, ssk, sm, work Steek Chart to BOR M—4 sts dec.

Rnd 4: Work est patt to M-A, sm, work Steek Chart to M-B, sm, work est patt to M-C, sm, work Steek Chart to M-D, sm, work est patt to M-E, sm, work Steek Chart to BOR M.

Rnd 5 (dec, neck): Work est patt to 2 sts before M-A, ssk, sm, work Steek Chart to M-B, sm, k2tog, work est patt to M-C, sm, work Steek Chart to M-D, sm, work est patt to M-E, sm, work Steek Chart to BOR M—2 sts dec.

8 sts dec; 127 sts rem:
16 Left and Right Front sts each side
71 Back sts
24 steek sts—8 at each underarm and 8 at the center front

SHAPING PART 4—SIZES - (-, -, -, -)[-, -, -, -] {-, -, 12, 13} ONLY:

Rnd 1 (dec, armholes): K2tog, work est patt to M-A, sm, work Steek Chart to M-B, sm, work est patt to 2 sts before M-C, ssk, sm, work Steek Chart to M-D, sm, k2tog, work est patt to 2 sts before M-E, ssk, sm, work Steek Chart to BOR M—4 sts dec.

Rnd 2: Work est patt to M-A, sm, work Steek Chart to M-B, sm, work est patt to M-C, sm, work Steek Chart to M-D, sm, work est patt to M-E, sm, work Steek Chart to BOR M.

Rnd 3 (dec, full): K2tog, work est patt to 2 sts before M-A, ssk, sm, work Steek Chart to M-B, sm, k2tog, work est patt to 2 sts before M-C, ssk, sm, work Steek Chart to M-D, sm, k2tog, work est patt to 2 sts before M-E, ssk, sm, work Steek Chart to BOR M—6 sts dec.

Rnds 4–5: Work est patt to M-A, sm, work Steek Chart to M-B, sm, work est patt to M-C, sm, work Steek Chart to M-D, sm, work est patt to M-E, sm, work Steek Chart to BOR M.

Rnd 6 (dec, full): K2tog, work est patt to 2 sts before M-A, ssk, sm, work Steek Chart to M-B, sm, k2tog, work est patt to 2 sts before M-C, ssk, sm, work Steek Chart to M-D, sm, k2tog, work est patt to

2 sts before M-E, ssk, sm, work Steek Chart to BOR M—6 sts dec.

16 sts dec; - (-, -, -, -)[-, -, -, -]{-, -, 131, 139} sts rem:

- (-, -, -, -)[-, -, -, -]{-, -, 16, 18} Left and Right Front sts each side

- (-, -, -, -)[-, -, -, -]{-, -, 75, 79} Back sts

24 steek sts—8 at each underarm and 8 at the center front

SHAPING PART 5— SIZES 1 (2, 3, 4, 5)[-, 7, 8, 9]{10, 11, 12, 13} ONLY:

Rnds 1–2: Work est patt to M-A, sm, work Steek Chart to M-B, sm, work est patt to M-C, sm, work Steek Chart to M-D, sm, work est patt to M-E, sm, work Steek Chart to BOR M.

Rnd 3 (dec, neck): Work est patt to 2 sts before M-A, ssk, sm, work Steek Chart to M-B, sm, k2tog, work est patt to M-C, sm, work Steek Chart to M-D, sm, work est patt to M-E, sm, work Steek Chart to BOR M—2 sts dec.

Rep [Rnds 1–3] 2 (2, 2, 1, 1)[-, 2, 3, 3]{2, 3, 1, 1} more times.

6 (6, 6, 4, 4)[-, 6, 8, 8]{6, 8, 4, 4} sts dec; 103 (103, 105, 107, 111)[-, 117, 119, 121]{121, 127, 127, 135} sts rem:

11 (11, 11, 11, 12)[-, 13, 13, 13]{13, 14, 14, 16} Left and Right Front sts each side

57 (57, 59, 61, 63)[-, 67, 69, 71]{71, 75, 75, 79} Back sts

24 steek sts—8 at each underarm and 8 at the center front

Sizes 1 (2, 3, 4, 5)[-, 7, 8, 9]{10, 11, 12, -} Only: Proceed to Finish Yoke.

Size 13 Only: Proceed to Shaping Part 6.

SHAPING PART 5— SIZE 6 ONLY:

Rnd 1: Work est patt to M-A, sm, work Steek Chart to M-B, sm, work est patt to M-C, sm, work Steek Chart to M-D, sm, work est patt to M-E, sm, work Steek Chart to BOR M.

Rnd 2 (dec, neck): Work est patt to 2 sts before M-A, ssk, sm, work Steek Chart to M-B, sm, k2tog, work est patt to M-C, sm, work Steek Chart to M-D, sm, work est patt to M-E, sm, work Steek Chart to BOR M—2 sts dec.

Rep [Rnds 1–2] 2 more times.

Rnds 7–8: Work est patt to M-A, sm, work Steek Chart to M-B, sm, work est patt to M-C, sm, work Steek Chart to M-D, sm, work est patt to M-E, sm, work Steek Chart to BOR M.

Rnd 9 (dec, neck): Work est patt to 2 sts before M-A, ssk, sm, work Steek Chart to M-B, sm, k2tog, work est patt to M-C, sm, work Steek Chart to M-D, sm, work est patt to M-E, sm, work Steek Chart to BOR M—2 sts dec.

Rep [Rnds 7–9] 2 more times.

12 sts dec; 113 sts rem:

12 Left and Right Front sts each side

65 Back sts

24 steek sts—8 at each underarm and 8 at the center front

Size 6 Only: Proceed to Finish Yoke.

SHAPING PART 6— SIZE 13 ONLY:

Rnds 1–3: Work est patt to M-A, sm, work Steek Chart to M-B, sm, work est patt to M-C, sm, work Steek Chart to M-D, sm, work est patt to M-E, sm, work Steek Chart to BOR M.

Rnd 4 (dec, neck): Work est patt to 2 sts before M-A, ssk, sm, work Steek Chart to M-B, sm, k2tog, work est patt to M-C, sm, work Steek Chart to M-D, sm, work est patt to M-E, sm, work Steek Chart to BOR M—2 sts dec.

2 sts dec; 133 sts rem:

15 Left and Right Front sts each side

79 Back sts

24 steek sts—8 at each underarm and 8 at the center front

Size 13 Only: Proceed to Finish Yoke.

FINISH YOKE— ALL SIZES

Cont in est patt with no further decreases until the yoke measures 8¾ (9, 9¼, 9¾, 9¾)[10¼, 10½, 10½, 10¾]{11, 11¼, 11¾, 12} in. / 22 (23, 23.5, 25, 25)[26, 26.5, 26.5, 27.5]{28, 28.5, 30, 30.5} cm from the separation at the underarms.

SEPARATE FRONT AND BACK SHOULDERS

Work est patt to M-A, rm, k1 steek st in pattern (this makes up the Left Front shoulder). BO 6 steek sts in pattern (the single st rem from the 6th bound off st is the 8th steek st; this will apply to all steek panel bind offs), rm, work est patt to M-C, rm, k1 steek st in pattern (this makes up the Right Front shoulder). BO 6 steek sts in pattern, rm, work 12 (12, 12, 12, 13)[13, 14, 14, 14]{14, 15, 15, 16} sts in est patt (this makes up the Right Back shoulder). BO 33 (33, 35, 37, 37)[39, 39, 41, 43]{43, 45, 45, 47} sts in pattern, work est patt to M-E, rm, k1 steek st in pattern (this makes up the Back Left shoulder). BO 6 steek sts in pattern, rm. Place the last st remaining (the final BO st) back onto the LHN as part of the Left Front shoulder—13 (13, 13, 13, 14)[14, 15, 15, 15]{15, 16, 16, 17} sts rem for each shoulder.

Break both yarns.

Make a note of which charted row is worked as your final row as you complete this round.

SHAPE SHOULDERS

Three additional rows will be worked on each shoulder, separately. You may continue in est patt, reading the WS Chart A rows from left to right and purling across the row, or work these 3 rows in MC only.

LEFT FRONT SHOULDER (AS WORN):

Place the 13 (13, 13, 13, 14)[14, 15, 15, 15]{15, 16, 16, 17} live sts of the Right Front, Right Back, and Left Back shoulders (as worn) on stitch holders or waste yarn. Only the

13 (13, 13, 13, 14)[14, 15, 15, 15]{15, 16, 16, 17} sts of the Front Left Shoulder remain on the working needle.
Beginning with the next row of the est patt, work 3 rows without any shaping: 1 RS row, 1 WS row, and 1 more RS row. Do not bind off any sts; place the sts onto a stitch holder or waste yarn. Break yarns, leaving a tail for weaving in.

RIGHT FRONT SHOULDER (AS WORN):

Place the 13 (13, 13, 13, 14)[14, 15, 15, 15]{15, 16, 16, 17} live sts of the Right Front Shoulder onto the working needle. Rejoin yarns.
Beginning with the next row of the est patt, work 3 rows without any shaping: 1 RS row, 1 WS row, and 1 more RS row. Do not bind off any sts; place the sts onto a stitch holder or waste yarn. Break yarns, leaving a tail for weaving in.

RIGHT BACK SHOULDER (AS WORN):

Work as for the Right Front Shoulder. Break CC yarn, leaving a tail for weaving in. Break MC yarn, leaving a 12 in. / 30.5 cm tail.

LEFT BACK SHOULDER (AS WORN):

Work as for the Right Front Shoulder. Break CC yarn, leaving a tail for weaving in. Break MC yarn, leaving a 12 in. / 30.5 cm tail.

REINFORCE AND CUT STEEKS

Using a needle and thread or a sewing machine, reinforce steek stitches as per the Steek Reinforcement Chart from the cast on edge to the bind off edge of the steeking panel at each location. The same method will be used at the neckline edge and both armholes.
Once complete, steam block the steek panels to smooth out the sts.
Carefully cut up the center of each panel as per the Steek Reinforcement Chart.

SHOULDER SEAMING

Turn the garment inside out so the WS is facing out and RS are together.
Place the live sts of the Right Front and Right Back Shoulders onto 2 gauge-size needles and hold the two needles parallel. Using a third needle and the 12 in. / 30.5 cm tail of MC yarn, graft the Front and Back Shoulder sts together using the Three-Needle bind off. Break yarn and pull tail through remaining loop to secure.
Repeat for the Left Shoulder.
Turn the garment back RS out.

NECKBAND

Using the smaller 16 in. / 40 cm circular needle and MC, starting at the left edge of the back neck bound off sts, pick up and knit 48 (50, 52, 56, 58)[60, 62, 66, 68]{70, 72, 76, 82} sts along the left edge of the neckline down to the single st on the locking marker. Place the single held st from the locking marker onto the LHN and knit this st placing the locking marker into the new loop on the RHN. Pick up and knit 48 (50, 52, 56, 58)[60, 62, 66, 68]{70, 72, 76, 82} sts along the right edge of the neckline. Pick up and knit 33 (33, 35, 37, 37)[39, 39, 41, 43]{43, 45, 45, 47} sts across the back neck bound off edge. Pm for BOR and join to work in the rnd—130 (134, 140, 150, 154)[160, 164, 174, 180]{184, 190, 198, 212} sts.
Rib Rnd (dec): (K1, p1) to 1 st before the marked center st, cdd and move the locking marker into the resulting st on the RHN, cont in est patt to end of rnd—2 sts dec.
Rep Rib Rnd 9 more times, continuing to align the knit and purl sts for contiguous ribbing on either side of the center decrease—110 (114, 120, 130, 134)[140, 144, 154, 160]{164, 170, 178, 192} sts rem.
BO in patt.

ARMHOLE FINISHING

Place the 12 (14, 16, 16, 18)[20, 22, 26, 28]{30, 32, 32, 34} live sts on hold at the bottom of one underarm onto the smaller 16 in. / 40 cm circular needle.
Slip the first 6 (7, 8, 8, 9)[10, 11, 13, 14]{15, 16, 16, 17} sts purlwise to the RHN. Place a BOR M on the RHN.
Join MC (this is at the center of the underarm sts).
K6 (7, 8, 8, 9)[10, 11, 13, 14]{15, 16, 16, 17} underarm sts, pick up and knit 45 (46, 48, 49, 51)[52, 54, 54, 55]{56, 58, 60, 61} sts evenly up the first edge of the armhole to the shoulder seam. Then pick up and knit 45 (46, 48, 49, 51)[52, 54, 54, 55]{56, 58, 60, 61} sts evenly down the second edge of the armhole to the live sts from the underarm. K6 (7, 8, 8, 9)[10, 11, 13, 14]{15, 16, 16, 17} underarm sts to the BOR M—102 (106, 112, 114, 120)[124, 130, 134, 138]{142, 148, 152, 156} sts.
Rib Rnd: *K1, p1; rep from * to end of rnd.
Rep Rib Rnd 9 more times.
BO in patt.
Repeat instructions for second armhole.

FINISHING

Weave in all loose ends.
Trim any waste steek sts neatly and fold the fabric to the WS. Tack down the steeked edges to the WS of the sweater with whipstitch if desired.
Wet block and carefully shape vest to measurements.
Trim all ends.

CHART A

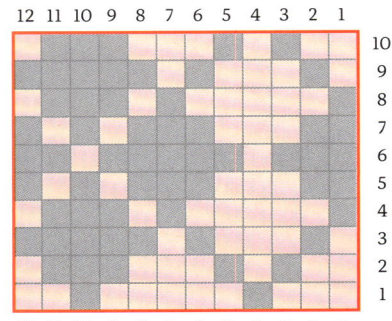

STEEK CHART

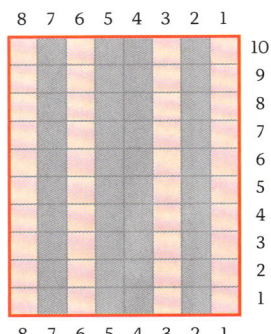

STEEK REINFORCEMENT CHART

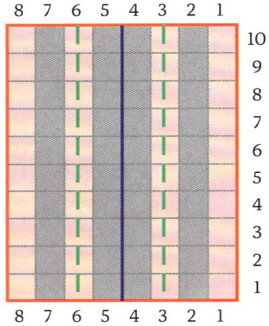

KEY

- ☐ knit
- ▨ MC
- ▨ CC
- – – Steek reinforcement
- — Steek cut line
- ☐ Pattern repeat

Coffee Talk

Alexis Bledel was born in Texas to Argentine and Mexican parents. Her first language is Spanish, and she didn't learn English until she began school. In Season 6, she pretended to speak broken Spanish to Esperanza, one of Emily's maids.

SCHEMATIC

Armhole, shoulder, and neckline dimensions do not include the ribbed finishings.

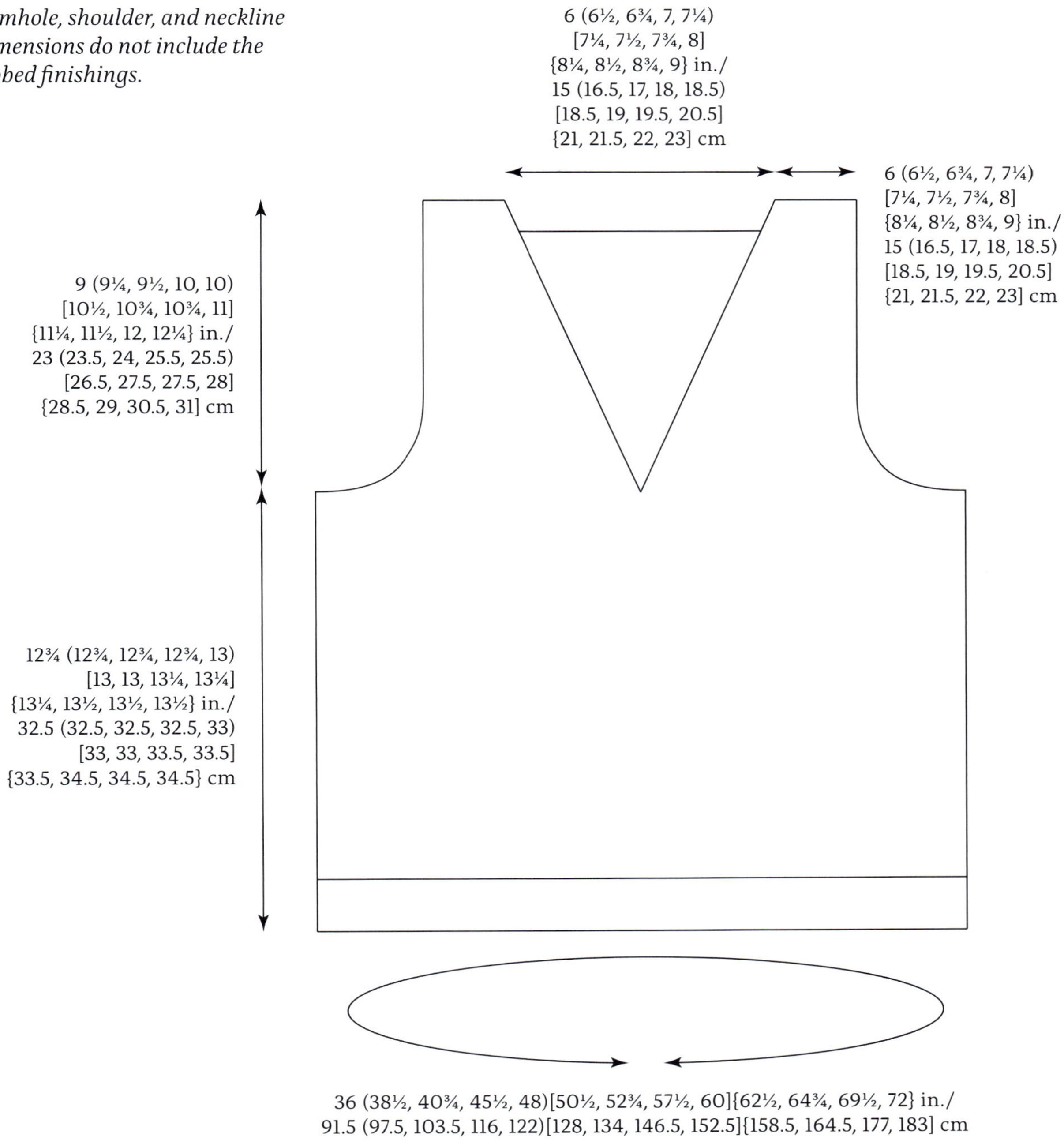

6 (6½, 6¾, 7, 7¼)
[7¼, 7½, 7¾, 8]
{8¼, 8½, 8¾, 9} in./
15 (16.5, 17, 18, 18.5)
[18.5, 19, 19.5, 20.5]
{21, 21.5, 22, 23} cm

6 (6½, 6¾, 7, 7¼)
[7¼, 7½, 7¾, 8]
{8¼, 8½, 8¾, 9} in./
15 (16.5, 17, 18, 18.5)
[18.5, 19, 19.5, 20.5]
{21, 21.5, 22, 23} cm

9 (9¼, 9½, 10, 10)
[10½, 10¾, 10¾, 11]
{11¼, 11½, 12, 12¼} in./
23 (23.5, 24, 25.5, 25.5)
[26.5, 27.5, 27.5, 28]
{28.5, 29, 30.5, 31} cm

12¾ (12¾, 12¾, 12¾, 13)
[13, 13, 13¼, 13¼]
{13¼, 13½, 13½, 13½} in./
32.5 (32.5, 32.5, 32.5, 33)
[33, 33, 33.5, 33.5]
{33.5, 34.5, 34.5, 34.5} cm

36 (38½, 40¾, 45½, 48)[50½, 52¾, 57½, 60]{62½, 64¾, 69½, 72} in./
91.5 (97.5, 103.5, 116, 122)[128, 134, 146.5, 152.5]{158.5, 164.5, 177, 183} cm

Luke's Diner Pullover

Designed by Jesie Ostermiller
SKILL LEVEL: ADVANCED

"The counter is a sacred space, my sacred space. You don't do yoga on the Dalai Lama's mat, and you don't come behind my counter. Period!"

—Luke to Sookie, Season 1, Episode 5

The Warner Bros. lot in Burbank, California, where *Gilmore Girls* was filmed, was previously used for films such as *The Music Man* and *Bonnie and Clyde* and shows like *The Dukes of Hazzard* and *Growing Pains*. However, the pilot was shot in a Toronto suburb in Ontario. This little Canadian town would have a big impact on how the Burbank set was styled. In Canada, Luke's Diner was shot at Williams Hardware store—something that carried over in the storyline about Luke's father. To maximize studio lot space, many locations had two or even three uses: Luke's Diner was also Taylor's soda shop, the flower shop, the library, bank, and Doose's Market stockroom. Weston's was also the arcade, the video store, high school classrooms, and Luke's apartment. Bootsy's newsstand doubled as the Yale bar. Fans of the show can still tour some of the facades from Stars Hollow on the studio lot, which is decorated festively during the holidays.

Knit flat from the bottom hems and cuffs up starting with a 2x2 ribbing, the sweater shows off Luke's iconic coffee cup logo worked in intarsia on the front. Once all the pieces are made, the front and back are then seamed at the shoulder, the sleeves are set in and seamed, and the undersides of the sleeves and the sides of the body are seamed. Stitches around the neck opening are picked up to work the collar. The classic drop-shoulder silhouette is easy to wear in an oversized or fitted way, depending on the wearer's preference. Come on, we're going to Luke's!

SIZES
1 (2, 3, 4)[5, 6, 7]{8, 9, 10}

FINISHED MEASUREMENTS
Chest Circumference: 36 (39½, 44½, 48)[51½, 56½, 60]{63½, 68, 71½} in. / 91.5 (100.5, 113, 122)[131, 143.5, 152.5]{161.5, 172.5, 181.5} cm
Garment is designed to be worn with 2–4 in. / 5–10 cm of positive ease.

YARN
Sport weight yarn, shown in 29 Bridges Studio *Sport* (3-ply; 100% superwash merino; 325 yd. / 297 m per 3½ oz. / 100 g hank)

COLORWAYS
Color A: Hot Metal, 4 (5, 6, 6)[7, 7, 8]{8, 9, 10} hanks
Color B: Little Miss Sunshine, 1 hank
Color C: Truffle, 1 hank

NEEDLES
US 1 / 2.25 mm, 16 in. / 40 cm and 32 in. / 80 cm long circular needle
US 2 / 2.75 mm, 32 in. / 80 cm long circular needle or size needed to obtain gauge

NOTIONS
Stitch markers
Row counter (optional)
Waste yarn or stitch holder
Tapestry needle

GAUGE
27 sts and 37 rows = 4 in. / 10 cm in St st worked flat on larger needle, taken after blocking
Make sure to check your gauge.

PATTERN NOTES
- The pieces of this pullover are knit flat from the bottom hems and cuffs up, using the smaller needle for all ribbing and changing to the larger needle for the body and sleeves. Once the pieces are complete, seam the shoulders together. Next, seam the sleeves to the body, centered on the shoulder seam. Once the sleeves are attached, the underarm and

Continued on page 124

side body seams are worked. After all seaming is complete, pick up stitches around the neck opening to work the collar.
- The logo chart (Chart A or B) is worked using the intarsia technique. While working the "Luke's" letters of the logo you will need 11 Color B yarn supplies and 8 Color C yarn supplies.
- Alternatively, the "Luke's" letters can be worked in duplicate stitch once the sweater front is complete. In this case, only the Color A and Color B portions of Chart A or B will be worked using the intarsia technique.
- As the front of the sweater is worked, the placement of Chart A will be lower down the body on some of the larger sizes than on some of the smaller sizes. This is due to the overall size of the chart that is being added. By the time the chart is complete, the placement on the front of the sweater should be equal across all sizes.
- Instructions for Size 1 are provided first, with instructions for Sizes 2–10 provided in parentheses/brackets. When only one set of numbers is provided, it applies to all sizes.
- Any references to Left and Right within this pattern are based on the garment as worn.

BACK CAST ON & HEM

Using the smaller needle and Color A, CO 122 (134, 150, 162)[174, 190, 202]{214, 230, 242} sts using the Long Tail cast on method. Do not join to work in the rnd.

Row 1 (RS): *K2, p2; rep from * to last 2 sts, k2.

Row 2 (WS): *P2, k2; rep from * to last 2 sts, p2.

Rep Rows 1–2 until the hem measures 2¼ in. / 5.5 cm from the CO edge, ending with a WS row.

BACK BODY

Switch to larger needles.
Work in St st until Back measures 21 (22, 24, 25)[26, 27, 28]{28, 29, 29} in. / 53.5 (56, 61, 63.5)[66, 68.5, 71]{71, 73.5, 73.5} cm from CO edge, ending with a WS row.

BACK NECKLINE

Neckline Bind Off Row (RS):
K45 (51, 57, 63)[67, 75, 80]{86, 92, 98}, place these just worked sts onto waste yarn or stitch holder (these sts make up the Right Back Shoulder). BO 32 (32, 36, 36)[40, 40, 42]{42, 46, 46} sts knitwise, knit to end of row—45 (51, 57, 63)[67, 75, 80]{86, 92, 98} sts rem on the working needle for the Left Back Shoulder (as worn).

LEFT BACK SHOULDER

Bind off all sts knitwise for this section.
Row 1 (WS, and each WS row): Purl.
Row 2 (RS, dec): BO 3 sts, knit to end—42 (48, 54, 60)[64, 72, 77]{83, 89, 95} sts rem.
Row 4 (dec): BO 2 sts, k to end—40 (46, 52, 58)[62, 70, 75]{81, 87, 93} sts rem.
Row 6 (dec): K2tog, k to end—39 (45, 51, 57)[61, 69, 74]{80, 86, 92} sts rem.
Row 7: Purl.
Note: At this time, the Back should measure approx. 22 (23, 25, 26)[27, 28, 29]{29, 30, 30} in. / 56 (58.5, 63.5, 66)[68.5, 71, 73.5]{73.5, 76, 76} cm from CO edge. If your row gauge is significantly different from the pattern gauge, you may need to work additional rows to reach the correct length. Be sure to end any extra length added with a WS row.
With RS facing, BO all sts knitwise.

RIGHT BACK SHOULDER

Bind off all sts purlwise for this section.
Place the live sts of the Right Back Shoulder onto the larger needle. Rejoin Color A with the RS facing.
Row 1 (RS, and each RS row): Knit.
Row 2 (WS, dec): BO 3 sts, purl to end—42 (48, 54, 60)[64, 72, 77]{83, 89, 95} sts rem.
Row 4 (dec): BO 2 sts, purl to end—40 (46, 52, 58)[62, 70, 75]{81, 87, 93} sts rem.
Row 6 (dec): P2tog, purl to end—39 (45, 51, 57)[61, 69, 74]{80, 86, 92} sts rem.
Row 7: Knit.
Note: If you added length to the Left Back Shoulder to reach the target length, add the same additional length here, ending with a RS row.
With WS facing, BO all sts purlwise.

FRONT CAST ON & HEM

Work as for Back Cast On & Hem section.

FRONT BODY

Switch to larger needles.
Work in St st until Front measures 9¼ (10¼, 12, 13)[13¾, 12½, 13¼]{13, 14, 14} in. / 23.5 (26, 30.5, 33)[35, 32, 33.5]{33, 35.5, 35.5} cm from CO edge, ending with a RS row.

Chart Setup Row (WS): P21 (27, 35, 41)[47, 44, 50]{56, 64, 70}, pm, p80 (80, 80, 80)[80, 102, 102]{102, 102, 102} sts, pm, purl to end.

FRONT INTARSIA CHART

Joining CCs as required to work the chart as intarsia, begin Chart A (A, A, A)[A, B, B]{B, B, B}, reading all RS (odd-numbered) rows from right to left and all WS (even-numbered) rows from left to right, as follows:

RS rows: Knit to M with Color A, sm, work chart to next M, sm, knit to end with Color A.

WS rows: Purl to M with Color A, sm, work chart to next M, sm, purl to end with Color A.

Work Rows 1–80 (80, 80, 80)[80, 102, 102]{102, 102, 102} once. When the chart is complete, break all CC yarn, leaving ends for weaving in, and remove all markers. Cont with Color A only.

COMPLETE FRONT BODY

Work in St st until Front measures 19½ (20½, 22¼, 23¼)[24, 25, 25¾]{25½, 26½, 26½} in. / 49.5 (52, 56.5, 59)[61, 63.5, 65.5]{65, 67.5, 67.5} cm from CO edge, ending with a WS row.

FRONT NECKLINE

Neckline Bind Off Row (RS): K50 (56, 63, 69)[74, 82, 87]{93, 100, 106}, place these just worked sts onto waste yarn or stitch holder (these sts make up the Left Front Shoulder). BO 22 (22, 24, 24)[26, 26, 28]{28, 30, 30} sts knitwise, knit to end of row—50 (56, 63, 69)[74, 82, 87]{93, 100, 106} sts rem on the working needle for the Right Front Shoulder (as worn).

RIGHT FRONT SHOULDER— SIZES 1–4 ONLY

Bind off all sts knitwise for this section.
Row 1 (WS and each WS row): Purl.
Row 2 (RS, dec): BO 3 sts, knit to end— 47 (53, 60, 66)[-, -, -]{-, -, -} sts rem.
Row 4 (dec): BO 2 sts, knit to end— 45 (51, 58, 64)[-, -, -]{-, -, -} sts rem.
Row 6 (dec): K2tog, knit to end— 44 (50, 57, 63)[-, -, -]{-, -, -} sts rem.
Rep [Rows 5–6] 5 (5, 6, 6)[-, -, -]{-, -, -} more times—39 (45, 51, 57)[-, -, -]{-, -, -} sts rem.
Proceed to Right Front Shoulder— All Sizes.

RIGHT FRONT SHOULDER— SIZES 5–10 ONLY

Bind off all sts knitwise for this section.
Row 1 (WS and each WS row): Purl.
Row 2 (RS, dec): BO 3 sts, knit to end— - (-, -, -)[71, 79, 84]{90, 97, 103} sts rem.
Row 4 (dec): BO - (-, -, -)[3, 3, 2]{2, 2, 2} sts, knit to end— - (-, -, -)[68, 76, 82]{88, 95, 101} sts rem.
Row 6 (dec): BO 2 sts, knit to end— - (-, -, -)[66, 74, 80]{86, 93, 99} sts rem.
Row 8 (dec): K2tog, knit to end— - (-, -, -)[65, 73, 79]{85, 92, 98} sts rem.
Rep [Rows 7–8] - (-, -, -)[4, 4, 5]{5, 6, 6} more times— - (-, -, -) [61, 69, 74]{80, 86, 92} sts rem. Proceed to Right Front Shoulder—All Sizes.

RIGHT FRONT SHOULDER— ALL SIZES

Work in St st until the Front measures approx. 22 (23, 25, 26) [27, 28, 29]{29, 30, 30} in. / 56 (58.5, 63.5, 66){68.5, 71, 73.5}{73.5, 76, 76} cm from the CO edge, ending with

a WS row. The total number of rows worked on the Front and Back from the CO to the shoulder BO should be the same.
With RS facing, BO all sts knitwise.

LEFT FRONT SHOULDER— SIZES 1–4 ONLY

Bind off all sts purlwise for this section.
Place the live sts of the Left Front Shoulder onto the larger needle. Rejoin Color A with the RS facing.
Row 1 (RS and each RS row): Knit.
Row 2 (WS, dec): BO 3 sts, purl to end—47 (53, 60, 66)[-, -, -]{-, -, -} sts rem.
Row 4 (dec): BO 2 sts, purl to end—45 (51, 58, 64)[-, -, -]{-, -, -} sts rem.
Row 6 (dec): P2tog, purl to end—44 (50, 57, 63)[-, -, -]{-, -, -} sts rem.
Rep [Rows 5–6] 5 (5, 6, 6)[-, -, -]{-, -, -} more times—39 (45, 51, 57)[-, -, -]{-, -, -} sts rem. Proceed to Left Front Shoulder—All Sizes.

LEFT FRONT SHOULDER— SIZES 5–10 ONLY

Bind off all sts purlwise for this section.
Place the live sts of the Left Front Shoulder onto the larger needle. Rejoin Color A with the RS facing.
Row 1 (RS and each RS row): Knit.
Row 2 (WS, dec): BO 3 sts, purl to end—- (-, -, -)[71, 79, 84]{90, 97, 103} sts rem.
Row 4 (dec): BO - (-, -, -)[3, 3, 2]{2, 2, 2} sts, purl to end—- (-, -, -)[68, 76, 82]{88, 95, 101} sts rem.
Row 6 (dec): BO 2 sts, purl to end—- (-, -, -)[66, 74, 80]{86, 93, 99} sts rem.
Row 8 (dec): P2tog, purl to end—- (-, -, -)[65, 73, 79]{85, 92, 98} sts rem.
Rep [Rows 7–8] - (-, -, -)[4, 4, 5]{5, 6, 6} *more* times— - (-, -, -)[61, 69, 74]{80, 86, 92} sts rem. Proceed to Left Front Shoulder—All Sizes.

LEFT FRONT SHOULDER— ALL SIZES

Work in St st until the Front measures approx. 22 (23, 25, 26)[27, 28, 29]{29, 30, 30} in. / 56 (58.5, 63.5, 66)[68.5, 71, 73.5]{73.5, 76, 76} cm from the CO edge, ending with a RS row. The total number of rows worked on the Front and Back from the CO to the shoulder BO should be the same.
With WS facing, BO all sts purlwise.

SLEEVES (MAKE 2 THE SAME)

SLEEVE CUFF

Using the smaller needle and Color A, CO 66 (66, 70, 70)[70, 70, 70]{74, 74, 74} sts using the Long Tail cast on method. Do not join to work in the rnd.
Row 1 (RS): *K2, p2; rep from * to last 2 sts, k2.
Row 2 (WS): *P2, k2; rep from * to last 2 sts, p2.
Rep Rows 1–2 until the cuff measures 2½ in. / 6.5 cm from the CO edge, ending with a WS row.

BODY OF SLEEVE

Switch to larger needle.
Beginning with a RS row, work 8 (8, 8, 6)[6, 6, 4]{4, 4, 4} rows in St st.
Inc Row (RS): K3, M1L, knit to last 3 sts, M1R, k3—2 sts inc.
Cont in St st until the sleeve measures 18.75 (19.25, 20.25, 20.75)[21.25, 21.75, 21.75]{22.25, 22.75,

Coffee Talk

The series *Pretty Little Liars* shared a Warner Bros. lot with *Gilmore Girls*. Luke's Diner became the Apple Rose Grille and got a complete interior makeover with white painted brick walls, chrome furniture, and wood paneling.

22.75} in. / 47.5 (49, 51.5, 52.5)[54, 55, 55]{56.5, 58, 58} cm from CO edge, or to desired length, ending with a WS row.

AT THE SAME TIME, work the Inc Row every 10 (10, 10, 8)[6, 6, 6]{6, 6, 4th row 11 (7, 3, 2)[22, 14, 11]{5, 1, 33} *more* time(s), then every 8 (8, 8, 6)[-, 4, 4]{4, 4, 2}th/nd row 2 (7, 12, 19)[-, 12, 17]{26, 32, 2} times—28 (30, 32, 44)[46, 54, 58]{64, 68, 72} sts inc; 94 (96, 102, 114)[116, 124, 128]{138, 142, 146} sts total.

With RS facing, BO all sts knitwise.

SEAMING

If desired, wet block all pieces per Schematic before seaming. Use Mattress stitch and Color A yarn for all seams. Seam Front and Back Body pieces at shoulders. Seam each sleeve cap to body, matching up the middle of the sleeve cap with the shoulder seam. Seam the underside of the sleeves and the sides of the body.

COLLAR

Using the smaller 16 in. / 40 cm circular needle and Color A, beginning in the middle of the back neckline BO sts, pick up and knit: 16 (16, 18, 18)[20, 20, 21]{21, 23, 23} back neck sts, 7 sts up the left back neckline edge, 22 (22, 25, 25)[28, 28, 28]{28, 31, 31} sts down the left front of the neckline edge, 22 (22, 24, 24)[26, 26, 28]{28, 30, 30} front neckline sts, 22 (22, 25, 25)[28, 28, 28]{28, 31, 31} sts up the right front of the neckline edge, 7 sts down the right back neckline edge, and 16 (16, 18, 18)[20, 20, 21]{21, 23, 23} rem back neck sts—112 (112, 124, 124)[136, 136, 140]{140, 152, 152} sts total. Pm for BOR and join to work in the rnd.

Rib Rnd: *K2, p2; rep from * to end of rnd.

Rep Rib Rnd until the collar measures 1 in. / 2.5 cm from the picked-up edge.

BO all sts loosely in patt.

FINISHING

If not previously blocked before seaming, wet block the garment per the Schematic. Weave in all ends.

SCHEMATIC

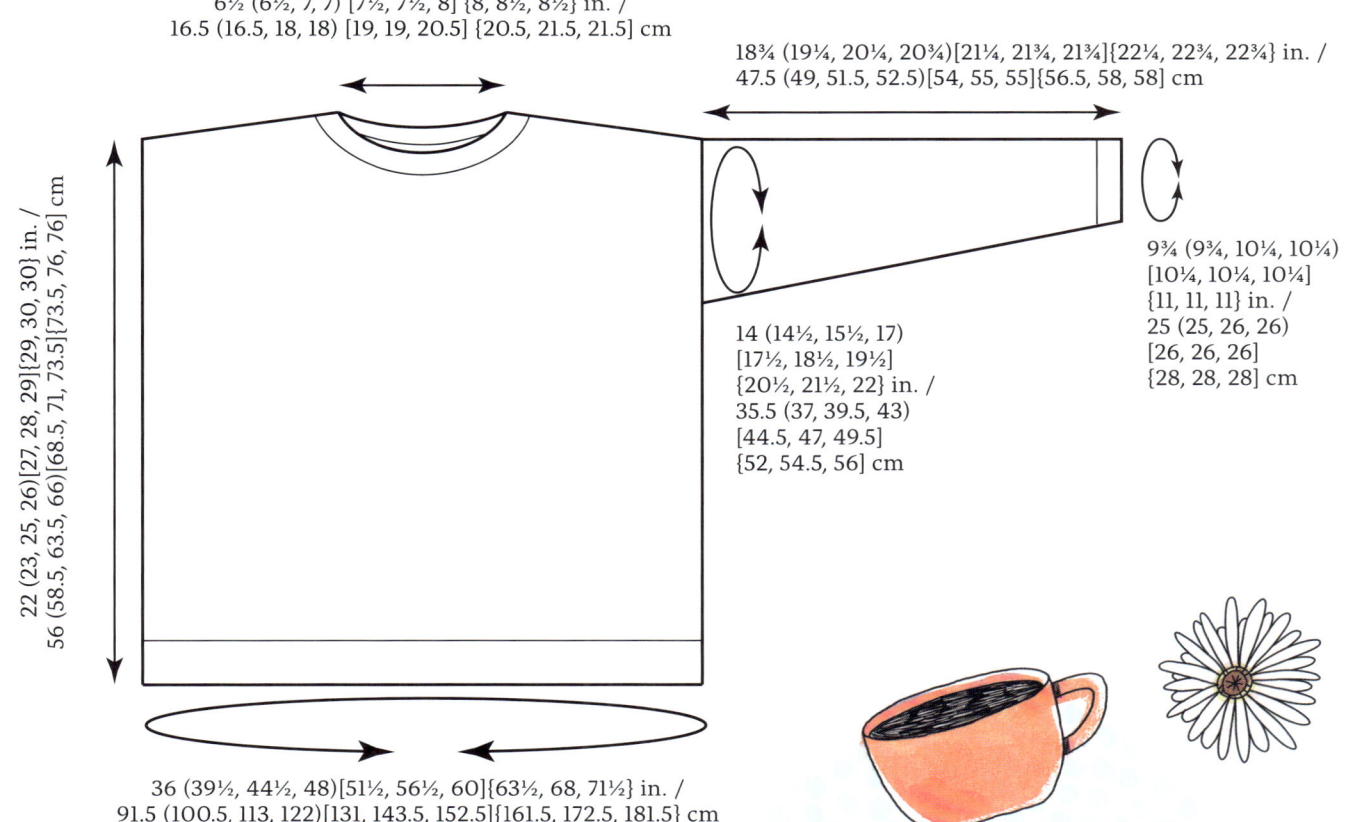

CHART A: SIZES 1–5 ONLY

KEY

☐ k on RS, p on WS
■ Color A
■ Color B
■ Color C

CHART B

Rory's Debutante Tunic

Designed by Nicole Reeves

SKILL LEVEL: ADVANCED

"I wanted my granddaughter to be presented to society in a beautiful, elegant ballroom, not a Shakey's."

—Emily, Season 2, Episode 6

To everyone's surprise, in Season 2, Episode 6, Rory allows Emily to arrange her début at the Debutante Ball. A popular society ritual performed from 1780 to 1914 where women wear white ball gowns and gloves, a "Deb Ball" was originally designed to show off unmarried women to bachelors looking for a potential wife. In Emily Gilmore's world, it's a way for grandparents to show off their accomplished grandchildren to their high-society friends, an experience they missed out on with Lorelai. Viewers learn through flashbacks that a sixteen-year-old Lorelai realized she was pregnant with Rory while unable to fit into her white debutante ball gown. What should have been a crowning achievement for the Gilmores—to present their top-of-her-class only child—ended in societal and self-imposed shame due to an unplanned teenage pregnancy. With a fight brewing between Emily and Richard over social obligations, anxiety between Rory and Dean arising from having to learn a dance and wear fancy clothing, and the stress between Lorelai and Christopher over his minimal presence in his daughter's life, history repeats itself and the Debutante Ball once again doesn't turn out the way the Gilmores plan.

Distinguish yourself from the other debutantes with this elegant sleeveless top inspired by Rory's white ball gown. The front and back pieces are worked flat identically with beautiful vines separated by vertical columns climbing up toward the neck on a background of reverse stockinette. The shoulders are joined with a Three-Needle bind off and the sides seamed, and finally stitches are picked up and worked in garter stitch detailing for the hem, neckline, and armholes.

SIZES
1 (2, 3, 4, 5)

FINISHED MEASUREMENTS
Chest Circumference: 31½ (40¾, 50½, 60, 69½) in. / 80 (103.5, 128.5, 152.5, 176.5) cm
Garment is designed to be worn with 0–4 in. / 0–10 cm of positive ease.

YARN
DK weight yarn, shown in Blue Sky Fibers *Skyland* (4-ply; 40% fine Highland wool, 30% baby alpaca, 30% silk; 210 yd. / 192 m per 3½ oz. / 100 g hank) in color 2407 Cumulus, 4 (6, 7, 8, 10) hanks

NEEDLES
US 6 / 4 mm, 16 in. / 40 cm and 24–32 in. / 60–80 cm long circular needles or size needed to obtain gauge

NOTIONS
Stitch marker
Waste yarn or stitch holders
Tapestry needle

GAUGE
23.5 sts and 30 rows = 4 in. / 10 cm over Chart A pattern worked flat, taken after blocking
Make sure to check your gauge.

PATTERN NOTES
- The tunic is worked from the bottom up, flat, in two identical pieces, then seamed together at the sides and shoulders. The neckline and armholes are trimmed in garter stitch after seaming.
- Selvedge sts are worked in garter stitch.
- Instructions for Size 1 are provided first, with instructions for Sizes 2–5 provided in parentheses. When only one set of numbers is provided, it applies to all sizes.

Continued on page 134

- During the neckline shaping, take care to maintain the proper stitch count of each row. To accomplish this: If a row on the lace chart has two yarn overs without two corresponding ssk sts, decrease one stitch at the beginning and end of the lace repeat. If it contains two ssk sts without two corresponding yarn overs, increase one stitch at the beginning and end of the lace repeat. This is to be done in addition to the bound off stitches that shape the neckline.

FRONT

Cast on 94 (122, 150, 178, 206) sts using the Long Tail cast on method. Do not join to work in the rnd.

Beginning with a RS row, work 13 rows of garter stitch (knit every row). You will end after completing a RS row.

Begin Chart A, reading all RS (odd-numbered) rows from right to left and all WS (even-numbered) rows from left to right. Work Setup Row (a WS row) once, then work [Rows 1–24] 4 times total to complete 96 rows (the pattern repeat is worked 3 (4, 5, 6, 7) times across each row).

ARMHOLE SHAPING

As the following armhole shaping is worked, increase and decrease sts as outlined in the Pattern Notes to maintain proper st count.

SIZE 1 ONLY:

Row 1 (RS, dec): BO 1 st knitwise, work est patt to end of row—1 st dec.
Row 2 (WS, dec): BO 1 st knitwise, work est patt to end of row—1 st dec.
Rep [Rows 1–2] 6 more times.
14 sts dec; 80 sts rem.
Proceed to All Sizes.

SIZE 2 ONLY:

Row 1 (RS, dec): BO 4 sts knitwise, work est patt to end of row—4 sts dec.
Row 2 (WS, dec): BO 4 sts knitwise, work est patt to end of row—4 sts dec.
8 sts dec; 114 sts rem.
Row 3 (RS, dec): BO 3 sts knitwise, work est patt to end of row—3 sts dec.
Row 4 (WS, dec): BO 3 sts knitwise, work est patt to end of row—3 sts dec.
6 sts dec; 108 sts rem.
Row 5 (RS, dec): BO 2 sts knitwise, work est patt to end of row—2 sts dec.
Row 6 (WS, dec): BO 2 sts knitwise, work est patt to end of row—2 sts dec.
4 sts dec; 104 sts rem.
Row 7 (RS, dec): BO 1 st knitwise, work est patt to end of row—1 st dec.
Row 8 (WS, dec): BO 1 st knitwise, work est patt to end of row—1 st dec.
Rep [Rows 7–8] 5 more times.
12 sts dec; 92 sts rem.
Proceed to All Sizes.

SIZE 3 ONLY:

Row 1 (RS, dec): BO 5 sts knitwise, work est patt to end of row—5 sts dec.
Row 2 (WS, dec): BO 5 sts knitwise, work est patt to end of row—5 sts dec.
Rep [Rows 1–2] 2 more times.
30 sts dec; 120 sts rem.

Row 7 (RS, dec): BO 4 sts knitwise, work est patt to end of row—4 sts dec.
Row 8 (WS, dec): BO 4 sts knitwise, work est patt to end of row—4 sts dec.
Rep [Rows 7–8] 1 more time.
16 sts dec; 104 sts rem.
Row 11 (RS, dec): BO 2 sts knitwise, work est patt to end of row—2 sts dec.
Row 12 (WS, dec): BO 2 sts knitwise, work est patt to end of row—2 sts dec.
4 sts dec; 100 sts rem.
Row 13 (RS, dec): BO 1 st knitwise, work est patt to end of row—1 st dec.
Row 14 (WS, dec): BO 1 st knitwise, work est patt to end of row—1 st dec.
Rep [Rows 13–14] 2 more times.
6 sts dec; 94 sts rem.
Proceed to All Sizes.

SIZE 4 ONLY:
Row 1 (RS, dec): BO 5 sts knitwise, work est patt to end of row—5 sts dec.
Row 2 (WS, dec): BO 5 sts knitwise, work est patt to end of row—5 sts dec.
Rep [Rows 1–2] 4 more times.
50 sts dec; 128 sts rem.
Row 11 (RS, dec): BO 4 sts knitwise, work est patt to end of row—4 sts dec.
Row 12 (WS, dec): BO 4 sts knitwise, work est patt to end of row—4 sts dec.
Rep [Rows 11–12] 1 more time.
16 sts dec; 112 sts rem.
Row 15 (RS, dec): BO 2 sts knitwise, work est patt to end of row—2 sts dec.
Row 16 (WS, dec): BO 2 sts knitwise, work est patt to end of row—2 sts dec.
Rep [Rows 15–16] 1 more time.
8 sts dec; 104 sts rem.
Row 19 (RS, dec): BO 1 st knitwise, work est patt to end of row—1 st dec.
Row 20 (WS, dec): BO 1 st knitwise, work est patt to end of row—1 st dec.
Rep [Rows 19–20] 1 more time.
4 sts dec; 100 sts rem.
Proceed to All Sizes.

SIZE 5 ONLY:
Row 1 (RS, dec): BO 5 sts knitwise, work est patt to end of row—5 sts dec.
Row 2 (WS, dec): BO 5 sts knitwise, work est patt to end of row—5 sts dec.
Rep [Rows 1–2] 6 more times.
70 sts dec; 136 sts rem.
Row 15 (RS, dec): BO 4 sts knitwise, work est patt to end of row—4 sts dec.
Row 16 (WS, dec): BO 4 sts knitwise, work est patt to end of row—4 sts dec.
Rep [Rows 15–16] 1 more time.
16 sts dec; 120 sts rem.
Row 19 (RS, dec): BO 2 sts knitwise, work est patt to end of row—2 sts dec.
Row 20 (WS, dec): BO 2 sts knitwise, work est patt to end of row—2 sts dec.
Rep [Rows 19–20] 1 more time.
8 sts dec; 112 sts rem.
Row 23 (RS, dec): BO 1 st knitwise, work est patt to end of row—1 st dec.
Row 24 (WS, dec): BO 1 st knitwise, work est patt to end of row—1 st dec.
Rep [Rows 23–24] 3 more times.
8 sts dec; 104 sts rem.
Proceed to All Sizes.

ALL SIZES:
Row 1 (RS): K1, work est patt to last st, k1.
Row 2 (WS): K1, work est patt to last st, k1.
Rep Rows 1–2 until the front yoke measures 6½ (6½, 7½, 9½, 11¼) in. / 16.5 (16.5, 19, 24, 28.5) cm from the underarm, ending after a WS row—80 (92, 94, 100, 104) sts.

NECKLINE SHAPING
As the following neckline shaping is worked, increase and decrease sts as outlined in the Pattern Notes to maintain proper st count.
Separation Row (RS): K1, work in est patt to center 22 (26, 26, 28, 30) sts, place these just worked sts onto waste yarn or st holder for the second shoulder. BO center 22 (26, 26, 28, 30) sts knitwise, work in est patt to last st, k1—29 (33, 34, 36, 37) sts rem for each shoulder.
Next Row (WS): K1, work est patt to end of row.

FIRST SHOULDER SHAPING
As the following shoulder shaping is worked, increase and decrease sts as outlined in the Pattern Notes to maintain proper st count.

SIZE 1 ONLY:
Row 1 (RS, dec): BO 3 sts knitwise, work est patt to last st, k1—3 sts dec.
Row 2 (WS): K1, work est patt to end of row.
Rep [Rows 1–2] 4 more times.
15 sts dec; 14 sts rem.
Row 11 (RS, dec): BO 2 sts knitwise, work est patt to last st, k1—2 sts dec.
Row 12 (WS): K1, work est patt to end of row.
Rep [Rows 11–12] 2 more times.
6 sts dec; 8 sts rem.
Row 17 (RS, dec): BO 1 st knitwise, work est patt to last st, k1—7 sts.
Row 18 (WS): K1, work est patt to end of row.
With RS facing, BO all sts knitwise.

SIZES 2–5 ONLY:
Row 1 (RS, dec): BO 5 sts knitwise, work est patt to last st, k1—5 sts dec.
Row 2 (WS): K1, work est patt to end of row.
Rep [Rows 1–2] 1 more time.

10 sts dec; - (23, 24, 26, 27) sts rem.
Row 5 (RS, dec): BO 4 sts knitwise, work est patt to last st, k1—4 sts dec.
Row 6 (WS): K1, work est patt to end of row.
Rep [Rows 5–6] - (0, 0, 1, 1) more time(s).
- (4, 4, 8, 8) sts dec; - (19, 20, 18, 19) sts rem.
Next Row A (RS, dec): BO 3 sts knitwise, work est patt to last st, k1—3 sts dec.
Next Row B (WS): K1, work est patt to end of row.
Rep [Next Rows A–B] - (0, 2, 1, 1) more time(s).
- (3, 9, 6, 6) sts dec; - (16, 11, 12, 13) sts rem.
Next Row C (RS, dec): BO 2 sts knitwise, work est patt to last st, k1—2 sts dec.
Next Row D (WS): K1, work est patt to end of row.
Rep [Next Rows C–D] - (3, 0, 1, 1) more time(s).
- (8, 2, 4, 4) sts dec; - (8, 9, 8, 9) sts rem.
Next Row E (RS, dec): BO 1 st knitwise, work est patt to last st, k1—1 st dec.
Next Row F (WS): K1, work est patt to end of row.
Rep [Next Rows E–F] - (0, 1, 0, 1) more time(s).
- (1, 2, 1, 2) sts dec; 7 sts rem.
With RS facing, BO all sts knitwise.

SECOND SHOULDER SHAPING

As the following shoulder shaping is worked, increase and decrease sts as outlined in the Pattern Notes to maintain proper st count.
Place the live sts of the second shoulder onto the working needle. Rejoin yarn with the WS facing.

SIZE 1 ONLY:
Row 1 (WS, dec): BO 3 sts purlwise, work est patt to last st, k1—3 sts dec.
Row 2 (RS): K1, work est patt to end of row.
Rep [Rows 1–2] 4 more times.
15 sts dec; 14 sts rem.

Row 11 (WS, dec): BO 2 sts purlwise, work est patt to last st, k1—2 sts dec.
Row 12 (RS): K1, work est patt to end of row.
Rep [Rows 11–12] 2 more times.
6 sts dec; 8 sts rem.
Row 17 (WS, dec): BO 1 st purlwise, work est patt to last st, k1—7 sts.
Row 18 (RS): K1, work est patt to end of row.
With RS facing, BO all sts purlwise.

SIZES 2–5 ONLY:
Row 1 (WS, dec): BO 5 sts purlwise, work est patt to last st, k1—5 sts dec.
Row 2 (RS): K1, work est patt to end of row.
Rep [Rows 1–2] 1 more time.
10 sts dec; - (23, 24, 26, 27) sts rem.
Row 5 (WS, dec): BO 4 sts purlwise, work est patt to last st, k1—4 sts dec.
Row 6 (RS): K1, work est patt to end of row.
Rep [Rows 5–6] - (0, 0, 1, 1) more time(s).
- (4, 4, 8, 8) sts dec; - (19, 20, 18, 19) sts rem.
Next Row A (WS, dec): BO 3 sts purlwise, work est patt to last st, k1—3 sts dec.
Next Row B (RS): K1, work est patt to end of row.
Rep [Next Rows A–B] - (0, 2, 1, 1) more time(s).
- (3, 9, 6, 6) sts dec; - (16, 11, 12, 13) sts rem.
Next Row C (WS, dec): BO 2 sts purlwise, work est patt to last st, k1—2 sts dec.
Next Row D (RS): K1, work est patt to end of row.
Rep [Next Rows C–D] - (3, 0, 1, 1) more time(s).
- (8, 2, 4, 4) sts dec; - (8, 9, 8, 9) sts rem.
Next Row E (WS, dec): BO 1 st purlwise, work est patt to last st, k1—1 st dec.
Next Row F (RS): K1, work est patt to end of row.
Rep [Next Rows E–F] - (0, 1, 0, 1) more time(s).
- (1, 2, 1, 2) sts dec; 7 sts rem.

Final WS Row: Work est patt to last st, k1.
With RS facing, BO all sts knitwise.

BACK
Work as for the Front.

BLOCKING & SEAMING
Weave in all ends to both pieces.
Wet block the Front and Back per the Schematic (dimensions provided are pre-seamed dimensions).
Once dry, seam the sides of the garment from underarm to bottom hem using Mattress stitch. Then seam the shoulders using the Horizontal Seaming method.

NECKLINE
Using the 16 in. / 40 cm circular needle, and starting at the left shoulder seam (as worn), pick up and knit sts evenly around the neckline edge: 1 st for every bound off st, and approx. 3 sts for every 4 rows up the edges of the neckline. Pm for BOR and join to work in the rnd.
Rnd 1: Knit.
Rnd 2: Purl.
Rep Rnds 1–2 once more.
BO all sts purlwise.

ARMHOLES
Using the 16 in. / 40 cm circular needle, and starting at the underarm seam, pick up and knit sts evenly around the armhole edge: approx. 1 st for every bound off st, and approx. 3 sts for every 4 rows. Pm for BOR and join to work in the rnd.
Rnd 1: Knit.
Rnd 2: Purl.
Rep Rnds 1–2 once more.
BO all sts purlwise.
Rep for second armhole.
To smooth out the Neckline and Armhole sts, steam block if desired.

CHART A

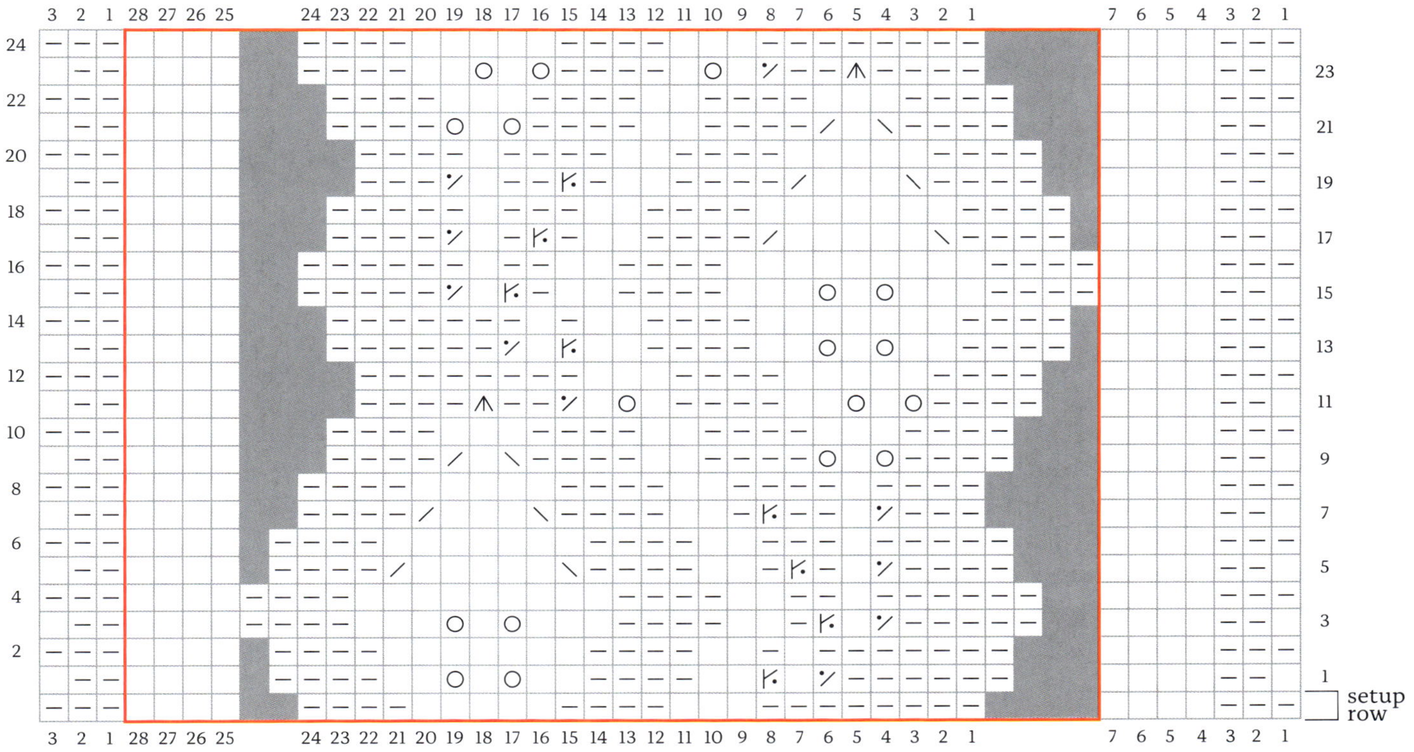

KEY

- ▨ No stitch
- ☐ k on RS, p on WS
- − p on RS, k on WS
- ╱ k2tog
- ╲ ssk
- ⌇ p2tog
- ⋀ s2kp
- ⱪ M1RP
- ○ yo
- ▭ Pattern repeat

SCHEMATIC

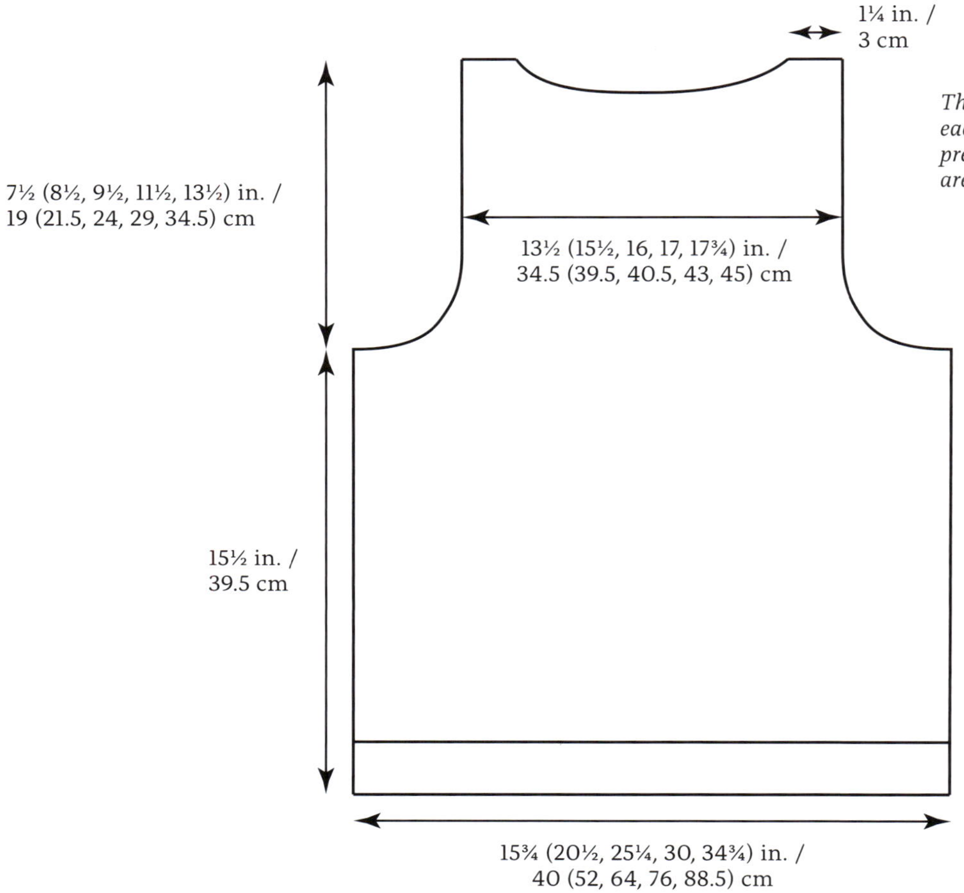

1¼ in. / 3 cm

The dimensions provided are for each flat piece of the garment, pre-seaming, before any edgings are applied.

7½ (8½, 9½, 11½, 13½) in. / 19 (21.5, 24, 29, 34.5) cm

13½ (15½, 16, 17, 17¾) in. / 34.5 (39.5, 40.5, 43, 45) cm

15½ in. / 39.5 cm

15¾ (20½, 25¼, 30, 34¾) in. / 40 (52, 64, 76, 88.5) cm

Coffee Talk

Both the Debutante Ball and the Chilton Dance were filmed at the Wilshire Ebell Women's Club in Los Angeles.

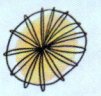

Paris's Mac & Cheese Cardigan

Designed by Sauniell Connally

SKILL LEVEL: ADVANCED

Paris: "Is that mac and cheese?"

Rory: "Sure is."

Paris: "I love mac and cheese."

—Season 2, Episode 16

Although she originally auditioned for the part of Rory, actor Liza Weil impressed the producers so much they created the character of Paris just for her. Creator Amy Sherman-Palladino said, "Liza was in my brain from auditioning for Rory. And I'm like, 'That girl is not right for Rory but she's unbelievably brilliant—she's like a master comedienne,' so I just wrote her in." Unsure if she could play such a role after reading Paris's lines, Weil admitted, "The younger version of myself was really freaked out that that's what they wrote. I couldn't fathom that they would think that they could do that! But now I think it's really flattering and I'm really glad . . . . Looking back at my time on *Gilmore Girls*, [I see] how fortunate I was to be a young actor and to be on a show that made it really cool for girls to be smart. I really don't think there were any other shows like that at that time that were portraying young girls like that." Rory helps Paris relax, gives her the support she lacks at home, and encourages her to ask Tristan out, eat her beloved mac and cheese, and loosen up. The two remain close and even become roommates while attending Yale—cementing their friendship for life.

Inspired by Paris's love of one of Rory and Lorelai's favorite comfort foods, mac and cheese, this oversized drop-shoulder cardigan is worked flat in pieces and then seamed, and features an allover macaroni noodle–style cable pattern. The ribbed placket is worked at the same time as the body until the shoulders. Once the pieces are blocked, the shoulders are seamed, the sleeves attached to the body, then the underarm seams joined. The collar is then seamed to the back neckline.

SIZES
1 (2, 3, 4, 5)[6, 7, 8, 9]{10, 11, 12, 13}

FINISHED MEASUREMENTS
Chest Circumference: 35½ (38¾, 41½, 44, 46¾)[51½, 54, 56¾, 59½]{62¾, 65½, 68, 70¾} in. / 90 (98.5, 105.5, 112, 119)[131, 137, 144, 151]{159.5, 166.5, 172.5, 180} cm

Garment is designed to be worn with 4–7½ in. / 10–19 cm of positive ease.

YARN
Worsted weight yarn, shown in The Lemonade Shop *House Worsted* (100% superwash merino; 212 yd. / 194 m per 3½ oz. / 100 g hank) in color Melt, 9 (10, 11, 12, 13)[14, 15, 16, 17]{18, 19, 20, 21} hanks

NEEDLES
US 7 / 4.5 mm, 24–32 in. / 60–80 cm long circular needles or size needed to obtain gauge

NOTIONS
Spare gauge-size needles (2)
Stitch markers
Stitch holders or waste yarn
Cable needle
Tapestry needle

GAUGE
24 sts and 28 rows = 4 in. / 10 cm in charted pattern worked flat, taken after blocking

Make sure to check your gauge.

PATTERN NOTES
- This cardigan is worked flat, in pieces, and then seamed. The ribbed placket up the front of the sweater is worked contiguously with the body up to the shoulders.
- Once the pieces are complete and blocked, seam the shoulders together. Next, seam the sleeves to the body, centered on the shoulder seam. Once the sleeves are attached, the underarm and side body seams are worked. After all seaming is complete, seam the collar to the back neckline.

Continued on page 142

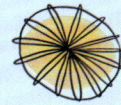

- Instructions for Size 1 are provided first, with instructions for Sizes 2–13 provided in parentheses/brackets. When only one set of numbers is provided, it applies to all sizes.
- Any references to Left and Right within this pattern are based on the garment as worn.

BACK

CAST ON & RIBBED HEM

CO 104 (116, 124, 132, 140)[152, 160, 168, 176]{188, 196, 204, 212} sts using the Long Tail cast on method.

Row 1 (RS): K1,*k2, p2; rep from * to last 3 sts, k3.

Row 2 (WS): P3, *k2, p2; rep from * to last st, p1.

Rep Rows 1–2 until the hem measures 2 in. / 5 cm from the CO edge, ending with a WS row.

On the final row, place a marker at each edge 4 (7, 5, 6, 4)[7, 5, 6, 4]{7, 5, 6, 4} sts in from the end.

BACK BODY

Row 1 (RS): K1, purl to M, sm, work Chart A (B, B, A, A)[B, B, A, A]{B, B, A, A} to M, sm, purl to last st, k1.

Row 2 (WS): P1, knit to M, sm, work Chart A (B, B, A, A)[B, B, A, A]{B, B, A, A} to M, sm, knit to last st, p1.

Rep Rows 1–2 until the back measures 22½ (23, 24, 24, 24½)[25, 25, 25½, 25½]{26, 26, 27, 27½} in. / 57 (58.5, 61, 61, 62)[63.5, 63.5, 65, 65]{66, 66, 68.5, 70} cm from the CO edge, ending with a WS row.

BACK NECKLINE

Separation Row (RS): Work in est patt over 30 (35, 38, 41, 44)[49, 52, 55, 58]{63, 66, 69, 72} sts. Place these just worked sts on waste yarn for the back right shoulder. BO 44 (46, 48, 50, 52)[54, 56, 58, 60]{62, 64, 66, 68} sts knitwise, work in est patt to the end of row—30 (35, 38, 41, 44)[49, 52, 55, 58]{63, 66, 69, 72} sts rem for back left shoulder.

BACK LEFT SHOULDER SHAPING

Row 1 (WS): Work est patt to end of row.

Short Row 2 (RS): Work est patt to last 10 (12, 13, 14, 15)[16, 17, 18, 19]{21, 22, 23, 24} sts, W&T.

Short Row 3: Work est patt to end of row.

Short Row 4: Work est patt to 10 (12, 13, 14, 15)[16, 17, 18, 19]{21, 22, 23, 24} sts before prev wrapped st, W&T.

Short Row 5: Work est patt to end of row.

Break yarn and place all sts on stitch holder or waste yarn. The W&T sts will remain unresolved and will be hidden on the inside of the garment once the shoulders are seamed.

BACK RIGHT SHOULDER SHAPING

Place the live sts of the Back Right Shoulder onto the working needle. Rejoin yarn with the WS facing.

Short Row 1 (WS): Work est patt to last 10 (12, 13, 14, 15)[16, 17, 18, 19]{21, 22, 23, 24} sts, W&T.

Short Row 2 (RS): Work est patt to end of row.

Short Row 3: Work est patt to 10 (12, 13, 14, 15)[16, 17, 18, 19]{21, 22, 23, 24} sts before prev wrapped st, W&T.

Short Row 4: Work est patt to end of row.

Short Row 5: Work est patt to end of row resolving wrapped sts as encountered.

Break yarn and place all sts on stitch holder or waste yarn.

RIGHT FRONT

CAST ON & RIBBED HEM

Note: The first stitch of the front placket is worked in garter st to make a tidy edge stitch.

CO 59 (63, 67, 71, 75)[83, 87, 91, 95]{99, 103, 107, 111} sts using the Long Tail cast on method.

Row 1 (RS): K2, (p1, k1) 5 times, pm-A, *k2, p2; rep from * to last 3 sts, k3.

Row 2 (WS): P3, *k2, p2; rep from * to M-A, sm, (p1, k1) 6 times.

Row 3: K2, (p1, k1) 5 times, sm, *k2, p2; rep from * to last 3 sts, k3.

Rep Rows 2–3 until the hem measures 2 in. / 5 cm from the CO edge, ending with a WS row.

RIGHT FRONT BODY

Row 1 (RS): K2, (p1, k1) 5 times, sm, p2 (1, 3, 2, 1)[2, 4, 3, 2]{1, 3, 2, 1}, pm-B, work Chart B (A, A, B, A)[B, B, A, B]{A, A, B, A} to last 3 (2, 4, 3, 2)[3, 5, 4, 3]{2, 4, 3, 2} sts, pm-C, purl to last st, k1.

Row 2 (WS): P1, knit to M-C, sm, work Chart B (A, A, B, A)[B, B, A, B]{A, A, B, A} to M-B, sm, purl to M-A, sm, (p1, k1) 6 times.

Row 3: K2, (p1, k1) 5 times, sm, purl to M-B, sm, work Chart B (A, A, B, A)[B, B, A, B]{A, A, B, A} to M-C, sm, purl to last st, k1.

Rep Rows 2–3 until the Right Front measures 16 (16, 17, 17, 17½)[17½, 17½, 17¾, 17¾]{18, 18, 19, 19½} in. / 40.5 (40.5, 43, 43, 44.5)[44.5, 44.5, 45, 45]{45.5, 45.5, 48.5, 50} cm from the CO edge, ending with a WS row.

Make a note of the last row worked so your Left Front can be knit to match.

RIGHT FRONT NECKLINE SHAPING

As the following shaping is worked, where you cannot complete a full cable due to the decrease sts, purl the sts to maintain the reverse St st fabric. Remove M-B as necessary to allow for the decreases to shift into the charted pattern.

Row 1 (RS, dec): K2, (p1, k1) 5 times, sm, k2tog-tbl, work est patt to end of row—1 st dec.

Row 2 (WS): Work est patt to M-A, sm, (p1, k1) 6 times.

Rep [Rows 1–2] 12 (8, 10, 12, 14)[19, 21, 23, 24]{21, 23, 25, 26} more times.

13 (9, 11, 13, 15)[20, 22, 24, 25]{24, 25, 26, 27} sts dec;

46 (54, 56, 58, 60)[63, 65, 67, 70]{77, 79, 81, 84} sts rem.

Sizes 1 (2, 3, 4, 5)[6, 7, -, -]{10, 11, -, -} Only: Proceed to Continue Right Front Neck Shaping.

Sizes - (-, -, -, -)[-, -, 8, 9]{-, -, 12, 13} Only: Proceed to All Sizes.

CONTINUE RIGHT FRONT NECK SHAPING

Row 1 (RS, dec): K2, (p1, k1) 5 times, sm, k2tog-tbl, work est patt to end of row—1 st dec.

Row 2 (WS): Work est patt to M-A, sm, (p1, k1) 6 times.

Row 3: K2, (p1, k1) 5 times, sm, work est patt to end of row.

Row 4: Work est patt to M-A, sm, (p1, k1) 6 times.

Rep [Rows 1–4] 3 (6, 5, 4, 3)[1, 0, -, -]{1, 0, -, -} more times.

4 (7, 6, 5, 4)[2, 1, -, -]{2, 1, -, -} sts dec;

42 (47, 50, 53, 56)[61, 64, -, -]{75, 78, -, -} sts rem.

Proceed to All Sizes.

All Sizes:

Row 1 (RS): K2, (p1, k1) 5 times, sm, work est patt to end of row.

Row 2 (WS): Work est patt to M-A, sm, (p1, k1) 6 times.

Rep Rows 1–2 until the Right Front measures 22½ (23, 24, 24, 24½)[25, 25, 25½, 25½]{26, 26, 27, 27½} in. / 57 (58.5, 61, 61, 62)[63.5, 63.5, 65, 65]{66, 66, 68.5, 70} cm from the CO edge when measured at the armhole edge, ending with a WS row.

RIGHT FRONT SHOULDER SHAPING

Row 1 (RS): K2, (p1, k1) 5 times, sm, work est patt to end of row.

Row 2 (WS): Work est patt to M-A, sm, (p1, k1) 6 times.

Short Row 3: K2, (p1, k1) 5 times, sm, work est patt to last 10 (12, 13, 14, 15)[16, 17, 18, 19]{21, 22, 23, 24} sts, W&T.

Short Row 4: Work est patt to M-A, sm, (p1, k1) 6 times.

Short Row 5: K1, (p1, k1) 5 times, sm, work est patt to 10 (12, 13, 14, 15)[16, 17, 18, 19]{21, 22, 23, 24} sts before prev wrapped st, W&T.

Short Row 6: Work est patt to M-A, sm, (p1, k1) 6 times.

Do not break yarn or place sts on hold. The W&T sts will remain unresolved and will be hidden on the inside of the garment once the shoulders are seamed.

RIGHT FRONT COLLAR

Setup Row (RS): K2, (p1, k1) 4 times, p1, kfb, rm, place the rem 30 (35, 38, 41, 44)[49, 52, 55, 58]{63, 66, 69, 72} sts on stitch holder or waste yarn—13 sts rem on working needle for collar.

Row 1 (WS): P2, (k1, p1) 5 times, p1.

Row 2 (RS): K2, (p1, k1) 5 times, k1.

Rep Rows 1–2 until the collar measures approx. 4¼ (4¼, 4½, 4½, 4¾)[5, 5, 5¼, 5½]{5½, 5¾, 6, 6} in. / 11 (11, 11.5, 11.5, 12)[12.5, 12.5, 13.5, 14]{14, 14.5, 15, 15} cm, ending with a WS row.

Break yarn and place all sts on stitch holder or waste yarn.

LEFT FRONT

CAST ON & RIBBED HEM

Note: The last stitch of the front placket is worked in garter st to make a tidy edge stitch.

CO 59 (63, 67, 71, 75)[83, 87, 91, 95]{99, 103, 107, 111} sts using the Long Tail cast on method.

Row 1 (RS): K3, *p2, k2; rep from * to last 12 sts, pm-A, (k1, p1) 5 times, k2.

Row 2 (WS): (K1, p1) 6 times, sm, *k2, p2; rep from * to last 3 sts, k3.

Row 3: K3, *p2, k2; rep from * to M-A, sm, (k1, p1) 5 times, k2.

Rep Rows 2–3 until the hem measures 2 in. / 5 cm from the CO edge, ending with a WS row.

LEFT FRONT BODY

Row 1 (RS): K1, p2 (1, 3, 2, 1)[2, 4, 3, 2]{1, 3, 2, 1}, pm-C, work Chart B (A, A, B, A)[B, B, A, B]{A, A, B, A} to 2 (1, 3, 2, 1)[2, 4, 3, 2]{1, 3, 2, 1} sts before M-A, pm-B, purl to M-A, sm, (k1, p1) 5 times, k2.

Row 2 (WS): (K1, p1) 6 times, sm, knit to M-B, work Chart B (A, A, B, A)[B, B, A, B]{A, A, B, A} to M-C, sm, knit to last st, p1.

Row 3: K1, purl to M-C, sm, work Chart B (A, A, B, A)[B, B, A, B]{A, A, B, A} to M-B, sm, purl to M-A, sm, (k1, p1) 5 times, k2.

Rep Rows 2–3 until the Left Front measures 16 (16, 17, 17, 17½)[17½, 17½, 17¾, 17¾]{18, 18, 19, 19½} in. / 40.5 (40.5, 43, 43, 44.5)[44.5, 44.5, 45, 45]{45.5, 45.5, 48.5, 50} cm from the CO edge, ending with a WS row. This length should match the Right Front.

LEFT FRONT NECKLINE SHAPING

As the following shaping is worked, where you cannot complete a full cable due to the decrease sts, purl the sts to maintain the reverse St st fabric. Remove M-B as necessary to allow for the decreases to shift into the charted pattern.

Row 1 (RS, dec): Work est patt to 2 sts before M-A, k2tog, sm, (k1, p1) 5 times, k2—1 st dec.

Row 2 (WS): (K1, p1) 6 times, sm, work est patt to end of row.

Rep [Rows 1–2] 12 (8, 10, 12, 14)[19, 21, 23, 24]{21, 23, 25, 26} more times.

13 (9, 11, 13, 15)[20, 22, 24, 25]{24, 25, 26, 27} sts dec;

46 (54, 56, 58, 60)[63, 65, 67, 70]{77, 79, 81, 84} sts rem.

Sizes 1 (2, 3, 4, 5)[6, 7, -, -]{10, 11, -, -} Only: Proceed to Continue Left Front Neck Shaping.

Sizes - (-, -, -, -)[-, -, 8, 9]{-, -, 12, 13} Only: Proceed to All Sizes.

CONTINUE LEFT FRONT NECK SHAPING

Row 1 (RS, dec): Work est patt to 2 sts before M-A, k2tog, sm, (k1, p1) 5 times, k2—1 st dec.

Row 2 (WS): (K1, p1) 6 times, sm, work est patt to end of row.

Row 3: Work est patt to M-A, sm, (k1, p1) 5 times, k2.
Row 4: (K1, p1) 6 times, sm, work est patt to end of row.
Rep [Rows 1–4] 3 (6, 5, 4, 3)[1, 0, -, -]{1, 0, -, -} more times.
4 (7, 6, 5, 4)[2, 1, -, -]{2, 1, -, -} sts dec; 42 (47, 50, 53, 56)[61, 64, -, -]{75, 78, -, -} sts rem.
Proceed to All Sizes.
All Sizes:
Row 1 (RS): Work est patt to M-A, sm, (k1, p1) 5 times, k2.
Row 2 (WS): (K1, p1) 6 times, sm, work est patt to end of row.
Rep Rows 1–2 until the front left measures 22½ (23, 24, 24, 24½)[25, 25, 25½, 25½]{26, 26, 27, 27½} in. / 57 (58.5, 61, 61, 62)[63.5, 63.5, 65, 65]{66, 66, 68.5, 70} cm from the CO edge when measured at the armhole edge, ending with a WS row.

LEFT FRONT SHOULDER SHAPING

Row 1 (RS): Work est patt to M-A, sm, (k1, p1) 5 times, k2.
Short Row 2 (WS): (K1, p1) 6 times, sm, work est patt to last 10 (12, 13, 14, 15)[16, 17, 18, 19]{21, 22, 23, 24} sts, W&T.
Short Row 3: Work est patt to M-A, sm, (k1, p1) 5 times, k2.
Short Row 4: (K1, p1) 6 times, sm, work est patt to 10 (12, 13, 14, 15)[16, 17, 18, 19]{21, 22, 23, 24} sts before prev wrapped st, W&T.
Short Row 5: Work est patt to M-A, sm, (k1, p1) 5 times, k2.
Short Row 6: (K1, p1) 6 times, sm, work est patt to end of row, resolving wrapped sts as encountered.
Break working yarn. With the RS facing, starting at the armhole edge, place the 30 (35, 38, 41, 44)[49, 52, 55, 58]{63, 66, 69, 72} sts before M-A on waste yarn or stitch holder. Remove M-A—12 sts rem on working needle for collar.

LEFT FRONT COLLAR

Rejoin the working yarn to the right edge of the Left Front Collar with the RS facing.
Setup Row (RS, inc): Kfb, (p1, k1) 5 times, k1—13 sts.
Row 1 (WS): P2, (k1, p1) 5 times, p1.
Row 2 (RS): K2, (p1, k1) 5 times, k1.
Rep Rows 1–2 until the collar measures 4¼ (4¼, 4½, 4½, 4¾)[5, 5, 5¼, 5½]{5½, 5¾, 6, 6} in. / 11 (11, 11.5, 11.5, 12)[12.5, 12.5, 13.5, 14]{14, 14.5, 15, 15} cm, ending with a WS row.
Break yarn and place all sts on stitch holder or waste yarn.

SLEEVES (MAKE 2 THE SAME)

RIBBED CUFF

CO 46 (46, 50, 50, 54)[54, 58, 58, 58]{62, 66, 70, 74} sts using the Long Tail cast on method.
Row 1 (RS): *K2, p2; rep from * to last 2 sts, k2.
Row 2 (WS): *P2, k2; rep from * to last 2 sts, p2.
Rep Rows 1–2 until the cuff measures 2 in. / 5 cm from the CO edge, ending with a WS row.

SLEEVE BODY

Row 1 (RS): K1, p4 (1, 3, 3, 2)[2, 4, 4, 4]{3, 2, 4, 3}, pm-A, work Chart A (B, B, B, A)[A, A, A, A]{B, A, A, B} to last 5 (2, 4, 4, 3)[3, 5, 5, 5]{4, 3, 5, 4} sts, pm-B, purl to last st, k1.
Row 2 (WS): P1, knit to M-B, work Chart A (B, B, B, A)[A, A, A, A]{B, A, A, B} to M-A, knit to last st, p1.
Row 3: K1, purl to M-A, work Chart A (B, B, B, A)[A, A, A, A]{B, A, A, B} to M-B, sm, purl to last st, k1.
Row 4: P1, knit to M-B, work Chart A (B, B, B, A)[A, A, A, A]{B, A, A, B} to M-A, knit to last st, p1.
Rep Rows 3–4 once more.

SLEEVE SHAPING

As the following shaping is worked, incorporate the stitch pattern in multiples of 6 (creating "half noodles"). Where you cannot complete a full cable, purl the sts to maintain the reverse St st fabric.

Inc Row (RS): K1, M1RP, work est patt to last st (sm as encountered), M1LP, k1—2 sts inc.
Cont in est patt, working the Inc Row every 6 (4, 4, 4, 2)[2, 2, 2, 2]{2, 2, 2, 2}th/nd row 18 (11, 14, 25, 10)[17, 18, 23, 26]{27, 29, 32, 33} more times. Then every 6 (6, 6, 4, 4)[4, 4, 4, 4]{4, 4, 4, 2}th/nd row 0 (10, 8, 0, 19)[14, 13, 10, 8]{6, 4, 1, 0} times.
38 (44, 46, 52, 60)[64, 64, 68, 70]{68, 68, 68, 68} sts inc; 84 (90, 96, 102, 114)[118, 122, 126, 128]{130, 134, 138, 142} sts total.
Cont in est patt, with no further increases, until the sleeve measures 22½ (21½, 21½, 21, 20¼)[19¼, 19, 18¾, 18½]{17½, 17, 16¼, 15¾} in. / 57 (54.5, 54.5, 53.5, 51.5)[49, 48.5, 47.5, 47]{44.5, 43, 41.5, 40} cm from the CO edge, or to desired length, ending with a WS row.
With RS facing, BO all sts loosely knitwise.

BLOCKING

Do not weave in ends prior to blocking.
Wet block pieces individually prior to seaming.

FINISHING

SHOULDER SEAMS

With the garment turned inside out (RS together, WS facing out), graft the live sts of each shoulder using the Three-Needle bind off.

SLEEVE TO BODY SEAMS

With the garment turned right side out, center the top of the sleeve over the shoulder seam. Seam each sleeve to the armhole edge of the body.

SIDE BODY AND UNDER-SLEEVE SEAMS

With the garment remaining right side out, seam sides of the body from the underarm to the hem using Mattress stitch. Seam the undersides of the sleeve from underarm to cuff using Mattress stitch.

COLLAR SEAMING

Place the live sts of each side of the collar onto 2 needles.
With the WS of the collar facing, graft the two sets of sts together using the Three-Needle bind off.
With the RS of the collar facing, seam the lower collar edge to the neckline edge using Mattress stitch.
Weave in all ends and trim.

CHART A

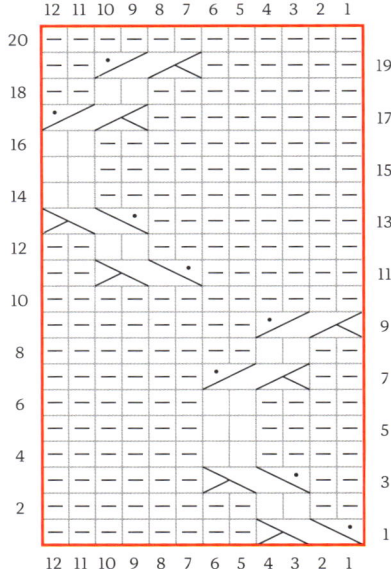

Coffee Talk

Liza Weil shared that for Season 3, Episode 11, where Paris and Rory take out their emotions through fencing, "They sent Alexis and I to fencing school. We had weeks of fencing lessons that were really involved.... When you watch the episode, it's not that long of a sequence. But they really invested the money and time for us to do that, which was amazing. It helped me so much as an actor."

CHART B

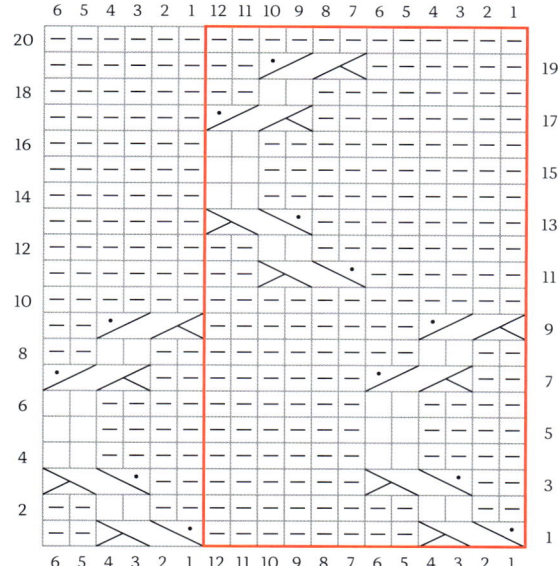

KEY

- ☐ k on RS, p on WS
- – p on RS, k on WS
- ⤫ 2/2 LPC
- ⤫ 2/2 RPC
- ▭ Pattern repeat

SCHEMATIC

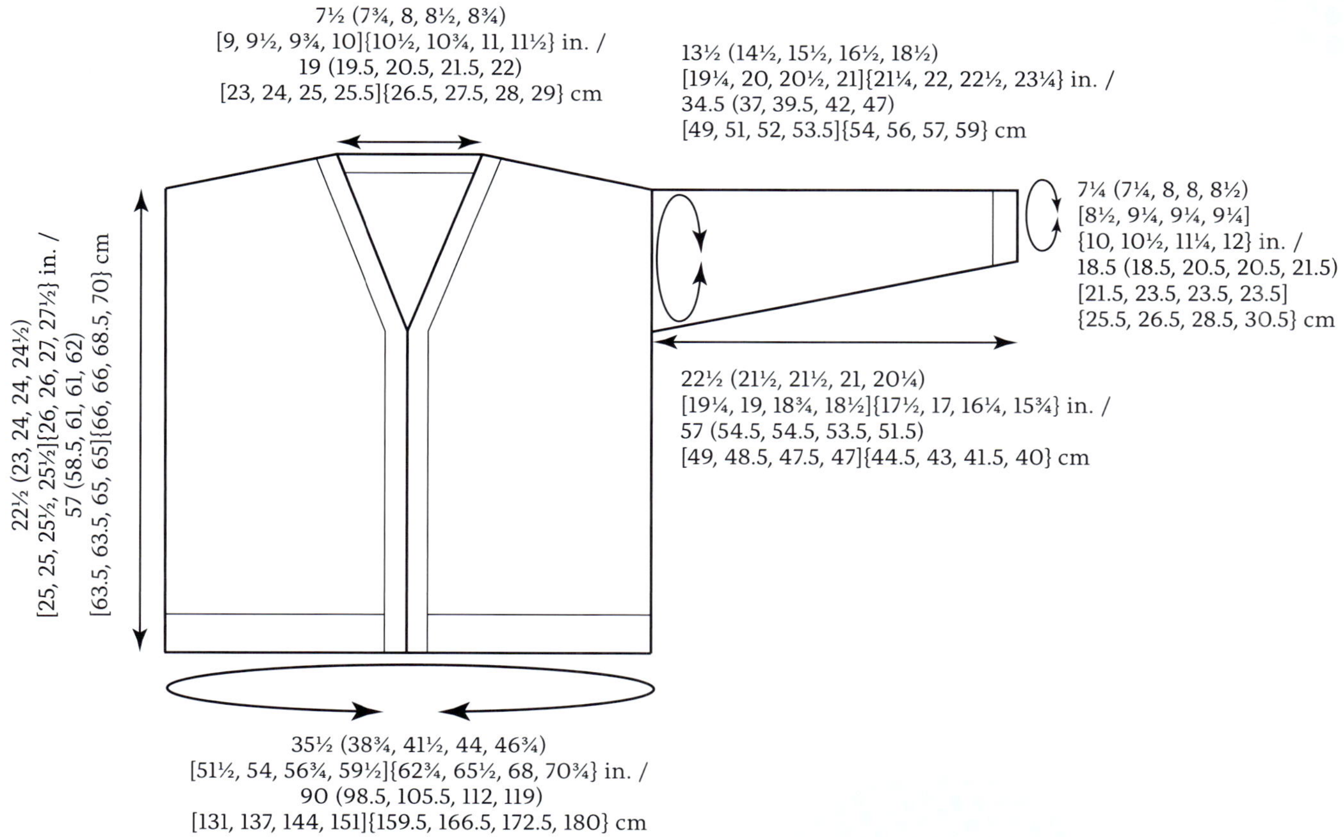

7½ (7¾, 8, 8½, 8¾)
[9, 9½, 9¾, 10]{10½, 10¾, 11, 11½} in. /
19 (19.5, 20.5, 21.5, 22)
[23, 24, 25, 25.5]{26.5, 27.5, 28, 29} cm

13½ (14½, 15½, 16½, 18½)
[19¼, 20, 20½, 21]{21¼, 22, 22½, 23¼} in. /
34.5 (37, 39.5, 42, 47)
[49, 51, 52, 53.5]{54, 56, 57, 59} cm

7¼ (7¼, 8, 8, 8½)
[8½, 9¼, 9¼, 9¼]
{10, 10½, 11¼, 12} in. /
18.5 (18.5, 20.5, 20.5, 21.5)
[21.5, 23.5, 23.5, 23.5]
{25.5, 26.5, 28.5, 30.5} cm

22½ (21½, 21½, 21, 20¼)
[19¼, 19, 18¾, 18½]{17½, 17, 16¼, 15¾} in. /
57 (54.5, 54.5, 53.5, 51.5)
[49, 48.5, 47.5, 47]{44.5, 43, 41.5, 40} cm

22½ (23, 24, 24, 24½)
[25, 25, 25½, 25½]{26, 26, 27, 27½} in. /
57 (58.5, 61, 61, 62)
[63.5, 63.5, 65, 65]{66, 66, 68.5, 70} cm

35½ (38¾, 41½, 44, 46¾)
[51½, 54, 56¾, 59½]{62¾, 65½, 68, 70¾} in. /
90 (98.5, 105.5, 112, 119)
[131, 137, 144, 151]{159.5, 166.5, 172.5, 180} cm

Rory's Boyfriends Pullover

Designed by Paul Haesemeyer
SKILL LEVEL: INTERMEDIATE

"Think how dull your life would be without me."
—Jess Mariano, Season 2, Episode 19

Throughout the series, viewers experience the loves of Rory's young life along with her. Jared Padalecki nailed his audition immediately. Newcomer Padalecki's Dean Forester from Stars Hollow High was liked by all and the first to tell Rory that he loved her, causing Rory to freeze up and freak out. Played by Milo Ventimiglia, Jess Mariano, Luke's nephew from New York, was a rule-breaker and was her intellectual equal in both books and music, but was unable to commit to her. Matt Czuchry landed the role of Logan Huntzberger. A fellow Yale student, Logan was adored by Rory's grandparents for his family's social status and provided her with the adventure and spontaneity she so desperately needed.

While very different people, each boyfriend fills a void left by Rory's absentee father, and each is instrumental in shaping her into the woman she will become. Actress Lauren Graham remembered, "It has all these points of entry in terms of how old [the characters are], and it never talked down to the audience. There was an aspect to [Stars Hollow] that was unique and unusual, and not everyone in the town was fifteen, seventeen, or twenty. As you would have in any town, there were people of all ages and sizes. I think Amy [Sherman-Palladino, the show's creator and executive producer] had a real talent for casting people that were interesting, who you believed were real people."

There's nothing like a cozy sweater to snuggle up in on a cold New England day! Inspired by Rory's comfy high school after-hours wardrobe when with her boyfriend Dean, this striped pullover is worked in the round from the bottom up. Beginning with ribbing on the torso, the body is worked in stockinette. Set-in sleeves are worked from picked up stitches in the round and shaped with German short rows. Different colors are used for the ribbed cuffs, with a matching ribbed collar added and folded over, then sewn in place at the end.

SIZES
1 (2, 3, 4, 5)[6, 7, 8, 9]

FINISHED MEASUREMENTS
Chest Circumference: 30¼ (34, 37½, 41¼, 44½)[48½, 51¾, 55½, 59] in. / 77 (86.5, 95.5, 105, 113)[123, 131.5, 141, 150] cm
Garment is designed to be worn with -2 to +2 in. / -5 to + 5 cm of ease.

YARN
Worsted weight yarn, shown in Ewe Ewe Yarns *Wooly Worsted* (100% superwash fine merino wool; 95 yd. / 86 m per 1¾ oz. / 50 g skein)

COLORWAYS
Color A: #23 Red Velvet, 9 (10, 11, 12, 13)[15, 16, 18, 19] skeins
Color B: #50 Pistachio, 1 skein
Color C: #95 Chocolate, 1 (1, 1, 1, 1) [1, 2, 2, 2] skein(s)
Color D: #20 Poppy, 1 skein

Color E: #30 Saffron, 1 skein

NEEDLES
US 6 / 4 mm, 16 in / 40 cm and 32–40 in. / 80–100 cm long circular needles and set of 5 double-pointed needles
US 8 / 5 mm, 32–40 in. / 80–100 cm long circular needles and set of 5 double-pointed needles or size needed to obtain gauge

NOTIONS
Stitch marker
Waste yarn
Tapestry needle

GAUGE
19 sts and 28.5 rows = 4 in. / 10 cm over St st worked in the round on larger needle, taken after blocking
Make sure to check your gauge.

PATTERN NOTES
- This pullover is worked in the round from the bottom up, using the small needle for all ribbing, and the large needle for the body and sleeves.

Continued on page 150

- The sleeves are worked in the round, outward from the body, using short rows to shape the sleeve cap.
- Instructions for Size 1 are provided first, with instructions for Sizes 2–9 provided in parentheses/brackets. When only one set of numbers is provided, it applies to all sizes.
- Any references to Left and Right within this pattern are based on the garment as worn.
- The small needle should be 2 needle sizes smaller than the large needle when gauge is met.
- All bind offs use the Sloped bind off method at the neck and shoulders.
- Set-in sleeves are picked up in the round, then shaped with German short rows.
- Use Magic Loop or dpns when circumference becomes too small.

CAST ON & RIBBING

Using smaller needle and Color B, CO 148 (166, 178, 196, 216)[234, 254, 272, 292] sts using the Alternating Cable cast on method. Pm for BOR and join to work in the rnd, being careful not to twist the sts.

Rib Rnd: *K1, p1; rep from * to end of rnd.

Rep Rib Rnd for 1½ in. / 4 cm.
Break Color B.

BODY OF SWEATER

Switch to larger needles.
Join Color C.
Rnds 1–6: Knit.
Break Color C.
Join Color D.
Rnds 7–10: Knit.
Break Color D.
Join Color E.
Rnds 11–12: Knit.
Break Color E.
Join Color A.

Work in St st until body measures 14 in. / 35.5 cm, or to desired total body length. On the final rnd, end 3 (3, 3, 4, 4)[4, 5, 5, 5] sts before BOR M.

Note: Adding length to the body will affect yardage requirements.

DIVIDE FOR ARMHOLES

Separation Row (RS): BO 6 (6, 6, 8, 8)[8, 10, 10, 10] sts (rm BOR M), k68 (77, 83, 90, 100) [109, 117, 126, 136] Front sts, BO 6 (6, 6, 8, 8)[8, 10, 10, 10] sts, knit to end of rnd (Back sts)—68 (77, 83, 90, 100) [109, 117, 126, 136] sts for Front and Back (each).

Place Front sts on waste yarn and turn work.

BACK—SECTION 1

Row 1 (WS): P all sts.
Row 2 (RS, dec): K2, k2tog, work to last 4 sts, ssk, k2—2 sts dec.
Rep [Rows 1–2] 2 (2, 2, 3, 3)[3, 3, 4, 4] more times.
6 (6, 6, 8, 8)[8, 8, 10, 10] sts dec;
62 (71, 77, 82, 92)[101, 109, 116, 126] sts rem.

BACK—SECTION 2

Row 1 (WS): Purl.
Row 2 (RS): Knit.
Row 3: Purl.
Row 4 (dec): K2, k2tog, work to last 4 sts, ssk, k2—2 sts dec.
Rep [Rows 1–4] 2 more times.
6 sts dec;
56 (65, 71, 76, 86)[95, 103, 110, 120] sts rem.

BACK—SECTION 3

Row 1 (WS): P all sts.
Row 2 (RS): K all sts.
Row 3: P all sts.
Row 4: K all sts.
Row 5: P all sts.
Row 6 (dec): K2, k2tog, work to last 4 sts, ssk, k2—54 (63, 69, 74, 84)[93, 101, 108, 118] sts rem.

Rep Rows 1–2 until the Back measures 6½ (7, 7½, 8, 8½)[9, 9½, 10, 10½] in. / 16.5 (18, 19, 20.5, 21.5) [23, 24, 25.5, 26.5] cm from the underarm bind off, ending with a WS row.

BACK SHOULDERS

BO sts knitwise on RS rows and purlwise on WS rows.

Row 1 (RS, dec): BO 4 (4, 5, 5, 6)[6, 7, 7, 8] sts, knit to end of row—50 (59, 64, 69, 78)[87, 94, 101, 110] sts rem.
Row 2 (WS, dec): BO 4 (4, 5, 5, 6)[6, 7, 7, 8] sts, purl to last st, sl1 wyif—46 (55, 59, 64, 72)[81, 87, 94, 102] sts rem.
Separation Row (RS): Sl2 wyib, pass first st over (1 st BO), BO 3 (3, 4, 4, 5)[5, 6, 6, 7] more sts, k8 (11, 12, 13, 14)[17, 17, 19, 21] sts, BO 21 (24, 26, 27, 31)[34, 38, 41, 43] sts, knit to last st, sl1 wyif.
9 (12, 12, 14, 15)[18, 18, 20, 22] sts rem for Right Back Shoulder; 13 (16, 17, 19, 21)[24, 25, 27, 30] sts rem for Left Back shoulder.

Place Right Back Shoulder sts on waste yarn and turn work.

LEFT BACK SHOULDER

BO sts knitwise on RS rows (at neckline edge) and purlwise on WS rows (at armhole edge).

Row 1 (WS, dec): Sl2 wyib, pass first st over (1 st BO), BO 3 (3, 4, 4, 5) [5, 6, 6, 7] more sts, purl to end of row—9 (12, 12, 14, 15)[18, 18, 20, 22] sts rem.
Row 2 (RS, dec): BO 2 (2, 2, 2, 3)[3, 3, 3, 4] sts, knit to last st, sl1 wyif—7 (10, 10, 12, 12)[15, 15, 17, 18] sts rem.
Row 3 (dec): Sl2 wyib, pass first st over (1 st BO), BO 2 (3, 3, 4, 4)[5, 5, 6,

7] more sts, purl to last st, sl1 wyif—4 (6, 6, 7, 7)[9, 9, 10, 10] sts rem.

Row 4 (dec): Sl2 wyib, pass first st over (1 st BO), BO 0 (1, 1, 1, 1)[2, 2, 2, 2] more st(s), knit to end of row—3 (4, 4, 5, 5)[6, 6, 7, 7] sts rem.

With WS facing, BO all sts purlwise.

RIGHT BACK SHOULDER

BO sts knitwise on RS rows (at armhole edge) and purlwise on WS rows (at neckline edge).

Place Right Back Shoulder sts onto working needle. Rejoin Color A with WS facing.

Row 1 (WS, dec): BO 2 (2, 2, 2, 3)[3, 3, 3, 4] sts, knit to last st, sl1 wyif—7 (10, 10, 12, 12)[15, 15, 17, 18] sts rem.

Row 2 (RS, dec): Sl2 wyib, pass first st over (1 st BO), BO 2 (3, 3, 4, 4)[5, 5, 6, 7] more sts, knit to last st, sl1 wyif—4 (6, 6, 7, 7)[9, 9, 10, 10] sts rem.

Row 3 (dec): Sl2 wyib, pass first st over (1 st BO), BO 0 (1, 1, 1, 1)[2, 2, 2, 2] more st(s), purl to last st, sl1 wyif—3 (4, 4, 5, 5)[6, 6, 7, 7] sts rem.

Row 4: Knit.

With WS facing, BO all sts purlwise.

FRONT

Place Front sts onto working needle. Rejoin Color A with WS facing.

Work as for Back—Sections 1 and 2.

Work Rows 1–6 of Back—Section 3, then rep Rows 1–2 of Back—Section 3 until the Front measures 5 (5½, 6, 6½, 7)[7½, 8, 8½, 9] in. / 12.5 (14, 15, 16.5, 18)[19, 20.5, 21.5, 23] cm from the underarm bind off, ending with a WS row.

FRONT SHOULDERS

Separation Row (RS): K23 (27, 29, 32, 35)[39, 42, 45, 49], place these just worked sts on waste yarn for the Left Front Shoulder. BO 8 (9, 11, 10, 14)[15, 17, 18, 20] sts knitwise, knit to end of row.

RIGHT FRONT SHOULDER

BO all sts knitwise in this section.

Row 1 (WS, and all WS rows unless otherwise noted): Purl to last st, sl1 wyif.

Row 2 (RS, dec): Sl2 wyib, pass first st over (1 st BO), BO 2 (2, 2, 2, 3)[3, 4, 4, 5] more sts, knit to end of row—20 (24, 26, 29, 31)[35, 37, 40, 43] sts rem.

Row 4 (dec): Sl2 wyib, pass first st over (1 st BO), BO 1 (1, 1, 2, 2)[2, 3, 3, 3] more sts, knit to end of row—18 (22, 24, 26, 28)[32, 33, 36, 39] sts rem.

Row 6 (dec): Sl2 wyib, pass first st over (1 st BO), BO 1 (1, 1, 1, 1)[2, 1, 2, 2] more st(s), knit to end of row—16 (20, 22, 24, 26)[29, 31, 33, 36] sts rem.

Row 8 (dec): Sl2 wyib, pass first st over (1 st BO), BO 0 (1, 1, 1, 1)[1, 1, 1, 1] more st(s), knit to end of row—15 (18, 20, 22, 24)[27, 29, 31, 34] sts rem.

Sizes 1–5 Only: Proceed to Right Shoulder Shaping.

Sizes 6–9 Only:

Row 9 (WS): Purl to last st, sl1 wyif.

Row 10 (dec): Sl2 wyib, pass first st over (1 st BO), BO 1 more st, knit to end of row—- (-, -, -, -)[25, 27, 29, 32] sts rem.

RIGHT SHOULDER SHAPING

BO sts knitwise on RS rows (at neckline edge) and purlwise on WS rows (at armhole edge).

Sizes 1 and 6–9 Only:

Row 1 (WS, dec): BO 4 (-, -, -, -)[6, 7, 7, 8] sts, purl to last st, sl1 wyif—11 (-, -, -, -)[19, 20, 22, 24] sts rem.

Row 2 (RS, dec): Sl2 wyib, pass first st over (1 st BO), knit to last st, sl1 wyif—10 (-, -, -, -)[18, 19, 21, 23] sts rem.

Row 3 (dec): Sl2 wyib, pass first st over (1 st BO), BO 3 (-, -, -, -)[5, 6, 6, 7] more sts, purl to end of row—6 (-, -, -, -)[12, 12, 14, 15] sts rem.

Row 4: Knit to last st, sl1 wyif.

Row 5 (dec): Sl2 wyib, pass first st over (1 st BO), BO 2 (-, -, -, -)[5, 5, 6, 7] more sts, purl to end of row—3 (-, -, -, -)[6, 6, 7, 7] sts remain.

Row 6: K all sts.

With WS facing, BO all sts purlwise.

Sizes 2–5 Only:

Row 1 (WS, dec): BO - (4, 5, 5, 6)[-, -, -, -] sts, purl to last st, sl1 wyif—- (14, 15, 17, 18)[-, -, -, -] sts rem.

Row 2 (RS, dec): Sl2 wyib, pass first st over (1 st BO), knit to last st, sl1 wyif—- (13, 14, 16, 17)[-, -, -, -] sts rem.

Row 3 (dec): Sl2 wyib, pass first st over (1 st BO), BO - (3, 4, 4, 5)[-, -, -, -] more sts, purl to last st, sl1 wyif—- (9, 9, 11, 11)[-, -, -, -] sts rem.

Row 4 (dec): Sl2 wyib, pass first st over (1 st BO), knit to last st, sl1 wyif—- (8, 8, 10, 10)[-, -, -, -] sts rem.

Row 5 (dec): Sl2 wyib, pass first st over (1 st BO), BO - (3, 3, 4, 4)[-, -, -, -] more sts, purl to end of row—- (4, 4, 5, 5)[-, -, -, -] sts rem.

Row 6: Knit.

With WS facing, BO all sts purlwise.

LEFT FRONT SHOULDER

BO all sts purlwise in this section.

Place Left Front Shoulder sts onto working needle. Rejoin Color A with WS facing.

Row 1 (WS, dec): BO 3 (3, 3, 3, 4)[4, 5, 5, 6] sts, purl to end of row—20 (24, 26, 29, 31)[35, 37, 40, 43] sts rem.

Row 2 (RS, and all RS rows unless otherwise noted): Knit to last st, sl1 wyif.

Row 3 (dec): Sl2 wyib, pass first st over (1 st BO), BO 1 (1, 1, 2, 2)[2, 3, 3, 3] more sts, purl to end of row—18 (22, 24, 26, 28)[32, 33, 36, 39] sts rem.

Row 5 (dec): Sl2 wyib, pass first st over (1 st BO), BO 1 (1, 1, 1, 1)[2, 1, 2, 2] sts, purl to end of row—16 (20, 22, 24, 26)[29, 31, 33, 36] sts rem.

Row 7 (dec): Sl2 wyib, pass first st over (1 st BO), BO 0 (1, 1, 1, 1)[1, 1, 1, 1] more st(s), purl to end of row—15 (18, 20, 22, 24)[27, 29, 31, 34] sts rem.

Sizes 1–5 Only: Proceed to Left Shoulder Shaping.

Sizes 6–9 Only:

Row 8 (RS): Knit to last st, sl1 wyif.

Row 9 (WS, dec): Sl2 wyib, pass first st over (1 st BO), BO 1 more st, purl to end of row—- (-, -, -, -)[25, 27, 29, 32] sts rem.

LEFT SHOULDER SHAPING

BO sts knitwise on RS rows (at armhole edge) and purlwise on WS rows (at neckline edge).

Sizes 1 and 6–9 Only:

Row 1 (RS, dec): BO 4 (-, -, -, -)[6, 7, 7, 8] sts, knit to last st, sl1 wyif—11 (-, -, -, -)[19, 20, 22, 24] sts rem.

Row 2 (WS, dec): Sl2 wyib, pass first st over (1 st BO), purl to last st, sl1 wyif—10 (-, -, -, -)[18, 19, 21, 23] sts rem.

Row 3 (dec): Sl2 wyib, pass first st over (1 st BO), BO 3 (-, -, -, -)[5, 6, 6, 7] more sts, knit to end of row—6 (-, -, -, -)[12, 12, 14, 15] sts rem.

Row 4: Purl to last st, sl1 wyif.

Row 5 (dec): Sl2 wyib, pass first st over (1 st BO), BO 2 (-, -, -, -)[5, 5, 6, 7] more sts, knit to end of row—3 (-, -, -, -)[6, 6, 7, 7] sts rem.

Row 6: Purl.

Row 7: Knit.

With WS facing, BO all sts purlwise.

Sizes 2–5 Only:

Row 1 (RS, dec): BO - (4, 5, 5, 6)[-, -, -, -] sts, knit to last st, sl1 wyif—- (14, 15, 17,18)[-, -, -, -] sts rem.

Row 2 (WS, dec): Sl2 wyib, pass first st over (1 st BO), purl to last st, sl1 wyif—- (13, 14, 16, 17)[-, -, -, -] sts rem.

Row 3 (dec): Sl2 wyib, pass first st over (1 st BO), BO - (3, 4, 4, 5)[-, -, -, -] more sts, knit to last st, sl1 wyif—- (9, 9, 11, 11)[-, -, -, -] sts rem.

Row 4 (dec): Sl2 wyib, pass first st over (1 st BO), purl to last st, sl1 wyif—- (8, 8, 10, 10)[-, -, -, -] sts rem.

Row 5 (dec): Sl2 wyib, pass first st over (1 st BO), BO - (3, 3, 4, 4)[-, -, -, -] more sts, knit to end of row—- (4, 4, 5, 5)[-, -, -, -] sts rem.

Row 6: Purl.

Row 7: Knit.

With WS facing, BO all sts purlwise.

CONSTRUCTION

Wet block to dimensions. Allow to dry. Seam shoulders using the Horizontal Invisible Seaming method.

SLEEVES (MAKE 2 THE SAME)

Using the larger needle in your preferred method for small circumference knitting, join Color A at the center of the underarm BO sts. Pick up and knit 60 (62, 66, 70, 78)[88, 96, 104, 104] sts around the armhole. Pm for BOR and join to work in the rnd.

Short Row 1 (RS): K35 (37, 39, 41, 46)[48, 53, 57, 57], turn.

Short Row 2 (WS): DS, p9 (11, 11, 11, 13)[7, 9, 9, 9], turn.

Short Row 3: DS, knit to prev DS, work kDS, k2 (2, 2, 2, 2)[4, 5, 5, 5], turn.

Short Row 4: DS, purl to prev DS, work pDS, p2 (2, 2, 2, 2)[4, 5, 5, 5], turn.

Short Row 5: DS, knit to prev DS, work kDS, k2, turn.

Short Row 6: DS, purl to prev DS, work pDS, p2, turn.

Short Row 7: DS, knit to prev DS, work kDS, k1 (1, 1, 1, 1)[2, 2, 2, 2], turn.

Short Row 8: DS, purl to prev DS, work pDS, p1 (1, 1, 1, 1)[2, 2, 2, 2], turn.

Rep [Short Rows 7–8] until 3 (3, 3, 4, 4)[4, 5, 5, 5] sts before BOR M.

Final Short Row (RS): DS, knit to BOR resolving rem DS as kDS.

Next Rnd: Knit resolving rem DS as kDS.

Cont in St st for 2 in. / 5 cm. On the final rnd, end 2 sts before BOR M.

ARM SHAPING

Dec Rnd: Ssk, sm, k1, k2tog, knit to end of rnd—2 sts dec.

*Knit 8 (7, 7, 7, 6)[5, 5, 5, 5] rnds, work Dec Rnd; rep from * 5 (6, 6, 7, 8)[9, 10, 11, 11] more times.

14 (16, 16, 18, 20)[22, 24, 26, 26] sts dec;

46 (46, 50, 52, 58)[66, 72, 78, 78] sts rem.

Cont in St st until sleeve measures 14 (14.5, 14.5, 15, 15)[15.5, 15.5, 16, 16] in. / 35.5 (37, 37, 38, 38)[39.5, 39.5, 40.5, 40.5] cm from the underarm picked up sts, or to 1½ in. / 4 cm short of desired length.

Break Color A.

Change to smaller needle.

Join Color E for Left Sleeve or Color D for Right Sleeve.

Knit 1 rnd.

Rib Rnd: *K1, p1; rep from * to end of rnd.

Rep Rib Rnd until the cuff measures 1½ in. / 4 cm.

BO all sts using the Sewn Tubular bind off.

COLLAR

Using the smaller 16 in. / 40 cm needle, join Color C at the left shoulder seam. Pick up and knit 33 (38, 40, 43, 48)[53, 57, 60, 65] sts along the front neckline edge and 29 (34, 36, 39, 42)[47, 51, 54, 57] sts along the back neckline edge—62 (72, 76, 82, 90)[100, 108, 114,122] sts. Pm for BOR and join to work in the rnd.

Rib Rnd: *K1, p1; rep from * to end of rnd.

Rep Rib Rnd until the collar measures 1½ in. / 4 cm.

BO loosely in patt. Cut tail approx. 3 times the length of the bound off edge. Fold collar in half, WS together, and sew into place to create a folded collar.

FINISHING

Weave in all ends. Block to finished measurements.

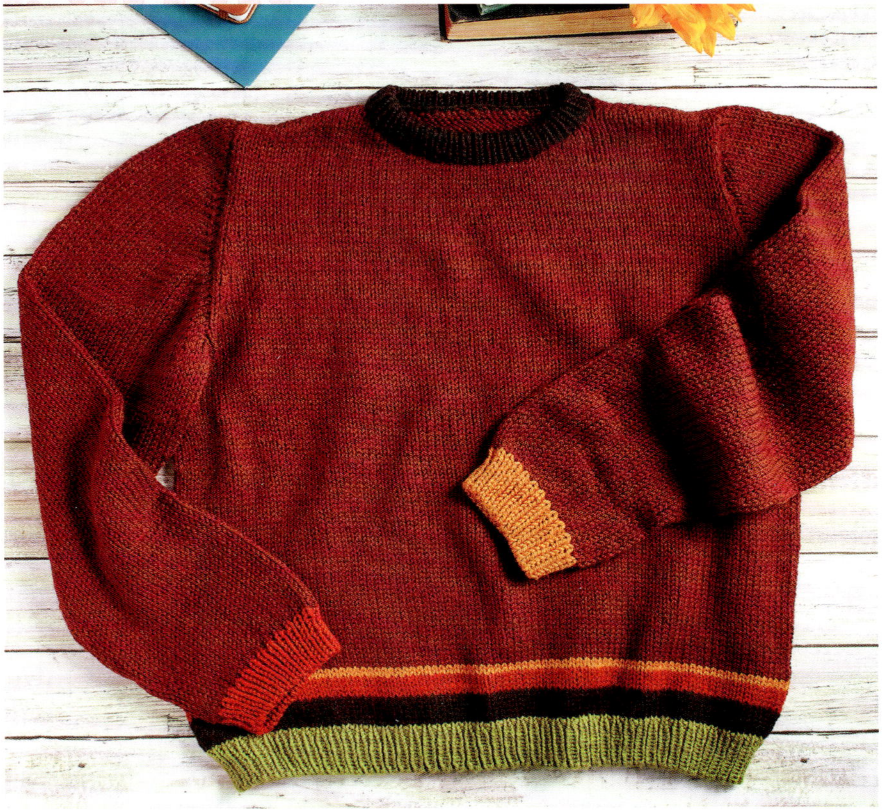

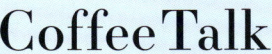

> **Coffee Talk**
>
> Jess Mariano's popularity with viewers made The WB interested in creating a spinoff series for Milo Ventimiglia called *Windward Circle*, taking place in Venice Beach, California.

SCHEMATIC

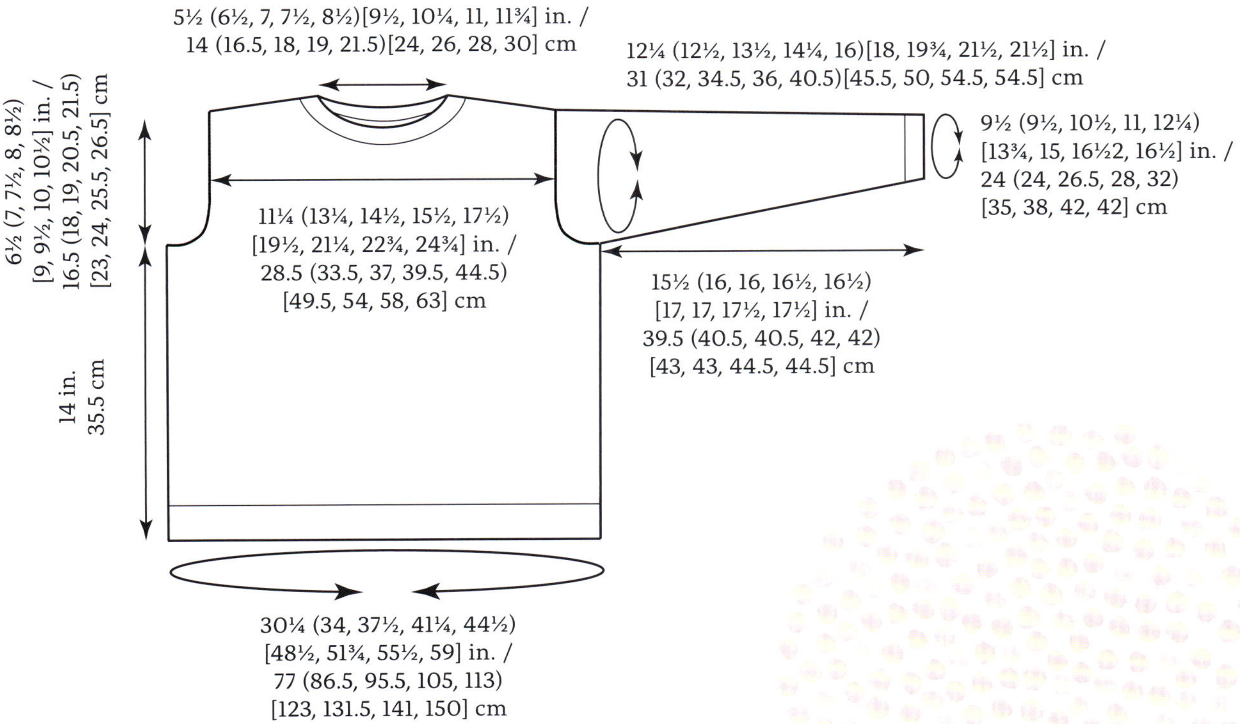

5½ (6½, 7, 7½, 8½)[9½, 10¼, 11, 11¾] in. / 14 (16.5, 18, 19, 21.5)[24, 26, 28, 30] cm
12¼ (12½, 13½, 14¼, 16)[18, 19¾, 21½, 21½] in. / 31 (32, 34.5, 36, 40.5)[45.5, 50, 54.5, 54.5] cm
6½ (7, 7½, 8, 8½) [9, 9½, 10, 10½] in. / 16.5 (18, 19, 20.5, 21.5) [23, 24, 25.5, 26.5] cm
9½ (9½, 10½, 11, 12¼) [13¾, 15, 16½2, 16½] in. / 24 (24, 26.5, 28, 32) [35, 38, 42, 42] cm
11¼ (13¼, 14½, 15½, 17½) [19½, 21¼, 22¾, 24¾] in. / 28.5 (33.5, 37, 39.5, 44.5) [49.5, 54, 58, 63] cm
15½ (16, 16, 16½, 16½) [17, 17, 17½, 17½] in. / 39.5 (40.5, 40.5, 42, 42) [43, 43, 44.5, 44.5] cm
14 in. 35.5 cm
30¼ (34, 37½, 41¼, 44½) [48½, 51¾, 55½, 59] in. / 77 (86.5, 95.5, 105, 113) [123, 131.5, 141, 150] cm

Chapter
5

Homey Decor and Gifts

Lorelai and Rory Dolls

Designed by Esther Braithwaite
SKILL LEVEL: EASY

"My mother never gave me any idea that I couldn't do whatever I wanted to do or be whomever I wanted to be. As she guided me through these incredible eighteen years, I don't know if she ever realized that the person I most wanted to be was her."

—Rory Gilmore, Season 3, Episode 22

Despite never having met in person until the first day of filming, actors Lauren Graham and Alexis Bledel had the perfect mother/daughter on-screen chemistry. While Graham was experienced in both TV and theater, Bledel was a fresh-faced film student at NYU Tisch School of the Arts and brand new to the acting scene. To help her stay in camera, the two would walk arm-in-arm with Graham guiding her young costar to her mark. Not only did this help the crew frame up the moving shot, but it also helped the two develop a relationship that was like sisters as well as mother and daughter. As the show continued to be renewed, the two remained arm-in-arm throughout the seven seasons. Creator Amy Sherman-Palladino recalls, "They developed this interesting camaraderie that was, you know, you can't cast that, it just shows up and then it happens."

These adorable little pocket-size Lorelai and Rory dolls are worked in the round from the bottom up in one piece. Their skirts are picked up and knit outward from the waist, embellished with details added with embroidery and duplicate stitching post-knitting. The dolls are then stuffed with poly stuffing, and simple running stitch is employed to define their arms and legs. Add the hairstyle of your choice and take them with you to Stars Hollow.

SIZES
One size

FINISHED MEASUREMENTS
Approx. 6½ in. / 16.5 cm tall

YARN
Worsted weight yarn, shown in Cascade Yarns *Cascade 220* (4-ply; 100% Peruvian highland wool; 220 yd. / 201 m per 3½ oz. / 100 g hank)

COLORWAYS
Color A: #8555 Black, 1 hank
Color B: #8021 Beige, 1 hank
Color C: #8686 Brown, 1 hank
Color D: #1068 Copper, 1 hank
Color E: #1010 Carob Brown, 1 hank
Color F: #8505 White, 1 hank
Color G: #2404 Atlantic, 1 hank
Color H: #9332 Sapphire, 1 hank
Color I: #1006 Sky Blue, 1 hank

NEEDLES
US 5 / 3.75 mm, set of 5 double-pointed needles or size needed to obtain gauge

NOTIONS
Stitch marker (optional)
Tapestry needle
Polyester stuffing (approx. 1 oz. / 30 g per doll)
US D-3 / 3.25 mm crochet hook

GAUGE
24 sts and 28 rows = 4 in. / 10 cm in St st worked in the rnd, taken before stuffing doll
Make sure to check your gauge.

PATTERN NOTES
- Each doll is worked in one piece, in the round, from the bottom up.
- The skirt is knit from stitches picked up and knit outward from the doll's body.
- Simple sewing techniques are used to define the arms and legs after knitting.
- Final details are added with embroidery and duplicate stitch.

Continued on page 158

- Written and charted instructions are provided for the entirety of the main body of the dolls. Note that the charts will also be used in the finishing of the doll for placement of arms, legs, and eyes.

LORELAI DOLL

BODY

Using Color A, CO 28 sts using the Long Tail cast on method, leaving a 16 in. / 40.5 cm long tail for seaming. Distribute sts evenly over 4 dpns (7 sts on each dpn). Pm for BOR (if desired) and join to work in the rnd, being careful not to twist sts.

BOOTS

Rnds 1–10: Knit.
Break Color A.

LEGS

Join Color B.
Rnds 11–18: Knit.
Break Color B.

SWEATER

Join Color A.
Rnd 19: Knit.
Rnd 20 (inc): K6, M1BL, k2, M1BL, k12, M1BL, k2, M1BL, k6—32 sts.
Rnds 21–30: Knit.
Break Color A.

FACE

Join Color B.
Rnds 31–38: Knit.
Break Color B.

HAIR

Join Color C.
Rnds 39–42: Knit.
Rnd 43 (dec): K1, *k4, k2tog; rep from * to last st, k1—27 sts.
Rnd 44 (and all even rnds): Knit.
Rnd 45 (dec): K1, *k3, k2tog; rep from * to last st, k1—22 sts.
Rnd 47 (dec): K1, *k2, k2tog; rep from * to last st, k1—17 sts.
Rnd 49 (dec): K1, *k1, k2tog; rep from * to last st, k1—12 sts.
Rnd 51 (dec): K1, *k2tog; rep from * to last st, k1—7 sts.
Break yarn, leaving an 8 in. / 20.5 cm tail. Thread the tapestry needle and weave tail through rem sts, cinch shut, and secure on WS.

SKIRT

Beginning at the back of the doll, at Rnd 21, pick up the right leg of the 32 sts across the rnd. Distribute sts so you have 8 sts on each of 4 dpns. Pm for BOR (if desired) and join to work in the rnd. Join Color D. With doll held upside down, continue working skirt as follows:
Rnd 1 (inc): *K4, M1BL; rep from * to end of rnd—40 sts.
Rnds 2–6: Knit.
Rnd 7: Purl.
Rnd 8: Knit.
BO all sts purlwise.

TURTLENECK SWEATER

Beginning at the back of the doll, at Rnd 31, pick up the right leg of the 32 sts across the rnd. Distribute sts so you have 8 sts on each of 4 dpns. Pm for BOR (if desired) and join to work in the rnd. Join Color E. With doll held right side up, continue working turtleneck as follows:
Rnd 1 (inc): *K4, M1BL; rep from * to end of rnd—40 sts.
Rnds 2–3: *K1, p1; rep from * to end of rnd.
BO all sts in patt.

RORY DOLL

BODY

Using Color F, CO 28 sts using the Long Tail cast on method, leaving a 16 in. / 40.5 cm long tail for seaming. Distribute sts evenly over 4 dpns (7 sts on each dpn). Pm for BOR (if desired) and join to work in the rnd, being careful not to twist the sts.

SHOES

Rnds 1–3: Knit.
Break Color F.

SOCKS

Join Color G.
Rnds 4–6: Knit.
Break Color G.
Join Color H.
Rnds 7–10: Knit.
Break Color H.

LEGS

Join Color B.
Rnds 11–16: Knit.
Break Color B.

SHIRT

Join Color G.
Rnd 17: Knit.
Rnd 18 (inc): K6, M1BL, k2, M1BL, k12, M1BL, k2, M1BL, k6—32 sts.
Rnds 19–30: Knit.
Break Color G.

FACE

Join Color B.
Rnds 31–38: Knit.
Break Color B.

HAIR

Join Color C.
Rnds 39–42: Knit.
Rnd 43 (dec): K1, *k4, k2tog; rep from * to last st, k1—27 sts.

Rnd 44 (and all even rnds): Knit.
Rnd 45 (dec): K1, *k3, k2tog; rep from * to last st, k1—22 sts.
Rnd 47 (dec): K1, *k2, k2tog; rep from * to last st, k1—17 sts.
Rnd 49 (dec): K1, *k1, k2tog; rep from * to last st, k1—12 sts.
Rnd 51 (dec): K1, *k2tog; rep from * to last st, k1—7 sts.
Break yarn, leaving an 8 in. / 20.5 cm tail. Thread the tapestry needle and weave tail through rem sts, cinch shut, and secure on WS.

SKIRT

Beginning at the back of the doll, at Rnd 20, pick up the right leg of the 32 sts across the rnd. Distribute sts so you have 8 sts on each of 4 dpns and join to work in the rnd. Pm for BOR if desired. Join Color H. With doll held upside down, continue working skirt as follows:

Rnd 1 (inc): *K2, M1BL; rep from * to end of rnd—48 sts.
Rnds 2–3: *K2, p2; rep from * to end of rnd. Do not break Color H; carry it loosely up the inside to Rnd 6.
Rnds 4–5: Join/with Color I, *k2, p2; rep from * to end of rnd. Do not break Color I; carry it loosely up the inside to Rnd 8.
Rnds 6–7: With Color H, *k2, p2; rep from * to end of rnd. Do not break Color H; carry it loosely up the inside to Rnd 10.
Rnds 8–9: With Color I, *k2, p2; rep from * to end of rnd. Break Color I.
Rnds 10–11: With Color H, *k2, p2; rep from * to end of rnd.
BO all sts in patt.
Threading the tapestry needle with approx. 24 in. / 61 cm of Color F, weave yarn vertically through the purl bumps in between each of the purl stitches in the skirt to create a plaid pattern.

FINISHING—BOTH DOLLS

Leaving CO tail at feet for sewing, weave in all other ends securely to the inside of the doll.
Use the charts as guides for the following instructions.

STUFF HEAD

Thread the tapestry needle with a length of Color B yarn approx. 24 in. / 61 cm long. Beginning at the back of the doll, sew a running st across the first face rnd (Rnd 31), then stuff the head firmly. Cinch the yarn to form neck and knot securely at the back of neck. Do not cut ends as you will use these to define arms as noted below.

STUFF BODY

Thread the tapestry needle with the 16 in. / 40 cm tail from the CO edge of the doll. Sew a running st across the CO edge, then stuff the body loosely. Cinch the yarn to close the bottom of doll and knot securely. Do not cut ends as you will use these to define the legs.

DEFINE LEGS

Using the tail remaining from the Stuff Body instructions, begin at the back middle seam and sew small vertical sts through to the front middle. Pull snugly to create leg definition as you continue to a few rows below doll's waist. Fasten yarn securely. Weave all remaining ends to the inside.

DEFINE ARMS

Using the tails of Color B remaining from the Stuff Head instructions, sew small vertical sts from back to front to create arms. Arms are 8 sts wide. Fasten yarn securely. Weave all remaining ends to the inside.

EMBROIDER EYES

Embroider eyes using Color A and the tapestry needle, using the appropriate chart for placement. Weave all remaining ends to the inside.

DUPLICATE STITCH SWEATER / SHIRT

Using color indicated on chart (Color E for Lorelai and Color F for Rory), embroider duplicate stitches for doll's sweater / shirt. Secure ends and weave to the inside of the doll.

LORELAI'S HAIR

Cut ten 10 in. / 25.5 cm strands of Color C. *Insert the crochet hook under the ladder between two stitches at the middle of the doll's head in the first knitted round of Color C (Rnd 39). Fold one strand of hair in half and pull through a knitted st, keeping the loop on your crochet hook. Wrap both ends of the strand of hair around the crochet hook and pull through the loop to secure. Rep from * 9 more times, attaching one strand of yarn per row, in a straight line up the middle of the doll's head. Arrange one strand of yarn to each side to create a part. Gather yarn at back of head and tie with waste yarn in Color C to create a ponytail.

RORY'S HAIR

Cut forty-eight 6 in. / 15 cm strands of Color C. *Insert the crochet hook under both legs of a knit st in the first rnd of hair (Rnd 39). Fold two strands of yarn in half and pull through a knitted st, keeping the loop on your crochet hook. Wrap both ends of the strands around the crochet hook and pull through

the loop to secure. Rep from *
23 more times, attaching two
strands of yarn per indicated stitch.
Style hair by pulling 4 strands of
yarn on each side of the face to the
back of the doll's head and securing
with a short length of Color H yarn,
tied in a bow.

RORY'S BOW TIE

Cut one 6 in. / 15 cm strand of Color
G. Thread yarn through both legs
of the 2 center sts of Color D at
Rory's neck. Tie into a bow and
trim ends to desired length.

Coffee Talk

Both Lauren Graham and Alexis Bledel appeared in all 153 original *Gilmore Girls* episodes.

LORELAI DOLL

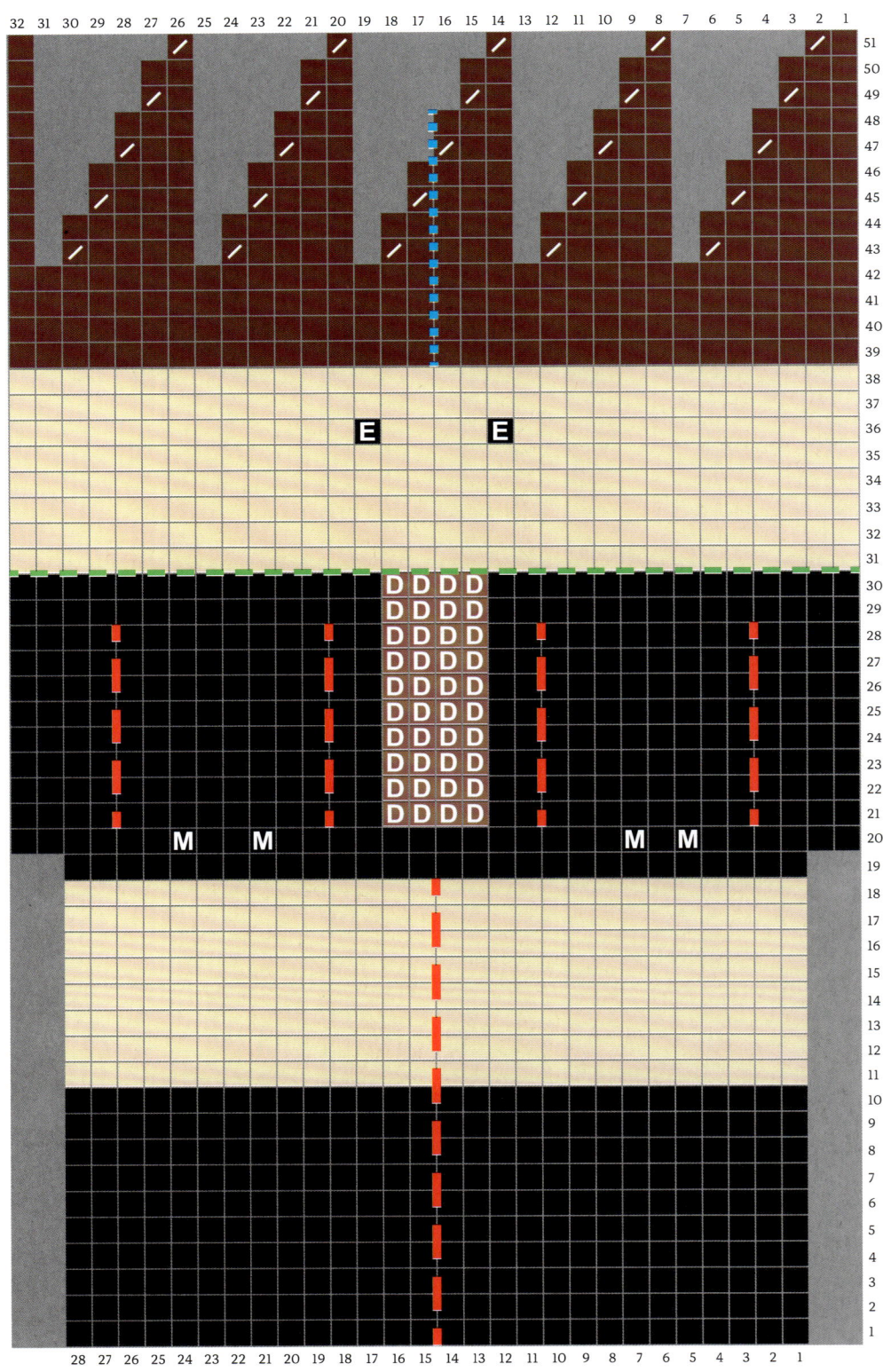

RORY DOLL

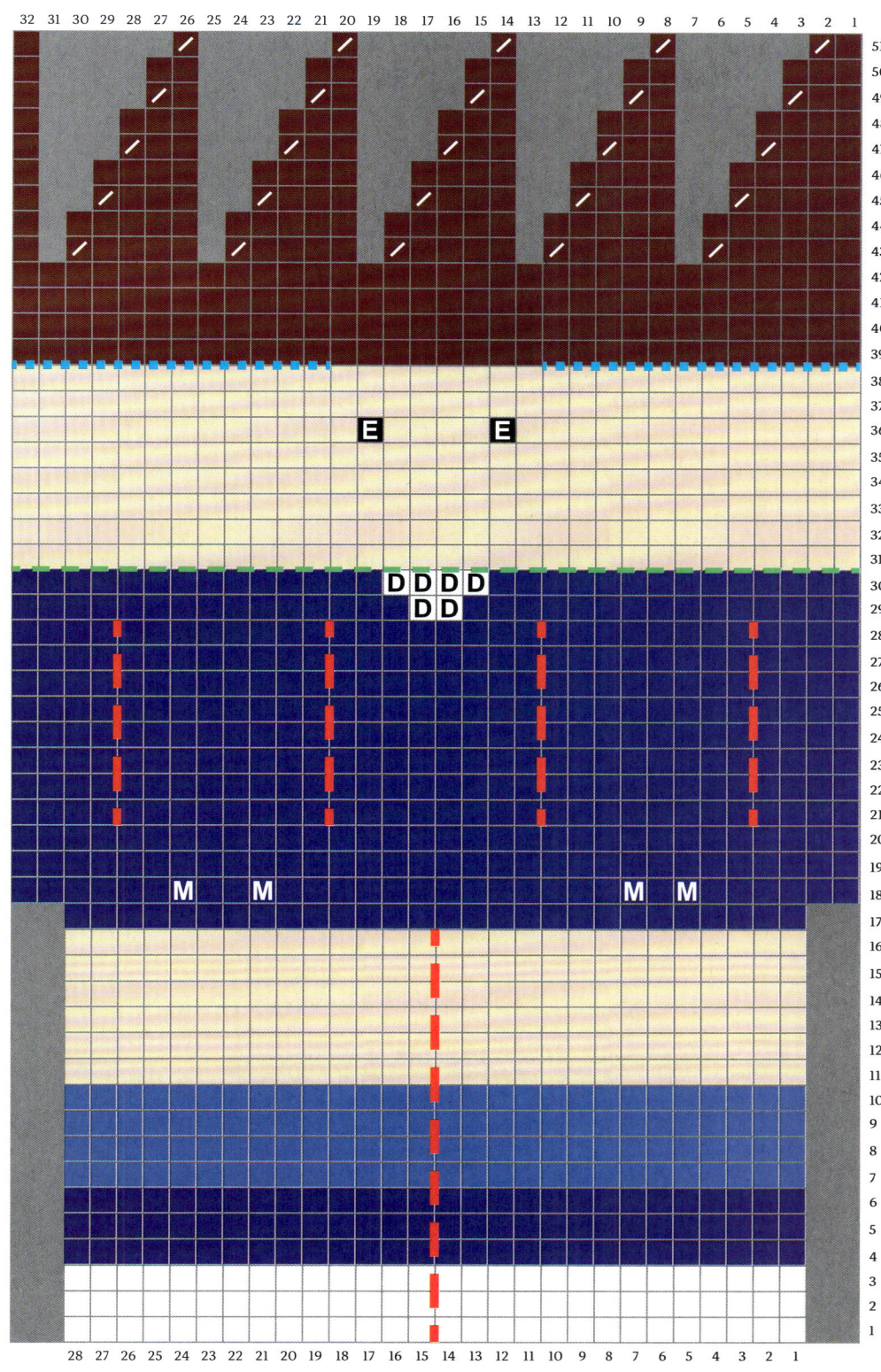

KEY

- knit
- No stitch
- Color A
- Color B
- Color C
- Color E
- Color F
- Color G
- Color H
- k2tog
- D Duplicate stitch
- E Eye
- M M1
- •••• Hair placement
- – – Running stitch for neck definition
- – – Stitch after stuffing for arm and leg definition

Lane's Drumstick Bag

Designed by Tanis Gray
SKILL LEVEL: EASY

"Remember two years ago, I got my mom that perfume? Okay, to me that said, 'Hey mom, you work hard, you deserve something fancy.' Now, to my mother it said, 'Hey mom, here's some smelly sex juice—the kind I use to lure boys with.' And resulted in me being sent to Bible camp all summer."

—Lane Kim, Season 1, Episode 10

Played by actor Keiko Agena, Lane Kim was the last character to be cast. Keiko was twenty-six years old when she won the role. In Season 1 of *Gilmore Girls*, she plays a fifteen-year-old. Raised in a strictly traditional and religious Korean household, Lane longs to be a typical American teenager who can listen to whatever music she likes, wear makeup, date non-Koreans, and dress how she chooses. Aided by her best friend since kindergarten, Rory, Lane leads a double life throughout the series. While Lorelai and Rory offer a haven to Lane to be herself at their home, she becomes adept at hiding her things, away from the prying eyes of her mother, Mrs. Kim. But when a music shop opens in Stars Hollow, Lane finds her calling at the drum set—she persistently persuades the shop owner, Sophie, to allow her band to practice quietly after hours.

Rock on, Hep Alien! Knit in the round from the top down, this self-striping drumstick bag would surely be one of the treasures Lane kept hidden from Mrs. Kim beneath her floorboards. Due to the nature of the chevron pattern, rainbow zigzags create bold striping and naturally wavy edges with just one skein of yarn. At the bottom, the bag is closed with a Three-Needle bind off. At the top, a double-yarnover eyelet round creates holes for a twisted rope cording to pass through and cinch shut. Although sized for standard drumstick length, the bag can effortlessly be lengthened or shortened for differently sized drumsticks or even knitting needles!

SIZES
One size

FINISHED MEASUREMENTS
Circumference: 8 in. / 20.5 cm
Height: 20 in. / 51 cm

YARN
DK weight yarn, shown in Must Stash Yarn *Everyday DK* (75% superwash merino, 25% nylon; 310 yd. / 283 m per 4½ oz. / 125 g hank) in color Lite Brite, 1 hank

NEEDLES
US 4 / 3.5 mm, set of double-pointed needles or size needed to obtain gauge
See Pattern Notes for needle options.

NOTIONS
Stitch marker
Tapestry needle

GAUGE
29 sts and 41 rnds = 4 in. / 10 cm over Chevon Stitch pattern worked in the round, taken after blocking
Make sure to check your gauge.

PATTERN NOTES
- The bag is worked from the top down.
- Due to the nature of the chevron stitch, the top and bottom edges will naturally become wavy.
- The bag is closed at the bottom using the Three-Needle bind off method.
- The cording is added through an eyelet round post-blocking. A double yarn over is created across the eyelet round to make holes large enough for the cording to pass through.
- If you prefer to avoid the use of dpns, for the entirety of the project, you can use gauge-size needles in your preferred construction method, such as Magic Loop, 2 Circulars, etc.

Continued on page 166

PATTERN STITCHES
Chevron Pattern (worked over a multiple of 16 sts)
Rnd 1: Kfb, k5, skp, k2tog, k5, *(kfb) 2 times, k5, skp, k2tog, k5; rep from * to last st, kfb.
Rnd 2: Knit.
Rep Rnds 1–2 for patt.

CAST ON & TOP EDGING
CO 64 sts using the Long Tail cast on method. Pm for BOR and join to work in the rnd, being careful not to twist the sts.
Rnd 1: Knit.
Rnd 2: Purl.
Rnd 3: Knit.
Rnd 4: Purl

BODY
Work Chevron Pattern until the bag measures 2½ in. / 6 cm from the tallest peak of the CO edge, ending with Rnd 2.
Eyelet Rnd (inc): *K6, double-yo, k2tog; rep from * to end—72 sts.
Next Rnd (dec): Knit, dropping extra yo as encountered—64 sts.
Beginning with Rnd 1, work Chevron Pattern until the bag measures 20 in. / 51 cm from the tallest peak of the CO edge, or to desired length, ending with Rnd 2.
Carefully turn the work inside out. Slip sts as necessary so that 32 sts are on each of 2 needles. Hold the 2 needles parallel and graft the bottom of the bag closed using the Three-Needle bind off method.

FINISHING
Weave in all loose ends to WS.
Turn bag right side out and wet block to dimensions. Allow to dry before adding cord.

Coffee Talk
Lane Kim was based on show creator Amy Sherman-Palladino's best friend growing up, Helen Pai. Amy gives her BFF—a producer on the show—a nod by naming Lane's band Hep Alien, an anagram of Helen Pai.

CORDING

Cut six 60 in. / 152 cm lengths of yarn.

Holding all 6 lengths together, tie an overhand knot at one end and hold in your hand.

Tape the unknotted ends to a surface such as a table or desk. Ensure the ends are secured so they won't come loose from under the tape when tension is applied to the yarn.

Twist the yarn counterclockwise, gently pulling the yarn to keep it taut as you twist.

When the length is fully twisted and feels like it wants to double back on itself, keeping the length taut, place your pointer finger on the midpoint of the twist, fold the end in your hand back toward the taped end, and then let go.

The two halves of the folded cording should twist together like a piece of rope.

Gently smooth out any bumps or inconsistencies in the rope.

Carefully remove the tape and tie a knot in the unsecured ends to prevent unraveling.

ADD CORDING TO BAG

Weave the cord through the eyelets created near the top of the bag and cinch shut.

Doose's Market Tote

Designed by Megan-Anne (Llama) Meyers

SKILL LEVEL: INTERMEDIATE

"I am merely a humble vessel for the municipal code."
—Taylor Doose, Season 5, Episode 4

Doose's Market, owned by Taylor Doose—who also sits on the Stars Hollow Tourist Board, the Stars Hollow Neighborhood Watch, The Stars Hollow Business Association, and the Stars Hollow Citizens for a Clean Stars Hollow, as well as owning and running Taylor's Olde Fashioned Soda Shoppe—seems to have everything a citizen of Stars Hollow needs. Doose's Market is where much of the town gossip occurs (in addition to a fake murder scene planted by Jess in Season 2), and where Rory has two big firsts: her first kiss and her first time shoplifting, and is also the store where Dean works. A rule-follower to the core, Taylor is a constant thorn in the side of anyone who needs to run something by the town selectman. With his deep passion for Stars Hollow, he quietly begins buying up all the town property, becoming even more controlling. Played by Michael Winters, the role of Taylor Doose was only supposed to be a four-episode arc, yet he continued to be asked back, eventually appearing in all seven seasons.

This market tote is a great way to show your love for Taylor and support Doose's Market and his Olde Fashioned Soda Shoppe. Worked from the bottom up, the bag is started with a flat panel for the base. Stitches are then picked up and knit around all four edges and worked in the round. The base, side panels, and handles are worked in garter stitch with the yarn doubled to reinforce the structure, and stranded colorwork advertises both of Taylor's businesses. While it can't transport you to Stars Hollow every time you need groceries, shopping with this bag in hand is certainly the next best thing.

SIZES
One size

FINISHED MEASUREMENTS
Width: 13 in. / 33 cm
Depth (not including handles): 10¾ in. / 27.5 cm
Handle Drop: 10 in. / 25.5 cm

YARN
Sport weight yarn, shown in Lattes & Llamas *Geek-A-Long Yarn* (3-ply; 80% superwash merino, 20% nylon; 328 yd. / 300 m per 3½ oz. / 100 g hank)

COLORWAYS
Main Color (MC): Evergreen Moonbeam, 1 hank
Contrast Color (CC): Gilded, 1 hank

NEEDLES
US 4 / 3.5 mm, 24 in. / 60 cm long circular needles or size needed to obtain gauge
Adjust needle length for comfort as needed.

NOTIONS
4 stitch markers (1 unique for BOR)
1 locking stitch marker (optional)
Tapestry needle
Waste yarn

GAUGE
27.5 sts and 35.5 rows = 4 in. / 10 cm in stranded colorwork in the round, taken after blocking
Make sure to check your gauge.

PATTERN NOTES
- Bag is worked bottom up, starting with a flat panel for the base of the bag. The body of the bag is worked by picking up stitches around all four edges of the base panel, before joining to work in the round.
- As you create the base of the bag, you may wish to clip a locking marker to the RS as the two sides of the garter stitch fabric will appear identical.

Continued on page 170

- The base and side panels are worked in garter stitch, holding both yarns together. This reinforces the structure of the bag.
- Dpns may be used in place of waste yarn to place stitches on hold, if preferred.
- Charts are provided for all colorwork portions of the bag. Written instructions are provided for the bag construction and for the base, side panels, and handles.
- Side panels have combined increases and decreases every other round to add visual interest and structure.
- Slip all markers when you come to them unless otherwise instructed. Slip all stitches purlwise unless otherwise instructed.

CAST ON & BASE

With MC and CC held together, CO 12 sts using the Long Tail cast on method. Do not join to work in the rnd. Cont to hold MC and CC together until instructed otherwise.
Setup Row (WS): Knit.
Cont in garter stitch for 148 rows. You will end with a WS row and have 75 garter ridges.
With RS facing, BO all sts knitwise but do not break yarns or finish off the final loop—1 st rem on RHN. Do not turn to WS.

BODY OF BAG

With the RS facing, rotate work 90 degrees. Pick up and knit 74 sts along the first long edge of the base. (K1, yo, k1) into the corner st. Pick up and knit 10 sts into the CO edge of the base. (K1, yo, k1) into the corner st. Pick up and knit 74 sts along the second long edge of the base. (K1, yo, k1) into the corner st. Pick up and knit 10 sts along the bound off edge. Kfb into the final corner stitch—180 sts.
Pm for BOR and join to work in the rnd, being careful not to twist the sts.
Setup Rnd: P77, pm-A, p13, pm-B, p77, pm-C, purl to end of rnd.
From this point forward, hold MC and CC together while working the 13 sts between M-A and M-B and between M-C and the BOR M. When working across Charts A, B, or C, hold MC and CC single, knitting all sts and changing colors as noted on the respective charts.
Begin Chart A, reading all rows from right to left as for working in the rnd as follows:
Rnd 1: Work Chart A to M-A (pattern repeat is worked 12 times), sm, holding MC and CC together: k1, M1R, k4, s2kp, k4, M1L, k1, sm, work Chart A to M-C (pattern repeat is worked 12 times), sm, holding MC and CC together: k1, M1R, k4, s2kp, k4, M1L, k1.
Rnd 2: Work Chart A to M-A, sm, holding MC and CC together: purl to M-B, sm, work Chart A to M-C, sm, holding MC and CC together: purl to end of rnd.
Rep [Rnds 1–2] 8 more times (18 rnds; 3 total repeats of Chart A).
Begin Charts B & C, reading all rows from right to left as for working in the rnd as follows:
Rnd 19: Work Chart B to M-A, sm, holding MC and CC together: k1, M1R, k4, s2kp, k4, M1L, k1, sm, work Chart C to M-C, sm, holding MC and CC together: k1, M1R, k4, s2kp, k4, M1L, k1.
Rnd 20: Work Chart B to M-A, sm, holding MC and CC together: purl to M-B, sm, work Chart A to M-C, sm, holding MC and CC together: purl to end of rnd.
Rep [Rnds 19–20] 23 more times (48 rnds; 1 total working of each chart).
Begin Chart A, reading all rows from right to left as for working in the rnd as follows:
Rnd 67: Work Chart A to M-A (pattern repeat is worked 12 times), sm, holding MC and CC together: k1, M1R, k4, s2kp, k4, M1L, k1, sm, work Chart A to M-C (pattern repeat is worked 12 times), sm, holding MC and CC together: k1, M1R, k4, s2kp, k4, M1L, k1.
Rnd 68: Work Chart A to M-A, sm, holding MC and CC together: purl to M-B, sm, work Chart A to M-C, sm, holding MC and CC together: purl to end of rnd.
Rep [Rnds 67–68] 5 more times (12 rnds; 2 total repeats of Chart A).
All charted colorwork is now complete. Do not break yarns.

HANDLES

Handles are worked holding MC and CC together throughout.
Setup Rnd 1: Knit.
Setup Rnd 2: Purl.
Rep Setup Rnds 1–2 once more.
Separation Rnd: **Rm (BOR), *k2tog, k2tog, pass the first k2tog over the second—1 st BO; rep from * to 1 st before M-A, sl1 wyib, rm (M-A), move slipped st back to LHN purlwise, k2tog, pass prev k2tog over—1 st BO, p5. Transfer the last 6 sts of your RHN to waste yarn. K2tog, p5. Transfer the last 6 sts of your RHN onto a second piece of waste yarn.
Rep from ** once more across M-B and M-C to end of rnd; do not transfer the final 6 sts to waste yarn. Without breaking the yarns, turn to the WS.

FIRST HANDLE

The handles are worked flat. Move the yarn between the needles between slipped sts to knit sts to avoid creating unwanted yo's.
Row 1: Sl1 wyif, k4, k1tbl.
Rep Row 1 (on RS and WS) until handle measures approx. 20 in. / 51 cm, or desired length, ending with a WS row. Take note of the

number of rows worked so the second handle will match.

Break yarns, leaving 10 in. / 25.5 cm for grafting.

With the Chart B side of the bag still facing, transfer 6 sts from the waste yarn on the other side of the bag to a spare working needle; 2 needles now hold 6 sts each.

Thread the tapestry needle with both tails and graft the two sets of sts together using Kitchener stitch.

Break yarn and secure end.

SECOND HANDLE

Transfer 6 live sts from one length of waste yarn to the working needle. Rejoin both MC and CC yarns with the WS facing.

Beginning with Row 1, work as for the First Handle, grafting to the remaining live sts with the Chart C side of the bag facing.

FINISHING

Weave in all ends. Block to dimensions, taking care not to overstretch the handles. Trim all ends.

Coffee Talk

During the seven-season run, viewers only see men working at Doose's Market.

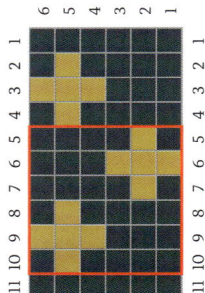

CHART A

CHART B

KEY
- ☐ knit 
- ■ MC
- ■ CC
- ▭ Pattern repeat

CHART C

"Babette Ate Oatmeal" Pillow

Designed by Tanis Gray

SKILL LEVEL: INTERMEDIATE

Rory: "You look nice today, Kirk."

Kirk: "Thanks, this is the suit they buried my dad in."

—*Gilmore Girls* Season 6, Episode 4

The character of Kirk Gleason, played by actor Sean Gunn, was inspired by creator Amy Sherman-Palladino's own father, Don Sherman, an actor and writer appearing on many well-known shows playing bit parts. While Gunn was originally cast for only one episode as a DSL installer named Mick, another small part came up as a swan delivery man, and he was cast once more. Sherman-Palladino thought it would be funny to continue to cast him in bit roles, soon making him a regularly featured permanent resident of Stars Hollow. Kirk is the youngest of twelve children. His eccentric ways, controlling mother, constant need to please Taylor Doose, intense night terrors, and entrepreneurship (creating his own hay-based skin care product line, or T-shirts with quotes from fellow residents) cemented his place as a fan favorite—ranking him #1 out of all Stars Hollow Townies in an *Entertainment Weekly* poll. Gunn says his character "became kind of part of the fabric of the town," and "I think you're always going to have a huge section of people in the audience who either know someone like Kirk or they feel like Kirk themselves sometimes."

This pillow begins with a provisional, or temporary, cast on, and is worked in the round seamlessly. The top and bottom edges are left open while "Babette ate oatmeal"—or your favorite phrase from Stars Hollow—is duplicate stitched onto the front. Access from both open ends makes the stitching an easier process. A pillow is then stuffed inside, and both the top and the bottom openings are grafted together.

SIZES
One size

FINISHED MEASUREMENTS
Height: 12 in. / 30.5 cm
Width: 20 in. / 51 cm

YARN
Worsted weight yarn, shown in Cascade Yarns 200 *Superwash Merino* (100% superwash merino wool; 220 yd. / 201 m per 3½ oz. / 100 g skein) in color #28 Black (MC), 2 skeins

NEEDLES
US 6 / 4 mm, 32 in. / 80 cm long circular needles or size needed to obtain gauge

NOTIONS
Approx. 5 yd. / 4.5 m of worsted weight white yarn (CC). Original design uses Cascade Yarns *220 Superwash Merino* in color #25 White (1 skein)
Waste yarn
Size J / 5.75 mm crochet hook
12 x 20 in. / 30.5 x 51 cm pillow form
Stitch marker
Tapestry needle
Spare gauge-size or below 24–32 in. / 60–80 cm long circular needle

GAUGE
19 sts and 27 rnds = 4 in. / 10 cm in St st in the round, taken after blocking
Make sure to check your gauge.

PATTERN NOTES
- Pillow is worked in the round beginning with a provisional cast on.
- Duplicate stitching is added post-blocking to create the writing on the pillow.
- The top and bottom edges of the pillow are grafted closed around the pillow form.

PILLOWCASE

Using waste yarn, CO 190 sts using the Crochet Provisional cast on method. Leaving a 36 in. / 91.5 cm tail of MC, knit across all the provisionally cast on sts. Pm for BOR and join to work in the rnd, being careful not to twist the sts.

Work in St st until the pillowcase measures 12 in. / 30.5 cm from the CO edge. Do not bind off. Break yarn, leaving a 36 in. / 91.5 cm tail. Place live sts on waste yarn for blocking.

BLOCKING

Weave in any ends that are not the 36 in. / 91.5 cm tails at the top and bottom of the pillowcase to the WS.

Wet block the pillowcase to dimensions, pinning out all edges to keep them straight. Align the BOR, indicated by the two long tails from the CO edge and the live sts at the top of the pillowcase, to the right. This edge will be an invisible "side seam." Allow to dry completely.

DUPLICATE STITCH MOTIF

Leave the pillowcase unseamed.

With the RS facing out, use removable stitch markers to find the center 87 sts by 8 rows across the face of the pillowcase. Be sure this is centered both horizontally and vertically across the face of your pillowcase.

With CC and tapestry needle, duplicate st the Chart A motif onto the pillowcase, being careful not to join the front and back together.

FINISHING

Weave in all loose CC ends to the WS.

Return the live sts from the top of the pillowcase to the working needle and a spare needle, dividing the sts evenly (95 sts on each needle); hold the two needles parallel with the RS facing out. Using the long tail from the top of the pillowcase, graft the sts together.

Insert the pillow form into the pillowcase.

Carefully remove the provisional cast on and place the live sts onto the working needle and a spare needle, dividing the sts evenly (95 sts on each needle); hold the two needles parallel with the RS facing out. Using the long tail from the cast on edge of the pillowcase, graft the sts together around the pillow form.

Weave in any loose ends to the inside of the pillowcase.

CHART A

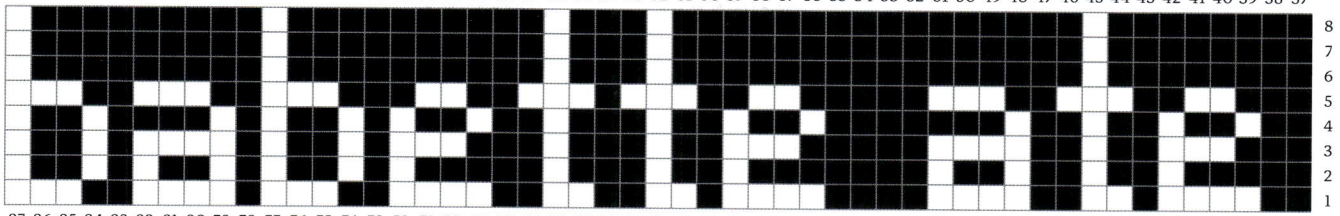

CHART A, CONTINUED

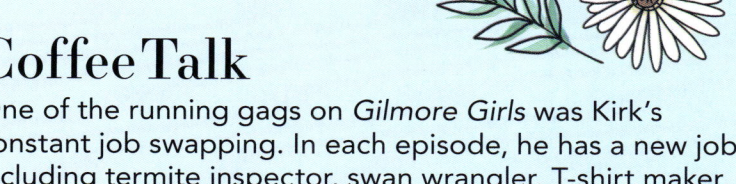

KEY

☐ Duplicate st with CC
■ Existing MC pillow sts

Coffee Talk

One of the running gags on *Gilmore Girls* was Kirk's constant job swapping. In each episode, he has a new job, including termite inspector, swan wrangler, T-shirt maker, beauty shop cashier, vintage ring seller, and movie theater projectionist, to name a few. Actor Sean Gunn reveals that his favorite job of Kirk's was hockey game announcer because he had always dreamed of being a sportscaster.

Sookie's Baby Blanket

Designed by Esther Braithwaite

SKILL LEVEL: INTERMEDIATE

Lorelai: "Everything okay?"

Sookie: "Sure. And I'm thrilled and delighted that Norman Mailer is coming in here every day and sitting at a table for four and ordering nothing at all, but tea!"

—*Gilmore Girls*, Season 5, Episode 6

Guest stars were in abundance during the seven-season run of *Gilmore Girls*, many going on to have illustrious careers or star in their own series after appearing on the show. Lane's guitar-playing crush Dave Rygalski was played by Adam Brody, who went on to star in *The O.C.* on the CW. Lorelai's boring date Peyton Sanders was played by Jon Hamm, who went on to be a lead in *Mad Men*, to name a few. Cameos were also fairly common on *Gilmore Girls*, with appearances by Secretary of State Madeleine Albright, *Family Guy* creator Seth MacFarlane, CNN's Christiane Amanpour, and two-time Pulitzer–Prize winning author Norman Mailer. Mailer's son Stephen was a friend of one of the *Gilmore* staff writers and played a reporter interviewing the famous curmudgeon at the Dragonfly Inn in Season 5. Mailer read the episode where he drives Sookie crazy by only ordering iced tea and taking up a table, and he thought it was "cute." A fan favorite, Episode 6, called "Norman Mailer, I'm Pregnant," is when Sookie realizes she's expecting her first child.

Made to resemble a sewn quilt, this garter stitch seamless modular baby blanket is worked from block to block. By picking up stitches from the previous square and working directly off it, 25 striped blocks fan out in a square shape that is easily made larger or smaller. Plan your stripes to make a pattern, work from leftover bits and bobs in your stash, go with all solids, or pick your colors as you go. Borders are then picked up and knit across each side individually.

SIZES
One size

FINISHED MEASUREMENTS
Width: 36 in. / 91.5 cm
Length: 36 in. / 91.5 cm

YARN
DK weight yarn, shown in The Plucky Knitter *Sweater DK* (90% superwash merino, 10% nylon; 270 yd. / 247 m per 4 oz. / 115 g hank)

COLORWAYS
Color A: Dive Bar, 1 hank
Color B: Chambray, 1 hank
Color C: Polar Dip, 3 hanks
Color D: Build Me Up, 1 hank
Color E: Like Sands Through the Hourglass, 1 hank

NEEDLES
US 6 / 4 mm, 32 in. / 80 cm long circular needles and pair of straight needles or size needed to obtain gauge

NOTIONS
Locking stitch marker (optional)
Tapestry needle

GAUGE
24 sts and 46 rows = 4 in. / 10 cm over garter stitch worked flat, taken after spray/dry blocking
Make sure to check your gauge.

PATTERN NOTES
- This blanket is worked by joining mitered squares together, each of which is knit in 2-color stripes.
- The cast on method for each square varies based on its position in the blanket.
- The MC and CC will differ for each square. Refer to the Schematic for placement and colors used for each square.
- It is recommended to swatch with Color A, C, or D to avoid running out of Colors B and E.

SQUARE #1 (BEGINS COLUMN 1)

With straight needles and MC, CO 61 sts using the Long Tail cast on method, marking the center stitch with a locking stitch marker if desired. The CO row counts as Row 1.

Row 2 (WS, MC): With MC, knit.
Row 3 (RS, CC, dec): Knit to 1 st before center st, s2kp, k to end—2 sts dec.
Row 4 (CC): Knit.
Row 5 (MC, dec): Work as for Row 2—2 sts dec.
Row 6 (MC): Knit.
Rep [Rows 3–6] 13 more times, then Rows 3–4 once more—3 sts.
Break MC.
Row 61 (RS, CC, dec): S2kp—1 st.
Break CC and pull tail through rem stitch to bind off.

SQUARES #2–5

With straight needles and MC, pick up and knit 30 sts evenly across top edge of the previous square, then cast on 31 sts using the Backwards Loop cast on method, marking the center stitch with a locking stitch marker if desired—61 sts. The pickup / CO row counts as Row 1.
Work Rows 2–61 of Square #1, using the appropriate colors for MC and CC.

SQUARE #6 (BEGINS COLUMN 2)

With straight needles and MC, CO 31 sts using the Long Tail cast on method, then pick up and knit 30 sts evenly up the right-hand side edge of Square #1 from bottom to top, marking the center stitch with a locking stitch marker if desired—61 sts. The pickup / CO row counts as Row 1.
Work Rows 2–61 of Square #1, using the appropriate colors for MC and CC.

SQUARES #7–10

With straight needles and MC, pick up and knit 31 sts evenly across the top of the previous square, then pick up and knit 30 sts from the right-hand side of the adjacent square, marking the center stitch with a locking stitch marker if desired—61 sts. The pickup / CO row counts as Row 1.
Work Rows 2–61 of Square #1, using the appropriate colors for MC and CC.

SQUARE #11 (BEGINS COLUMN 3)

With straight needles and MC, CO 31 sts using the Long Tail cast on method, then pick up and knit 30 sts evenly up the right-hand side edge of Square #6 from bottom to top, marking the center stitch with a locking stitch marker if desired—61 sts. The pickup / CO row counts as Row 1.
Work Rows 2–61 of Square #1, using the appropriate colors for MC and CC.

SQUARES #12–15

Work as per Squares #7–10, using the appropriate colors for MC and CC.

SQUARE #16 (BEGINS COLUMN 4)

With straight needles and MC, CO 31 sts using the Long Tail cast on method, then pick up and knit 30 sts evenly up the right-hand side edge of Square #11 from bottom to top, marking the center stitch with a locking stitch marker if desired—61 sts. The pickup / CO row counts as Row 1.
Work Rows 2–61 of Square #1, using the appropriate colors for MC and CC.

SQUARES #17–20

Work as per Squares #7–10, using the appropriate colors for MC and CC.

SQUARE #21 (BEGINS COLUMN 5)

With straight needles and MC, CO 31 sts using the Long Tail cast on method, then pick up and knit 30 sts evenly up the right-hand side edge of Square #16 from bottom to top, marking the center stitch with a locking stitch marker if desired—61 sts. The pickup / CO row counts as Row 1.
Work Rows 2–61 of Square #1, using the appropriate colors for MC and CC.

SQUARES #22–25

Work as per Squares #7–10, using the appropriate colors for MC and CC.

BORDER A

With circular needles and Color C, pick up and knit 150 sts evenly across the left-hand side edges of Squares #5 through #1. The pickup row counts as Row 1.
Row 2 (WS): Knit.
Row 3 (RS): Knit.
Row 4 (WS): Knit.
Rep [Rows 3–4] 13 more times (15 garter ridges total).
With RS facing, BO all sts knitwise.

BORDER B

With circular needles and Color C, pick up and knit 150 sts evenly across the right-hand side edges of Squares #21 through #25. The pickup row counts as Row 1.
Work Rows 2–4, subsequent repeats, and bind off, as per Border A.

BORDER C

With circular needles and Color C, pick up and knit 180 sts evenly across the top edges of Border B, Squares #25, 20, 15, 10, and 5, and Border A. The pickup row counts as Row 1.
Work Rows 2–4, subsequent repeats, and bind off, as per Border A.

BORDER D

With circular needles and Color C, pick up and knit 180 sts evenly across the bottom edges of Border A, Squares #1, 6, 11, 16, and 21, and Border B. The pickup row counts as Row 1.

Work Rows 2–4, subsequent repeats, and bind off, as per Border A.

FINISHING

Weave in all ends to the WS. Spray/dry block the blanket to measurements. Allow to dry completely. Trim all ends.

Coffee Talk

Creator Amy Sherman-Palladino admired the Algonquin Round Table—a group of famous authors, actors, and critics who met daily at the Algonquin Hotel in New York City in the 1920s to have lunch together—and wanted to have her own version at the Dragonfly Inn. Sherman-Palladino said, "Ya' know, we should get Tony Kushner, Stephen Sondheim, and Norman Mailer, and have our own Algonquin Round Table at Lorelai's inn. . . . We had a legend for two days in Stars Hollow." One of the most famous members of the original New York group was writer Dorothy Parker, whom Sherman-Palladino named her production company, Dorothy Parker Drank Here Productions, after.

SCHEMATIC

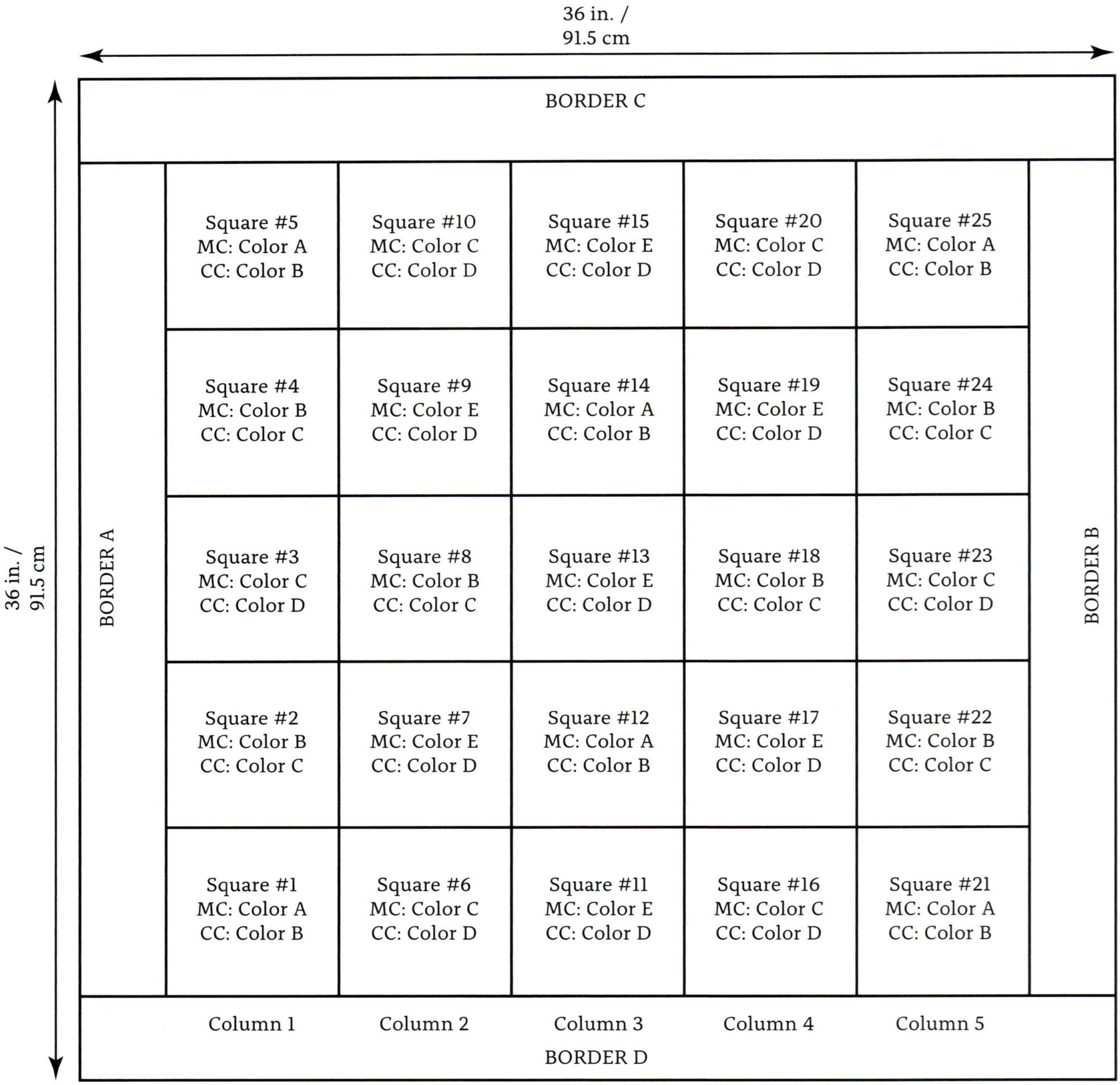

36 in. / 91.5 cm (width)

36 in. / 91.5 cm (height)

BORDER C (top)
BORDER A (left)
BORDER B (right)
BORDER D (bottom)

	Column 1	Column 2	Column 3	Column 4	Column 5
Row 5 (top)	Square #5 MC: Color A CC: Color B	Square #10 MC: Color C CC: Color D	Square #15 MC: Color E CC: Color D	Square #20 MC: Color C CC: Color D	Square #25 MC: Color A CC: Color B
Row 4	Square #4 MC: Color B CC: Color C	Square #9 MC: Color E CC: Color D	Square #14 MC: Color A CC: Color B	Square #19 MC: Color E CC: Color D	Square #24 MC: Color B CC: Color C
Row 3	Square #3 MC: Color C CC: Color D	Square #8 MC: Color B CC: Color C	Square #13 MC: Color E CC: Color D	Square #18 MC: Color B CC: Color C	Square #23 MC: Color C CC: Color D
Row 2	Square #2 MC: Color B CC: Color C	Square #7 MC: Color E CC: Color D	Square #12 MC: Color A CC: Color B	Square #17 MC: Color E CC: Color D	Square #22 MC: Color B CC: Color C
Row 1 (bottom)	Square #1 MC: Color A CC: Color B	Square #6 MC: Color C CC: Color D	Square #11 MC: Color E CC: Color D	Square #16 MC: Color C CC: Color D	Square #21 MC: Color A CC: Color B

Firelight Festival Blanket

Designed by Sauniell Connally
SKILL LEVEL: INTERMEDIATE

"... A beautiful girl from one county; a handsome boy from another. They meet and they fall in love. Separated by distance and by parents who did not approve of the union, the young couple dreamed of a day that they could be together. ... So, one night, cold and black with no light to guide them, they both snuck out of their homes and ran away as fast as they could ... right where the town gazebo is today. ... And that, my friends, is the story of how Stars Hollow came to be. ..."

—Miss Patty, Season 1, Episode 16

A town that loves a good shindig, Stars Hollow is home to various events throughout the year, such as the Old Muddy River Bridge Knit-a-Thon, Bid-on-a-Basket Festival, Winter Carnival, End of Summer Madness Festival, 24-Hour Dance-a-Thon, Movie Night in the Square, Spring Fling Festival, Battle of Stars Hollow Reenactment, Festival of Living Art, and, of course, Founders Firelight Festival. Taking place in late winter, this festival celebrates the founding of the town: two lovers were kept apart by their families but, brought together by fate, met under the stars where the town gazebo was built.

In celebration of Stars Hollow's annual Firelight Festival, this blanket captures the beautiful fire and warm starlight of the evening. The blanket is worked flat and seed stitch borders with embossed flame motifs surround the star stitch center panel. Not meant to be a perfect square, as the star stitch panel creates a slight bias, the blanket features fire motifs that encourage wavy edges and extreme comfort.

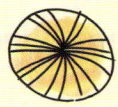

SIZES
One size

FINISHED MEASUREMENTS
Width: 36 in. / 91.5 cm
Length: 44 in. / 112 cm

YARN
Bulky weight yarn, shown in 316 Dye Studio *House Bulky* (single ply; 80% superwash merino, 20% nylon; 76 yd. / 69.5 m per 100 g hank) in color Marigold, 11 hanks

NEEDLES
US 11 / 8.0 mm, 40 in. / 100 cm long circular needle or size needed to obtain gauge

NOTIONS
Stitch markers
Tapestry needle

GAUGE
11 sts and 17 rows = 4 in. / 10 cm over St st worked flat, taken after steam blocking
Make sure to check your gauge.

PATTERN NOTES
- This blanket is worked flat from bottom to top.
- When working the Embossed Flame pattern, the number of stitches will increase over Rows 3–9, and then decrease again over Rows 13–29. When the flame is complete, the motif will return to a count of 11 stitches. This will give the embossed effect. The flames should not be blocked in a way as to flatten the embossing.
- All stitches of the flame are twisted on the RS only.
- Written instructions are provided for the entirety of the pattern.

Continued on page 186

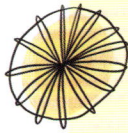

PATTERN STITCHES

EMBOSSED FLAME—WORKED OVER 11 STS
Row 1 (RS): P4, k3, p4.
Row 2 (WS): K4, p3, k4.
Row 3 (inc): P4, (k1tbl, yo) 2 times, k1tbl, p4—13 sts.
Row 4: K4, p5, k4.
Row 5 (inc): P4, k2tbl, yo, k1tbl, yo, k2tbl, p4—15 sts.
Row 6: K4, p7, k4.
Row 7 (inc): P4, k3tbl, yo, k1tbl, yo, k3tbl, p4—17 sts.
Row 8: K4, p9, k4.
Row 9 (inc): P4, k4tbl, yo, k1tbl, yo, k4tbl, p4—19 sts.
Row 10: K4, p11, k4.
Row 11: P4, k11tbl, p4.
Row 12: K4, p11, k4.
Row 13 (dec): P4, k3tbl, k2tog-tbl, k6tbl, p4—18 sts.
Row 14: K4, p10, k4.
Row 15 (dec): P4, k3tbl, k2tog-tbl, k5tbl, p4—17 sts.
Row 16: K4, p9, k4.
Row 17 (dec): P4, k3tbl, k2tog-tbl, k4tbl, p4—16 sts.
Row 18: K4, p8, k4.
Row 19 (dec): P4, k3tbl, k2tog-tbl, k3tbl, p4—15 sts.
Row 20: K4, p7, k4.
Row 21 (dec): P4, k3tbl, k2tog-tbl, k2tbl, p4—14 sts.
Row 22: K4, p6, k4.
Row 23 (dec): P4, k3tbl, k2tog-tbl, k1tbl, p4—13 sts.
Row 24: K4, p5, k4.
Row 25 (dec): P4, k3tbl, k2tog-tbl, p4—12 sts.
Row 26: K4, p4, k4.
Row 27 (dec): P4, k2tbl, k2tog-tbl, p4—11 sts.
Row 28: K4, p3, k4.
Row 29 (dec): P4, k1tbl, k2tog-tbl, p4—10 sts.
Row 30: K4, p2, k4.
Row 31 (inc): P3, yo, p1, k2tog-tbl, p1, yo, p3—11 sts.
Row 32: Knit.
Row 33: Purl.
Row 34: Knit.
Row 35: Purl.
Row 36: Knit.
Rep Rows 1–36 for patt.

STAR STITCH—WORKED OVER A MULTIPLE OF 3 + 1 STS
Row 1 (RS): K1, *yo, k3, pass first stitch of the 3 knit stitches over 2 sts and off the needle; rep from * to end.
Row 2 (WS): Purl.
Row 3: *Yo, k3, pass first stitch of the 3 knit stitches over 2 sts and off the needle; rep from * to last st, k1.
Row 4: Purl.
Row 5: K2, *yo, k3, pass first stitch of the 3 knit stitches over 2 sts and off the needle; rep from * to last 2 sts, yo, k2tog.
Row 6: Purl.
Rep Rows 1–6 for patt.

HORIZONTAL LACE—WORKED OVER A MULTIPLE OF 2 STS
Row 1 (RS): Knit.
Row 2 (WS): Purl.
Row 3: *Yo, k2tog; rep from * to end.
Row 4: Purl.
Rows 5–6: Knit.
Rep Rows 1–6 for patt.

CAST ON & BOTTOM BORDER
CO 97 sts using the Knitted cast on method.
Row 1 (RS): *K1, p1; rep from * to last st, k1.
Row 2 (WS): *K1, p1; rep from * to last st, k1.
Rep Rows 1–2 once more.

BOTTOM FLAME MOTIF
Setup Row 1 (RS): (K1, p1) 2 times, k1tbl, pm, purl to last 5 sts, pm, k1tbl, (p1, k1) 2 times.
Setup Row 2 (WS): (K1, p1) 2 times, p1tbl, sm, knit to M, sm, p1tbl, (p1, k1) 2 times.
Row 1 (RS): (K1, p1) 2 times, k1tbl, sm, p1, work Embossed Flame over 11 sts, p2, *work Embossed Flame over 11 sts, p1; rep from * 4 more times, p1, work Embossed Flame over 11 sts, p1, sm, k1tbl, (p1, k1) 2 times.
Row 2 (WS): (K1, p1) 2 times, p1tbl, sm, k1, work Embossed Flame over 11 sts, k2, *work Embossed Flame over 11 sts, k1; rep from * 4 more times, k1, work Embossed Flame over 11 sts, k1, sm, p1tbl, (p1, k1) 2 times.
Rep [Rows 1–2] 17 more times to complete the entire Embossed Flame motif.

BOTTOM HORIZONTAL LACE
Row 1 (RS): (K1, p1) 2 times, k1tbl, sm, p1, work Embossed Flame over 11 sts, pm, k1tbl, k1, work Horizontal Lace to 13 sts before M, k1tbl, pm, work Embossed Flame over 11 sts, p1, sm, k1tbl, (p1, k1) 2 times.
Row 2 (WS): (K1, p1) 2 times, p1tbl, sm, k1, work Embossed Flame over 11 sts, sm, p1tbl, work Horizontal Lace to 2 sts before M, p1, p1tbl, sm, work Embossed Flame over 11 sts, k1, sm, p1tbl, (p1, k1) 2 times.
Row 3: (K1, p1) 2 times, k1tbl, sm, p1, work Embossed Flame over 11 sts, sm, k1tbl, k1, work Horizontal Lace to 1 st before M, k1tbl, sm, work Embossed Flame over 11 sts, p1, sm, k1tbl, (p1, k1) 2 times.
Row 4: (K1, p1) 2 times, p1tbl, sm, k1, work Embossed Flame over 11 sts, sm, p1tbl, work Horizontal Lace to 2 sts before M, p1, p1tbl, sm, work Embossed Flame over 11 sts, k1, sm, p1tbl, (p1, k1) 2 times.
Rep [Rows 3–4] 1 more time to complete the Horizontal Lace 1 time vertically.

CENTER PANEL

Note: The Embossed Flame motif at the left and right edges will begin on Row 7.

Row 1 (RS): (K1, p1) 2 times, k1tbl, sm, p1, work Embossed Flame over 11 sts, sm, k1tbl, work Star Stitch to 1 st before M, k1tbl, sm, work Embossed Flame over 11 sts, p1, sm, k1tbl, (p1, k1) 2 times.

Row 2 (WS): (K1, p1) 2 times, p1tbl, sm, k1, work Embossed Flame over 11 sts, sm, p1tbl, work Star Stitch to 1 st before M, p1tbl, sm, work Embossed Flame over 11 sts, k1, sm, p1tbl, (p1, k1) 2 times.

Rep [Rows 1–2] 46 more times (94 rows total). Your final WS row will be Row 28 of Embossed Flame and Row 4 of Star Stitch in their respective sections.

Row 95 (RS): (K1, p1) 2 times, k1tbl, sm, p1, work Row 29 of Embossed Flame over 11 sts, sm, k1tbl, work Row 5 of Star Stitch to 1 st before M, k1tbl, sm, work Row 29 of Embossed Flame over 11 sts, p1, sm, k1tbl, (p1, k1) 2 times.

Row 96 (WS): (K1, p1) 2 times, p1tbl, sm, k1, work Row 30 of Embossed Flame over 11 sts, sm, p1tbl, knit to 1 st before M, p1tbl, sm, work Row 30 of Embossed Flame over 11 sts, k1, sm, p1tbl, (p1, k1) 2 times.

TOP HORIZONTAL LACE

Note: The Embossed Flame motif at the left and right edges will begin on Row 31.

Row 1 (RS): (K1, p1) 2 times, k1tbl, sm, p1, work Embossed Flame over 11 sts, sm, k1tbl, k1, work Horizontal Lace to 1 st before M, k1tbl, sm, work Embossed Flame over 11 sts, p1, sm, k1tbl, (p1, k1) 2 times.

Row 2 (WS): (K1, p1) 2 times, p1tbl, sm, k1, work Embossed Flame over 11 sts, sm, p1tbl, work Horizontal Lace to 2 sts before M, p1, p1tbl, sm, work Embossed Flame over 11 sts, k1, sm, p1tbl, (p1, k1) 2 times.

Rep [Rows 1–2] 2 more times to complete the Horizontal Lace 1 time vertically, and complete the Embossed Flame motif.
Remove center markers on final repeat; only the markers 5 sts in from each edge should remain.

TOP FLAME MOTIF

Row 1 (RS): (K1, p1) 2 times, k1tbl, sm, p1, work Embossed Flame over 11 sts, p2, *work Embossed Flame over 11 sts, p1; rep from * 4 more times, p1, work Embossed Flame over 11 sts, p1, sm, k1tbl, (p1, k1) 2 times.

Row 2 (WS): (K1, p1) 2 times, p1tbl, sm, k1, work Embossed Flame over 11 sts, k2, *work Embossed Flame over 11 sts, k1; rep from * 4 more times, k1, work Embossed Flame over 11 sts, k1, sm, p1tbl, (p1, k1) 2 times.

Rep [Rows 1–2] 17 more times to complete the entire Embossed Flame motif. Remove rem markers on final repeat.

TOP BORDER

Row 1 (RS): *K1, p1; rep from * to last st, k1.
Row 2 (WS): *K1, p1; rep from * to last st, k1.
Rep Rows 1–2 once more.
With RS facing, BO all sts loosely knitwise.

FINISHING

Weave in all ends and steam block.

Coffee Talk

Gilmore Girls received one Emmy during its seven-season run, in 2004 for Outstanding Makeup for a Series for "The Festival of Living Art" episode in Season 4. Rory plays Antea from *A Young Girl Named Antea* by Parmigianino and Lorelai plays a dancing woman from Renoir's *The Dance at Bougival*.

Glossary

CAST ONS

ALTERNATING CABLE CAST ON

This is a variation of the Cable cast on method that is geared towards projects that begin with a ribbed edge: stitches are cast on alternately knitwise and purlwise to mimic that of the subsequent ribbing.

Make a slipknot and place it on the needle. Holding the needle with the slipknot in your left hand, insert the right needle into the stitch. Knit but do not drop the stitch from the left needle; place this new stitch onto the left needle (1 new stitch made).

*Step 1: Insert the right needle between the first two stitches on the left needle from the back and purl, place the new stitch on the left needle (1 new stitch made).

Step 2: Insert the right needle between the first two stitches on the right needle from the front and knit, place the new stitch on the left needle (1 new stitch made). Repeat from * until the required number of stitches are on the needle.

BACKWARDS LOOP CAST ON

*Holding the yarn over your left thumb with the end coming from the ball held by your last three fingers and at the outside of the thumb, insert the needle up under the yarn next to the outside of your thumb. Remove your thumb from the loop, and pull the end to tighten the yarn slightly to snug the yarn up on the needle.

Repeat from * until the required number of stitches has been cast on.

CABLE CAST ON

TO START A PROJECT:
Make a slipknot and place it on the needle. Holding the needle with the slipknot in your left hand, insert the right needle into the stitch. Knit but do not slip stitch from the left needle. Place this new stitch on the left needle.

*Insert the right needle between the first two stitches on the left needle and knit, place the new stitch on the left needle.

Repeat from * until the required number of stitches are on the needle.

MID-ROW:
*Insert the right needle between the first two stitches on the left needle and knit, place the new stitch on the left needle.

Repeat from * until the required number of stitches are on the needle.

KNITTED CAST ON

TO START A PROJECT:
Place a slipknot onto the left-hand needle (this will be the first stitch cast on).

*Insert the right-hand needle into the first stitch on the left-hand needle and knit, place the new stitch on the left needle.

Repeat from * until the required number of stitches are on the needle.

MID-ROW:
With the wrong side facing, holding the needle with the live stitches in your left hand, *insert the right needle into the first stitch. Knit but do not slip the stitch from the left needle. Place this new stitch on the left needle.

Repeat from * until the required number of stitches are on the needle.

AT END OF ROW:
After completing the previous row, turn the work so the opposite side of the work is facing. Holding the needle with the live stitches in your left hand, *insert the right needle into the first stitch. Knit but do not slip the stitch from the left needle. Place this new stitch on the left needle.

Repeat from * until the required number of stitches are on the needle.

LONG TAIL CAST ON

Make a slipknot with the yarn, leaving a tail long enough to cast on the required number of stitches (usually about 1 in. / 2.5 cm per stitch), and place the slipknot onto the needle. Holding the needle in your right hand, clasp both strands in your lower three fingers with the long tail over your thumb and the end coming from the ball over your index finger.

*Spread your thumb and index finger apart to form a V. Insert the needle tip up between the two strands on your thumb. Bring the needle tip over the top of the first strand around your index finger, then down to draw a loop between the strands on your thumb. Remove your thumb and tighten the stitch on the needle—1 stitch cast on. Place your thumb and index finger between the strands of yarn again.

Repeat from * until the required number of stitches has been cast on.

CIRCULAR CAST ON

Stitches are cast on over/around a large loop that is subsequently pulled tight to close any gap. This is best worked over double-pointed needles. *Note: Stitches will be cast onto one double-pointed needle, then transferred to the remaining needles as noted in the pattern.*

Create a loop of yarn that is approximately 1 to 2 in. / 2.5 to 5 cm in diameter by crossing the working yarn (the yarn attached to the working ball) in front of the short tail (enough to weave in at the end) and pinch this crossing point between the thumb and middle finger of the left hand. Tension the working yarn over the top of the pointer finger and under the ring finger of the left hand so that your fingers look like they are creating a lowercase "b."

Step 1: Insert the right-hand needle through the front of the loop, and yarn over counterclockwise around the needle with the working yarn; pull the needle back through the loop towards you (1 loop is on the right-hand needle).

Step 2: Leave the right-hand needle outside/above the loop and yarn over counterclockwise around the needle; pull this second loop through the first created on Step 1; 1 stitch is now cast on.

Step 3: Insert the right-hand needle through the front of the loop, and yarn over counterclockwise around the needle with the working yarn; pull the needle back through the loop toward you (1 additional loop is on the right-hand needle).

Step 4: Leave the right-hand needle outside/above the loop and yarn over counterclockwise around the needle; pull this second loop through the first created on Step 3; a new stitch is now cast on. Repeat Steps 3 and 4 until the required number of stitches are on the needle. Once all the stitches are cast on, transfer the stitches to the required number of double-pointed needles. Pull the short tail to cinch up the loop. As the stitches are worked on the first few rounds, the loop may loosen; you can cinch the loop closed again by pulling the short tail and securing it to the wrong side once enough fabric is established.

TWISTED GERMAN CAST ON

Make a slipknot with the yarn, leaving a tail long enough to cast on the required number of stitches (usually about 1 in. / 2.5 cm per stitch), and place the slipknot onto the needle. *Holding the needle and yarn as for a Long Tail cast on, bring the needle toward you, under both strands around your thumb. Swing the tip up and toward you again, then down into the loop on your thumb, then up in front of the loop on your thumb. Then swing it over the top of the loops and over the first strand on your index finger, catch that strand, and bring the needle back down through the thumb loop and to the front, turning your thumb as needed to make room for the needle to pass through. Remove your thumb from the loop, then pull the strands to tighten the stitch. Repeat from * until the required number of stitches has been cast on.

TWO-COLOR ITALIAN CAST ON

Also known as the two-color tubular cast on, this method provides a stretchy but stable cast on edge that flows seamlessly into 1x1 ribbed fabric. The following instructions cast on a purl stitch first, followed by a knit stitch. To cast on a knit stitch first, reverse the order of Steps 3 and 4.

Step 1: Using Color A and Color B held together, create a slipknot and place the slipknot onto the working needle. The two loops of the slipknot will count as extra stitches and will be removed before any work begins. Hold the needle with the slipknot in our right hand, with the tip pointing to the left (as if ready to knit). Secure this slipknot onto the working needle by placing your index finger on top of the knot (to prevent it from sliding off the needle).

Step 2: With your index finger and thumb of your left hand positioned to an "L" shape, drape the DC yarn over your index finger and the LC yarn over your thumb. Secure both tails to the palm of your left hand by holding them with your lower three fingers. This provides tension for the cast on. The yarn now appears to create a triangle shape: the right tip of the triangle is the slipknot secured to the knitting needle in your right hand and the two lower points of the triangle are where the yarns drape over your index finger and thumb. The yarn over the thumb will be used to add stitches purlwise and the yarn over the index finger will be used to add stitches knitwise.

Step 3: Create a Purl Stitch—swing the knitting needle away from you, over the top of the DC yarn on your index finger, then point the needle tip down and toward you, catching the DC yarn. Swing the needle toward you, over the top of the LC yarn on your thumb, then point the needle tip down and away from you, catching the LC yarn. Continue the motion of moving the needle tip away from you, under the DC yarn, then back into the original position. One purl stitch has been created with the LC yarn.

Step 4: Create a Knit Stitch—swing the needle point toward you, over the top of the LC yarn on your index finger, then point the needle tip down and away from you, catching the LC yarn. Swing the needle upward between the LC and DC yarns, away from you, over the top of the DC yarn on your index finger, then point the needle tip down and toward you, catching the DC yarn. Continue the motion of moving the needle toward you, under the LC yarn, then back into the original position. One knit stitch has been created with the DC yarn.

Repeat Steps 3 and 4 until the required number of stitches has been cast on (be sure not to count the slipknot in your total stitches).

Work the final two setup rows one time before beginning work (reverse the order of the slipped and knit / purl stitches if you reversed Steps 3 and 4 during the cast on).

Setup Row 1 (RS): With LC, (sl1 wyif, k1tbl) to end. Drop slipknot off the needle. Slide.

Setup Row 2 (RS): With DC, (p1, sl1 wyib) to end of row. Do not turn.

PROVISIONAL CAST ONS

CROCHET PROVISIONAL CAST ON—AROUND KNITTING NEEDLE

With waste yarn, make a slipknot and place on the crochet hook. Hold the needle in your left hand, the waste yarn over your left index finger, and the crochet hook in your right hand.

*Hold the needle above the yarn coming from the hook. With the crochet hook, reach over the top of the needle and make a chain, making sure the yarn goes around the needle—1 stitch cast on.

Repeat from * until the required number of stitches has been cast on. Cut the yarn and fasten off the last chain, being careful not to tighten the stitch.

Change to the working yarn, ready to work across the cast on stitches per pattern.

When going to finish the edge or pick up the stitches to continue working in the other direction, pull the waste yarn tail out of the last stitch cast on, and pull carefully to unzip the edge, placing the resulting stitches onto the needle as you go.

BIND OFFS

ICELANDIC BIND OFF

The Icelandic bind off is a stretchy bind off method that pairs nicely with garter stitch fabric.

Step 1: Knit 1 stitch loosely.
Step 2: Transfer the remaining stitch purlwise from the right hand to left hand needle.
Step 3: Insert the right-hand needle purlwise through the first stitch on the left-hand needle (almost as if to slip the stitch), then knit the next stitch from the left-hand needle through the first stitch. As you knit the second stitch and remove it from the left-hand needle, allow the slipped stitch to fall off the needle tip at the same time. The slipped stitch has now dropped off over thr top of the stitch just knit, binding off 1 stitch.

Repeat Steps 2 and 3 until 1 stitch remains on the right-hand needle.

Break the working yarn and pull the tail through the remaining stitch, pulling tight to cinch closed.

SEWN TUBULAR BIND OFF

Also known simply as the Tubular bind off, this method creates a seamless yet stretchy edge to ribbed fabric. This method uses two working needles and a tapestry needle to graft the live stitches together.

Cut a tail of working yarn that is four times the length of the stitches to be bound off.

Tubular Setup Round 1: *K1, sl1 wyif; rep from * to end of rnd.
Tubular Setup Round 2: *Sl1 wyib, p1; rep from * to end of rnd.

Slipped Stitch Round: Without knitting any stitches, slip all of the stitches purlwise onto two needles, placing all of the knit stitches on the original working needle and all of the purl stitches on a second circular needle that will be inside/behind the working needle. Each needle will now hold half of the stitches.

Thread a tapestry needle with the tail and graft all of the stitches between the two needles (see Grafting technique).

THREE-NEEDLE BIND OFF

The three-needle bind off is a way of joining two sets of live stitches in a bound off edge, creating a firm seam. This method of seaming is ideal for seams that need the firmness to support the weight of the body and sleeves of a garment.

Place each set of stitches to be joined on separate needles, making sure the needle tips are at the right-hand edge of the stitches to be bound off.

Hold both needles in your left hand with the needle tips pointing to the right.

Insert the right needle knitwise into the first stitch on both needles, then knit them together—1 stitch from each needle has been joined. *Knit the next stitch on both needles together, lift the first stitch worked over the stitch just worked and off the needle—1 stitch bound off.

Repeat from * until all stitches have been worked and 1 stitch remains on the right needle. Cut yarn and fasten off the remaining stitch.

MATTRESS STITCH

Mattress stitch creates an invisible seam along two adjoining edges.

Place the pieces being sewn together side by side on a flat surface with the right sides facing you. Thread a piece of yarn about three times longer than the seam to be sewn into a tapestry needle.

Beginning at the bottom edge, insert the tapestry needle under one bar between the edge stitches on one piece, then under the corresponding bar on the other piece.

*Insert the tapestry needle under the next two bars of the first piece, then under the next two bars of the other piece. Repeat from *, alternating sides, until the seam is complete, ending on the last bar or pair of bars on the first piece. Weave in ends on the wrong side to secure.

GRAFTING

Grafting joins two sets of live stitches without a visible seam. This seaming method is not well suited for joining shoulder seams, which need to support the weight of the body and sleeves of the garment. It should be used for smaller seamed areas or for joining sections of a cowl or the toe of a sock that is expected to be stretched.

Work a few stitches at a time, pulling the yarn loosely, then adjust the length of each stitch to match the tension on each side of the join.

Place each set of stitches to be joined onto two separate needles, making sure the needle tips are at the right-hand edge of the stitches to be joined.

Hold both needles in your left hand, parallel, with the needle tips pointing to the right.

Step 1: Insert a tapestry needle purlwise through first stitch on the front needle and pull the yarn through, leaving the stitch on the front needle.

Step 2: Insert a tapestry needle knitwise through the first stitch on the back needle and pull the yarn through, leaving the stitch on the back needle.

Step 3: Insert a tapestry needle knitwise through the first stitch on the front needle, slip the stitch off the front needle, and pull the yarn through.

Step 4: Insert a tapestry needle purlwise through the next stitch on the front needle and pull the yarn through, leaving the stitch on the front needle.

Step 5: Insert a tapestry needle purlwise through the first stitch on the back needle, slip the stitch off the back needle, and pull the yarn through.

Step 6: Insert a tapestry needle knitwise through the next stitch on the back needle and pull the yarn through, leaving the stitch on the back needle.

Repeat Steps 3–6 until the yarn has been threaded through the last stitch of each needle once. Insert a tapestry needle knitwise into the last stitch on the front needle, slip the stitch off the front needle, and pull the yarn through. Then insert a tapestry needle purlwise into the last stitch on the back needle, slip the stitch from the needle, and pull the yarn through. Weave in the ends on the wrong side to secure.

STEEKING—SEWN REINFORCEMENT

Steeking is a method of reinforcing columns of stitches on a project that was worked in the round so that you may cut the work without the columns of work unraveling. This converts a project that was worked in the round into a flat piece, such as converting a pullover into a cardigan. Or, it may be used to create openings in a project that is otherwise worked seamlessly in the round.

Reinforcement may be done one of two ways: by hand, using a sewing needle and thread, or with a sewing machine.

When reinforcing your columns of stitches to be steeked, you may use any color of thread cause the reinforcement won't be visible from the right side of the work when the project is complete.

[Optional] If you would like to make a visual line of where you will cut the project, choose a contrasting color of thread to be highly visible to mark the column you will cut. Threading your sewing needle with a length of this contrasting color thread, run the needle alternately over then under the horizontal bars running between the stitches in columns 4 and 5 of the steek panel. This is just a visual and does not impact the reinforced stitches.

TO REINFORCE YOUR STEEKING COLUMNS BY HAND

Thread your needle with a length of thread and work a column of back stitch up the center of the stitch in columns 3 and 6 of your steek panel. For extra security, you may repeat the back stitch on the adjacent stitch in columns (2 and 7).

TO REINFORCE YOUR STEEKING COLUMNS USING A SEWING MACHINE

Option 1: Using the zigzag stitch set to the same width as one column of stitches, zigzag stitch up columns 3 and 6 of your steek panel.

Option 2: Using straight stitch set to a length of one row of stitches, straight stitch up columns 3 and 6 of your steek panel. Two passes is recommended for this method.

BACK STITCH

The back stitch is a hand-sewing technique used to reinforce stitches, often for the purpose of steeking your work.

*With a sewing needle and thread, insert the needle under two middle bars between the legs of a stitch; pull through. Then insert the tapestry needle back under the first bar, pull through. Repeat from * until all stitches have been secured.

HORIZONTAL INVISIBLE SEAMING

This is a method of seaming two horizontal pieces of knit fabric together, such as a cast on edge to a bind off edge (or two cast on/two bind off edges).

Align the two edges to be seamed so that they are lined up, stitch by stitch, with the right side facing up.

With a threaded tapestry needle with a length of yarn approximately three times the length of the seamed edges, insert the needle under both legs of the first stitch of one piece and pull the yarn through (leaving a tail for weaving in).

Insert the needle under both legs of the lined-up stitch on the opposite edge (the piece you are joining to) and pull the yarn through.

Repeat these two steps (without leaving a tail for weaving in on each subsequent stitch) until all the stitches are seamed. Once the seaming is complete, you may adjust the tension of the seaming yarn so it lies flat and the stitches appear the same size as the joined edges. Trim the ends and weave in.

DOUBLE KNITTING

Double knitting is a method of creating two-sided fabric, such as for a scarf or a coaster, without having an exposed wrong side. The front and back of the fabric are created simultaneously, knitting all stitches with one color, and purling all adjacent stitches with the opposite color, so that the front and back of the project are mirrors of one another. As such, double knitting is done in multiples of two stitches. Colorwork charts provided for double knitting indicate the color of the stitch that will be knit; the opposite color will be worked on all purl stitches and is not charted.

TO WORK IN THE ROUND:

*Move both yarns to the back between the needles as if to knit (if not already in position) and knit 1 stitch using the color indicated in the chart square. After completing the knit stitch, move both yarns to the front between the needles as if to purl and purl the next stitch with the opposite color as what is indicated for the knit stitch. Repeat from * to end of round.

TO WORK FLAT:

With the RS facing: *Move both yarns to the back between the needles as if to knit (if not already in position) and knit 1 stitch using the color indicated in the chart square. After completing the knit stitch, move both yarns to the front between the needles as if to purl and purl the next stitch with the opposite color as what is indicated for the knit stitch. Repeat from * to end of row.

With the WS facing: *Move both yarns to the back between the needles as if to knit (if not already in position) and knit 1 stitch using the opposite color indicated in the chart square. After completing the knit stitch, move both yarns to the front between the needles as if to purl and purl the next stitch with the color indicated in the chart square. Repeat from * to end of row.

APPLYING/PLACING BEADS

CROCHET HOOK METHOD

Using abbreviated letters to indicate the color of bead, (i.e.: G—green, R—Red, or Y—yellow), AB-X indicates to apply a bead to the fabric.

Using a crochet or bead hook appropriate for the size of bead being used, insert the hook through the bead and leave the bead on the hook. Pick up the loop of the stitch over which you want to place the bead with the crochet hook and let it drop off your knitting needle. Pull this loop through the bead and place the loop back onto the left-hand needle and remove the crochet hook. Knit this stitch in pattern to secure the bead.

JOGLESS STRIPES

Knitting in the round is a coil; the end of a round pushes up on top of the previous round rather than ending at the marker. As such, when you change to a new color when striping a project worked in the round, you will see a jog in the colors. This technique minimizes this jog and allows for a smoother color transition.

Knit one round with your new color. Move the beginning of the round marker to the right needle.

Use the tip of the right needle to pick up the right leg of the stitch below the first stitch of the new round (the leg will be the color of the old yarn) from back to front; place this new stitch on the left needle right beside the first stitch of the new round. Knit these two stitches together. Knit to the end of the round as normal.

RUNNING STITCH

Running stitch can be used to decorate knitted fabric such as adding eyes or mouths as a visible technique, or it can be used to cinch sections of work and be less visible.

DECORATIVE RUNNIING STITCH

Thread the tapestry needle with the working yarn. Starting at the right-most point of the designated embroidery location, from the wrong side, push the tapestry needle through to the RS of the work, carry it across the front of the work over the required number of stitches, and then push it back through to the wrong side. Ensure the yarn isn't loose or saggy, but isn't so tight that it puckers. Cut the yarn and weave the tails to the wrong side to secure.

RUNNING STITCH (FOR CINCHING)

Thread the tapestry needle with the working yarn. Starting at the right-most point of the designated cinching section, with the RS facing, pick up the right leg of each of the required stitches. At the stopping point, remove the working yarn from the tapestry needle and pull the tails tight to cinch the section. Secure with an overhand knot. Trim the tails or secure to the wrong side.

STRANDED COLORWORK

Sometimes referred to as Fair Isle knitting, stranded colorwork uses two (or more) colors per round, with the color not currently being used being stranded, or carried, loosely across the wrong side of the work. Both yarns can be held in either the right or left hand, however you prefer to knit, or with one color in each hand. Whichever method you use, make sure to maintain even tension and keep the position vertically to maintain color dominance. The bottom strand carried will have more dominance than the top; it's best practice to carry the contrast colors as the dominant (or bottom) yarn.

When rounds of stranded colorwork are placed between rounds of stockinette, make sure to check both gauges before you begin; most knitters will work the stranded colorwork section more tightly than plain stockinette. Adjust your needle size when switching to the stranded section as needed to match gauge and remember to change back to the smaller needle(s) when beginning the next section of plain stockinette.

As you work across a round of the pattern, spread the stitches just worked apart slightly before knitting the next stitch with the color that has been carried across the wrong side. The float across the back should be relaxed, not sagging, but should also not be tight, as to avoid puckering of the fabric.

If floats between color changes will be more than ½ to ¾ in. / 1 to 2 cm long, it's a good idea to catch the unused/floating color to reduce the risk of snagging the float later. The easiest way to do this is to hold the color to be "caught" in your left hand and the working color in your right hand. Insert the right needle into the next stitch and under the floated yarn, then knit as usual, allowing the floated yarn to come back down behind the needles so the working yarn will lie over the top of it on the next stitch. Catching floats more regularly than is necessary uses more yarn and can create a stiffer fabric.

INTARSIA COLORWORK

Unlike stranded colorwork, where long strands of color are carried across the back of the work while creating rows of multiple color stitch motifs, intarsia colorwork uses the "supply" or "bobbin" method.

When working the intarsia technique, primarily worked flat, each section of a new color across a row uses a new length of yarn. As such, if you have multiple sections of blue, and multiple sections of red across a given pattern row, you will have multiple red and multiple blue supplies or bobbins of each yarn across the row.

At each color change, the two abutting colors are twisted once, to secure the work, and then the "old" color is dropped so the required number of stitches can be worked using the "new" color.

Intarsia colorwork can be worked across multiple different types of knitted fabric but is most commonly found across stockinette stitch. Regardless of the type of fabric being knit, the twist at each color change should occur on the wrong side of the work. In the case where your working yarn may be in the front of the work, such as when purling on the right-side, move the yarn to the back between the needles, twist the two yarns, and then move the new working yarn to the front between the needles.

DUPLICATE STITCH

Duplicate stitch is a way of adding sections of color to a knitted piece without having to work stranded knitting or intarsia. The technique covers each stitch completely. Large areas can become thick and stiff, so it's best used in small areas. With the color to be stitched threaded into a tapestry needle, insert the needle from the wrong side to the right–side in the stitch below the first stitch to be covered.

*Insert the tapestry needle under both legs of the stitch in the row above the stitch to be covered, and pull the yarn through, being careful not to pull the yarn too tightly. Insert the needle back into the same spot where you initially brought it to the right side, and pull the yarn through to completely cover the first stitch. Bring the needle up through the stitch below the next stitch to be covered.

Repeat from * to continue covering stitches.

I-CORD

An I-cord is a long, narrow knitted tube that mimics knitting in the round but is worked flat with just two needles. It is best worked on double-pointed needles or a circular (a needle with tips at each end; a straight needle with a stopper at one end will not work).

Cast on the number of stitches listed in the pattern (usually between two and four stitches). Slide the stitches to the right edge of the needle and pull the working yarn behind the back of the work ready to knit the first stitch closest to the right needle tip. This will create a tube.

Row 1: Knit, then slide stitches back to right end of needle. Do not turn; pull the working yarn behind.

Repeat Row 1 until the cord is the desired length. Finish off the cord as directed in the pattern.

SPRAY / DRY BLOCKING

Unlike wet blocking, where a project is fully submerged in water until fiber saturation before being placed on a drying surface, dry blocking is worked in the reverse order. This avoids the project from growing or changing shape in unexpected ways when moving from a water bath to a drying surface, and reduces drying time. It is especially useful for large projects like blankets.

After weaving in all of the ends of your finished project, place the project onto the drying surface of your choice. Pin out the project to the required dimensions while dry. Then, using a spray bottle, spray the surface of the piece until it is evenly wet, but not soaking. This allows the fibers to relax and bloom without changing the size or shape of the project. If the water beads on the surface of the project, gently press the water into the fabric with the flat of your hand.

Allow to dry fully and then unpin.

SHORT ROWS

WRAP AND TURN (W&T) SHORT ROWS

Slip all stitches purlwise in the following sequences.

On knit rows: Knit to instructed turning point. With the yarn in back, slip the next st to the right needle, move the yarn to the front between needles, slip the stitch back to the left needle and move the yarn back between needles to the purl side. Turn work.

On purl rows: Purl to the instructed turning point. With the yarn in front, slip the next stitch to the right needle, move the yarn to the back between needles, slip the stitch back to the left needle and move the yarn to the front between needles to the purl side. Turn work.

To process the wrap on a subsequent row: Work to the wrapped stitch, pick up the wrap from front to back for a knit stitch (and from back to front for a purl stitch), and place the wrap on the left needle. Work the wrap together with the stitch as a k2tog or p2tog.

GERMAN SHORT ROWS

Double stitches are creating by distorting the stitch at the end of the previously turned row.

On knit rows (following a turn): Move the working yarn to the front between the needles. Slip the first stitch purlwise to the right-hand needle. To create the ddouble stitch (DS), pull the working yarn up and over the back of the right-hand needle so the stitch now looks like an upside-down V, with 2 legs. Keep the yarn in back, ready to knit the next stitch, and work across the row in pattern.

On purl rows (following a turn): With the working yarn still in front, slip the first stitch purlwise to the right-hand needle. To create the double stitch (DS), pull the working yarn up and over the back of the right-hand needle so the stitch now looks like an upside-down V with 2 legs. Move the working yarn to the front between the needles, ready to purl the next stitch, and work across the row in pattern.

To process a double stitch on a subsequent row: Work to the double stitch and knit (or purl) the two legs together as if it were one stitch as a k2tog (kDs) or p2tog (pDS).

Abbreviations

2/2 LPC - slip 2 stitches to cable needle and hold to front, purl 2; knit 2 from cable needle

2/2 RC - slip 2 stitches to cable needle and hold to back, knit 2; knit 2 from cable needle

2/2 RPC - slip 2 stitches to cable needle and hold to back, knit 2; purl 2 from cable needle

approx. - approximately

BO - bind off

BOR - beginning of round

CC – contrast color

cdd – slip 2 stitches knitwise, knit 1, pass slipped stitches over (2 stitches decreased)

circ - circular(s)

cm - centimeter(s)

CO - cast on

cont – continue

dec - decrease(s/d)

double-yo - yarn over 2 times consecutively (2 stitches increased)

dpn(s) – double pointed needle(s)

DS - Double stitch (used in German Short Rows)

est - established

in. - inch(es)

inc - increase(s/d)

k - knit

k2tog - knit 2 stitches together (1 stitch decreased)

k2tog-tbl - knit 2 stitches together through the back loops (1 stitch decreased)

k3tog - knit 3 stitches together (2 stitches decreased)

kApB – double-knit pair; knit front layer stitch with Color A, bring both yarns forward, purl back layer stitch with Color B, bring both yarns backward

kBpA – double-knit pair; knit front layer stitch with Color B, bring both yarns forward, purl back layer stitch with Color A, bring both yarns backward

kBpC – double-knit pair; knit front layer stitch with Color B, bring both yarns forward, purl back layer stitch with Color C, bring both yarns backward

kCpB – double-knit pair; knit front layer stitch with Color C, bring both yarns forward, purl back layer stitch with Color B, bring both yarns backward

kDS – knit double stitch (used in German short rows)

kfb - knit into front and back of same stitch (1 stitch increased)

LHN - left hand needle

LLI (Left Lifted Increase): Using the tip of your left-hand needle, lift the left leg of the stitch 2 rows below the last stitch on the right-hand needle, knit this through the back loop - 1 stitch increased.

M – marker

m – meter(s)

M-A (B, C, etc.) – marker A (B, C, etc.)

M1BL - cast on 1 stitch using the Backwards Loop cast on method (1 stitch increased)

M1L - insert the left-hand needle under the running thread from front to back, knit this new loop through the back loop (1 stitch increased)

M1LP - insert the left-hand needle under the running thread from front to back, purl this new loop through the back loop (1 stitch increased)

M1R - insert the left-hand needle under the running thread from back to front, knit this new loop (1 stitch increased)

M1RP - insert the left-hand needle under the running thread from back to front, purl this new loop (1 stitch increased)

MC – main color

N1 (2, 3, etc,) – Needle 1 (2, 3, etc.)

p – purl

p2tog - purl 2 stitches together (1 stitch decreased)

p2tog-tbl - purl 2 stitches together through the back loops (1 stitch decreased)

patt – pattern

pDS – purl double stitch (used in German short rows)

pm – place marker

prev – previous/ly

rem - remain(s)

rep – repeat

RHN - right hand needle

RLI (Right Lifted Increase): Using the tip of your right-hand, lift the right leg of the stitch below the first stitch on the left-hand needle, place this lifted stitch onto the left-hand needle, knit this through the front loop - 1 stitch increased.

rm – remove marker

rnd(s) - round(s)

RS - right side

s2kp – slip 2 stitches knitwise, knit 1, pass slipped stitches over (2 stitches decreased)

sk2p – slip 1 stitch knitwise, knit 2 stitches together, pass slipped stitch over (2 stitches decreased)

skp - slip 1 stitch knitwise, knit 1, pass slipped stitch over (1 stitch decreased)

sl - slip stitch purlwise (unless otherwise noted)

slide - slide stitches from one end of the needle to the other

sm – slip marker

ssk - slip, slip, knit: slip 1 stitch knitwise, slip second stitch knitwise, move these 2 stitches back to left-hand needle purlwise and knit 2 together through the back loop (1 stitch decreased)

ssp – slip, slip, purl: slip 1 stitch knitwise, slip second stitch knitwise, move these 2 stitches back to left-hand needle purlwise and purl 2 together through the back loop (1 stitch decreased)

St st – stockinette stitch

st(s) - stitch(es)

tbl – through back loop(s)

turn - turn work so opposite side of work is facing

w&t – wrap and turn (short row method)

WS - wrong side

wyib - with yarn in back

wyif - with yarn in front

yd. - yard(s)

yo - yarn over (1 stitch increased)

* (*) - used to indicate the beginning of a length of instructions to be repeated

( ) or [ ] - used to indicate a set of instructions to be repeated or differentiate between sizes

Yarn Resource Guide

29 BRIDGES STUDIO
29bridges.com

316 DYE STUDIO
316dyestudio.com

A WHIMSICAL WOOD YARN CO.
Awhimsicalwoodyarnco.com

BERROCO
Berroco.com

BROOKLYN TWEED
Brooklyntweed.com

BLUE SKY FIBERS
Blueskyfibers.com

CASCADE YARNS
Cascadeyarns.com

EMMA'S YARN
Emmasyarn.com

EWE EWE YARNS
Eweewe.com

FIBER SEED
Thefiberseed.com

HAZEL KNITS
Hazelknits.com

JAMIESON'S OF SHETLAND
Jamiesonsofshetland.co.uk

KEENAN HAND DYED YARN
Keenanyarn.com

KIM DYES YARN
Kimdyesyarn.com

LATTES & LLAMAS
Lattesandllamas.com

THE LEMONADE SHOP
Thelemonadeshopyarns.com

LITTLE FOX YARN
Littlefoxyarn.com

MUST STASH YARN
Muststashshop.com

OINK PIGMENTS
Oinkpigments.com

THE PLUCKY KNITTER
Thepluckyknitter.com

QUEEN CITY YARN
Queencityyarn.com

SWEETGEORGIA YARNS
Sweetgeorgiayarns.com

TEAL TORCH KNITS
Tealtorchknits.com

URBAN GIRL YARNS
urbangirlyarns.com

WOOL & VINYL
Woolandvinyl.com

YARN CAFÉ CREATIONS
Yarncafecreations.com

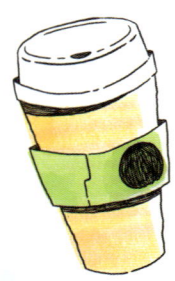

For The Gensheimer Girls:
Marcia, Emily, and Beth

Where you lead, I will follow.

As always, I wouldn't be here without the encouragement and support of my family—Roger, Callum, and Astrid. Roger, from taking the kids to the playground so I could get my knitting done, to bringing me snacks during late night writing sessions, I couldn't have done this without you. I know how lucky I am, and I love the three of you more than Lorelai loves caffeine.

Mom and Dad, you never batted an eye when I asked for more books or cared that I would rather hang out at the bookstore than go to a party. You've always accepted me for who I am, and I'm forever grateful.

Much gratitude to my esteemed honorary *Gilmore*, editor Sammy Holland. You're the first person I would call if I hit a deer, and I'm up for a road trip to an ivy league with you any time.

To my magnificent technical editor, Meaghan Schmaltz, your attention to detail is unparalleled. I salute your hard work and I'm up for an around-the-world adventure with you always.

My deepest thanks to the extraordinarily talented knitting designers within these pages. You're an absolute delight to work with, and I love our book adventures together—past, present, and future. Thank you for letting me be your Cruise Director and continuing to put your faith in me and meet your deadlines. Thank you to sample knitter Beth Leath, who always comes through in a knitting emergency.

Kudos to the talented dyers who offered yarn support and encouragement. Thank you for your confidence in my projects—your support is better than the finest cashmere.

To the marvelous people at Insight Editions, it means everything to me that you continue to call my name, letting me be there on the next train. Thank you for your unwavering support with beloved fandoms.

Published by Titan Books, London, in 2024.

A division of Titan Publishing Group Ltd
144 Southwark Street
London SE1 0UP
www.titanbooks.com

Find us on Facebook: www.facebook.com/TitanBooks
Follow us on X: @titanbooks

 Copyright © 2024 Warner Bros. Entertainment Inc.
GILMORE GIRLS and all related characters and elements are
© & ™ Warner Bros. Entertainment Inc. WB SHIELD: TM & © WBEI. (s24)

Published by arrangement with Insight Editions, San Rafael, California.
www.insighteditions.com

No part of this publication may be reproduced, stored in a retrieval system, or transmitted, in any form or by any means without the prior written permission of the publisher, nor be otherwise circulated in any form of binding or cover other than that in which it is published and without a similar condition being imposed on the subsequent purchaser.

A CIP catalogue record for this title is available from the British Library.

ISBN: 9781835412770

Publisher: Raoul Goff
SVP, Group Publisher: Vanessa Lopez
VP, Creative: Chrissy Kwasnik
VP, Manufacturing: Alix Nicholaeff
Editorial Director: Lia Brown
Art Director: Stuart Smith
Senior Designer: Judy Wiatrek Trum
Senior Editor: Samantha Holland
Assistant Editor: Emma Merwin
Executive Project Editor: Maria Spano
Senior Production Manager: Greg Steffen
Senior Production Manager, Subsidiary Rights: Lina s Palma-Temena

Technical Editor: Meaghan Schmaltz

Photographer: Ted Thomas
Prop Stylist: Elena P. Craig

Thanks to our models: Adam, Alisa, Emma, Jenni, Justin, Kristi and Sammy
And thanks to Mishi and Ted for your perfect Stars Hollow locations.

Insight Editions, in association with Roots of Peace, will plant two trees for each tree used in the manufacturing of this book. Roots of Peace is an internationally renowned humanitarian organization dedicated to eradicating land mines worldwide and converting war-torn lands into productive farms and wildlife habitats. Roots of Peace will plant two million fruit and nut trees in Afghanistan and provide farmers there with the skills and support necessary for sustainable land use.

Manufactured in China by Insight Editions

10 9 8 7 6 5 4 3 2 1